The Work of Cities

Globalization and Community
Dennis R. Judd, Series Editor

The Work of Cities

Susan E. Clarke and Gary L. Gaile

Globalization and Community / Volume 1
University of Minnesota Press
Minneapolis • London

Published by the University of Minnesota Press
111 Third Avenue South, Suite 290
Minneapolis, MN 55401-2520
http://www.upress.umn.edu

Library of Congress Cataloging-in-Publication Data

Clarke, Susan E., 1945–
   The work of cities / Susan E. Clarke and Gary L. Gaile.
     p.   cm. — (Globalization and community ; v. 1)
   Includes bibliographical references and index.
   ISBN 0-8166-2892-0 (hc : alk. paper). — ISBN 0-8166-2893-9 (pbk. : alk. paper)
   1. Community development, Urban.   2. Urban economics.   3. Community development, Urban—Case studies.   I. Gaile, Gary L.   II. Title.   III. Series.
   HN49.C6C573   1998
   307.1′416′0973—dc21   98-10858

10 09 08 07 06 05 04 03 02 01 00 99 98   10 9 8 7 6 5 4 3 2 1

To our parents
Harry F. and Elayne M. Clarke
Stanley V. and Helen A. Gaile

Contents

Acknowledgments

We share an interest in communities. Until recently, we've pursued this common interest independently—in the United States and Africa—and from the different disciplinary perspectives of political science and geography. But as globalization trends became more visible, we began to compare notes on how local leaders and citizens were responding to these trends and making choices about their communities' future. Asking community leaders about these choices seemed to us the best way to understand the reality of the big talk about globalization, territoriality, sovereignty, localism, and citizenship that academics like to engage in among themselves. Thanks to a grant from the U.S. Department of Commerce, Economic Development Administration (EDA) (Grant 99-07-13709), we were able to do so. John Fieser at EDA encouraged us to apply for a research grant to study these changes in American cities; he was especially supportive of our efforts and a patient guide to the intricacies of sponsored research. A subsequent grant from the National Science Foundation (Grant SES-9112359) allowed Susan Clarke to return to eight of the cities in our original EDA study to analyze neighborhood and minority voices in local economic development processes.

The more we talked to local leaders, the more we realized they were grappling with the issues Robert Reich (1989) addresses in *The Work of Nations*: changing production systems, global linkages, new geographies of human capital, institutional transformations, and rethinking citizenship in a global era. In many important ways, local officials and community leaders understood the gravity and consequences of these trends sooner and better than national policy makers and academics—not because they were necessarily smarter or more reflexive, but because they had no choice: in a climate of national retrenchment of aid to cities and rapid transformation of local conditions, community leaders are truly on the front lines of change. *The Work of Cities* emerged from these conversations with each other and with many, many others. We can acknowledge only a few of these others here.

Since beginning the EDA grant in 1989 and realizing we had completely different styles of collaboration, not to mention ideas about sampling, interviewing, data analysis, and expectations for revisions, our efforts to work together have been a continuous source of amazement and amusement to our friends, family, colleagues, and students. A sense of humor is critical: our marriage is intact and our friendships stronger. We especially appreciate comments on our work from Michael Pagano, Dennis Judd, Ed Goetz, Michael Rich, Terry Nichols Clark, Martin Saiz, Cynthia Horan, Lewis Randolph, Ann O'M. Bowman, Bill Barnes, Tim Grendell, Lynn Staeheli, Jim Huff, Anne Huff, W. A. V. Clark, Ed Malecki Jr., Rodney Hero, Robyne Turner, Norman Krumholz, Hal Wolman, Beth Mitchneck, Rod Erickson, Etienne Nel, and the many graduate students who helped us with the surveys: Jeni James Arndt, Susan Iott, Anne Moss, Martin Saiz, Caroline Tolbert, Elisa Rosen, Brad Hall, John Larsen, and especially Mara Sidney and Laura Brunell. The friendly, polite, but skeptical response to our findings from our colleagues at the University of Essex forced us to clarify the arguments; colleagues at Lund, Cambridge, Berlin, and Bristol also helped us refine our perspective. Luzie Mason at the Center for Public Policy, University of Colorado at Boulder, arranged the trips, kept the budgets, and made a complicated project go as smoothly as possible.

Finally, Carrie Mullen at the University of Minnesota Press and Dennis Judd, series editor, provided the best possible editorial and intellectual climate for bringing the book to its final stages. Their enthusiasm often outweighed our own—at least at those critical moments when the tedium and annoyances of polishing a manuscript seemed insurmountable. Without them, we'd still be arguing, cutting, pasting, and revising; thanks to them, we have a book. Thanks to Judy Selhorst, our copy editor, it is a more readable and accurate book than our "final" version of the manuscript.

The questions we are interested in and find important can be answered only in such places as Tulsa, Macon, Cleveland, Tacoma, Harare, Murewa, Kutus, Nairobi, Njabini, Machakos, Tot, Mbale, Masaka, Durban, Grahamstown, and Port Elizabeth. Both of us have spent most of our academic lives teaching but also doing research outside the university, in communities like these and others around the world. We can't imagine it otherwise. Others involved in this type of research will understand the importance of our final acknowledgments. Over the years, we've made several visits to the following cities and owe special thanks to the people listed below for taking time from their schedules to talk to us about local issues. Their information and insights have been invaluable, although we understand they may not agree with our interpretations. Inevitably, this is an imperfect list: we apologize for omitting names or misspelling the ones listed; affiliations and organizations change, but this is the record we've reconstructed as best we could from our logs and files. It surely underestimates our debt and appreciation.

Cleveland, Ohio
Dick Bingham, Cleveland State University
Charles Brown, Department of Finance
Tom Cox, Neighborhood Progress Inc.
Claire Felbinger, Cleveland State University
David Garrison, Cleveland State University
Ned Hill, Cleveland State University
Chris Johnson, Midtown Corridor
Dennis Keating, Cleveland State University
Kathy Kiesling, reporter, *Plain Dealer*
Jack Krumhansl, Division of Neighborhood Revitalization
Norm Krumholz, Cleveland State University
Vincent J. Lombardi, Economic Development, Department of Community
    Development
Luis Martinez, Neighborhood Planning, Division of Neighborhood
    Revitalization
Mary Ellen Mazey, Wright State University
Hunter Morrison, Department of Planning
John Purcell, Mayor's Office
Terry Racik, Neighborhood Commercial Development, Department of Community Development
Keith Rasey, Cleveland State University
William Reesberger, Department of Community Development
Joe Romano, Cleveland Tomorrow
Terrance A. Ross, Division of Neighborhood Revitalization
Richard A. Shatten, Cleveland Tomorrow
Gregory A. Shumate, Economic Development, Department of Community
    Development
Glenn Smith, Planning and Policy Development, Division of Neighborhood
    Revitalization
Joseph F. Smith, Division of Redevelopment
Philip D. Starr, Cleveland Center for Neighborhood Development
Paul Weiner, Department of Finance
William A. Whitney, Detroit Shoreway CDC

Dayton, Ohio
John Blair, Wright State University
Robert Bradley, Department of Economic Development
Janet Henry, Dayton Foundation
Jeffery A. Klank, Dayton Citywide Development Corporation
Barbara LaBrier, Office of Management and Budget
Dean Lovelace, Priority Board and Parity 2000
Leo Lucas, Priority Board and Black Political Assembly
Phyllis Mitchell, Neighbor to Neighbor Project
Lawrence Nelson, Black Political Assembly
Ray Reynolds, Department of Urban Development
Tim Riordon, Finance Office
Mike Schierloh, Assistant City Manager for Urban Redevelopment
Jill Triwush, Dayton Citywide Development Corporation

Columbus, Ohio
Maria Caprio, Office of Management and Budget
Patrick Grady, Economic Development Division, Development Department
Ray Lorello, Development Department
Paula J. Trout, Office of Management and Budget

Oklahoma City, Oklahoma
Edward R. Bee, Chamber of Commerce
Debbie Blackburn, Neighborhood Alliance
Don Bown, Finance Department
Paul H. Brum, Public Works Department
Lisa Crowell, Neighborhood Alliance
Mike Deming, Planning and Economic Development
Tiana P. Douglas, Second Century Development Corporation
Carl Friend, Neighborhood and Community Planning
H. D. "Bud" Heiser, Neighborhood and Community Planning
Beverly Hodges, City Council and Classen Beautiful
Ron Mason, Finance Department
Danny Terrell, Neighborhood Initiative Program
James E. Thompson, Assistant City Manager
John Yokel, Paseo CDC

Tulsa, Oklahoma
Willie Adams, Tulsa Economic Development Corporation
Gene E. Bread, Indian Health Care Resource Center
Paul D. Chapman, Tulsa Development Authority
Steve Childress, Downtown Tulsa Unlimited, Inc.
Mike Davidsson, Metropolitan Tulsa Chamber of Commerce
Michael P. Kier, Treasury/Budget Department
Brenda Kay Miller, Urban Redevelopment Department
Troy Paton, Minority Business Development Center
Ron Payne, Department of Finance
Susan Savage, Mayor's Office

Andrew Skeeter, American Indian Heritage Center
Emily Warner, Department of City Development
Terry Young, Tulsa Economic Development Corporation
HelenMarie Zachritz, Department of Finance

Columbus, Georgia
Greg Clark, Department of Economic and Community Development
E. Gregory Dawson, Minority Business Development Center
R. Dedwylder, Columbus Uptown Inc.
Rev. Johnny Flakes, 4th Avenue Baptist Church
Kay House, Finance Department
Patty Howard, Historic Columbus Foundation
Stan Keen, Columbus Housing Authority
Roger Secrest, Internal Auditor

Macon, Georgia
Maryel Battin, Macon Heritage Foundation
Reginald Bell, City Administration Office
Albert Billingslea, Bibb County Commissioner and Macon-Bibb County
    Planning and Zoning Commission
Valerie Binford, City Administration Office
Sid Cherry, Macon Urban Development Authority
Carson Flournoy, neighborhood associations
Alex C. Habersham, Macon-Bibb County Board of Tax Assessors
Rev. Charles Jones, Bellevue Baptist Church
Robert A. Loveland, Finance Officer
David M. Luckie, Greater Macon Chamber of Commerce
Catherine M. Maness, Economic and Community Development Department
Tom Moody, Macon Industrial Development Authority
Vernon B. Ryle III, Macon-Bibb County Planning and Zoning Commission
Israel G. Small, Assistant Chief Administrative Officer
Chester A. Wheeler III, Economic and Community Development Department

Miami, Florida
Frank Casteneda, Department of Community Development
Margarita G. Cordovi, Planning Department
Ernest L. Martin, Metro Dade County Community and Economic
    Development Department
Otis Pitts, Tacolcy Economic Development Corporation
Manohar S. Surana, Department of Management and Budget
Bert Waters, Planning Department
Arleen Weintraub, Department of Development

Jacksonville, Florida
Scott D. Adams, Downtown Development Authority
Richard L. Bowers, City Department of Housing and Urban Development
Al Ray, Finance/Budget Department
Jesse B. Smith, Economic Development Coordinator, Mayor's Office

David Swain, Jacksonville Community Council, Inc.
Bert Swanson, University of Florida
Robyne Turner, Florida Atlantic University

Syracuse, New York
Reed Dolberg, Department of Economic Development
David Kreider, City Planning Commission and Greater Syracuse Chamber of
    Commerce
David Mankewietz, Metropolitan Development Association
William S. McIntyre, Commissioner, Finance
David Michel, Commissioner, Community Development
Samuel W. Williams, Greater Syracuse Business Incubator Center

Albany, New York
Elaine Amodeo, Department of Economic Development
Anthony J. Ferrara, Commissioner, Department of Economic Development
John Martin, Center for Economic Growth, Inc.
Charles Newland, Department of Economic Development
Janet O'Brian, Capital Cities Renaissance Corp.
David S. Riker, Department of Community Redevelopment

Fort Wayne, Indiana
Mark D. Becker, Department of Economic Development
Ronald R. Fletcher, Department of Redevelopment
C. James Owen, Indiana University/Purdue University at Fort Wayne
Greg Purcell, Department of Community Development
Beverly S. Rippy, City Clerk
John Stafford, Mayor's Office

Indianapolis, Indiana
Fred Armstrong, Controller
John Labal, Economic Development and Housing, Metropolitan
    Development Department
Ron Miller, Budget Officer
Sheila Pahud, Greater Indianapolis Progress Committee
Kathryn H. Snedeker, Mayor's Office

Seattle, Washington
David Bloom, Council of Churches
John Braden, Department of Economic Development
Thomas Brunton, Department of Community Development
Susan C. Cary, Southeast Effective Development
Norm Chamberlain, Rainier Valley Chamber of Commerce
Patricia Chemnick, Southeast Effective Development
Mike Dickerson, Washington Association for Community Economic
    Development
John Forbes, South End Seattle Community Organization
Claude Forward, Genesee Merchant's Association
Bill Mayhern, Central Puget Sound Economic Development
Mary Jean Ryan, Evergreen CDA

Phyllis M. Sato, Urban Enterprise Center, Greater Seattle Chamber of
Commerce
Steve Shepard, Department of Neighborhoods
Tacoma, Washington
Martha Anderson, Economic Development, Planning and Development
Services
John Austin, Economic Development Board for Tacoma-Pierce County
Alberta Canada, Hilltop Housing Consortium
Mariza Craig, Neighborhood Business District Revitalization Program
Thomas Dickson, Urban League of Tacoma
Elton Gatewood, Neighborhood Council Office
Sharon Hansen, Tacoma-Pierce County Commission on Children, Youth &
Their Families
Don Hines, Department of Community and Economic Development
Rod Kerslake, Economic Development, Planning and Development Services
Barbara Levy, Union Station District Development Association
Peter Luttrop, Finance Department
Erling Mork, Economic Development Corporation
Keith Palmquist, Community Development Department
Glenn Peterson, Economic Development, Planning and Development
Services Department
Keith Peterson, Finance Office
Judy Sheridan, Legislative Liaison
Bill Smitherman, Upper Tacoma Renaissance Association
Daisy Stallworth, Economic Development Council, Pierce County
Nancy Troop, Economic Development, Planning and Development Services

In addition, we appreciate the information provided by economic development officials in the following cities in response to our mail surveys in 1989 and/or 1996: Akron, Albany, Alexandria, Allentown, Anchorage, Ann Arbor, Atlanta, Aurora, Austin, Bakersfield, Beaumont, Birmingham, Boise, Buffalo, Canton, Cedar Rapids, Charlotte, Chattanooga, Chesapeake, Chicago, Cincinnati, Cleveland, Colorado Springs, Columbus (Ohio), Corpus Christi, Dallas, Davenport, Denver, Durham, El Paso, Eugene, Evansville, Flint, Fort Worth, Fremont, Fullerton, Garden Grove, Garland, Grand Rapids, Greensboro, Hammond, Hampton, Hartford, Hollywood (Florida), Houston, Huntsville, Independence, Indianapolis, Irving, Jacksonville, Jersey City, Kansas City (Kansas), Kansas City (Missouri), Knoxville, Lansing, Las Vegas, Lexington, Lincoln, Little Rock, Livonia (Michigan), Los Angeles, Louisville, Lubbock, Madison, Mesa, Miami, Milwaukee, Minneapolis, Newport News, New York, Norfolk, Oklahoma City, Orlando, Oxnard, Peoria, Pittsburgh, Portland (Oregon), Portsmouth, Providence, Raleigh, Richmond, Roanoke,

Rochester, Rockford, St. Louis, St. Paul, St. Petersburg, Salt Lake City, San Antonio, San Diego, Santa Ana, Savannah, Seattle, Spokane, Springfield (Illinois), Springfield (Massachusetts), Stamford, Stockton, Sunnyvale, Syracuse, Tacoma, Tampa, Tempe, Topeka, Tulsa, Virginia Beach, Waco, Waterbury, Wichita, Winston-Salem, Worcester, Yonkers, Youngstown.

Introduction

To many of us, local economic development is an arcane world of revenue bonds, roads, dubious revitalization projects, and, even worse, corrupt deals over tax breaks for private investors. But in the 1990s this agenda includes world trade centers in Durham and Lubbock, "internationally friendly" infrastructure and thirty sister cities in Portland, training software specialists in Ann Arbor and Stamford, and setting up public-private partnerships for telecommunications in cities like Milpitas. What is going on?

It's simple—cities are adapting to restructuring and globalization trends with a range of policy choices unanticipated by scholars and unheard of just a few years ago. No longer is the work of cities centered on delivering services, providing public order, and luring investment to their communities. In a rapidly transforming world, America's cities occupy a strategic position in the global web and play an increasing role in determining the quality of local citizenship. Thinking locally and acting globally suddenly matter for local officials. In this book, we move beyond scholarly debates and political disputes to survey the remarkable transformations in local economies as local citizens and leaders face the twenty-first century.

The role of cities in the twenty-first century is a matter of some scholarly debate but dwindling public interest in the United States. Globalization and restructuring processes raise important questions about the functions and viability of any particular location in a global economy.[1] But as nations become increasingly competitive on a global scale, many officials believe that any public investment in subnational economies diverts resources better used to increase national productivity. Most significantly, the majority of Americans now dwell in suburban communities; an even higher proportion of the voting public lives outside central cities and gives declining support for the spending of public funds on areas that seem distant and remote from their daily lives.

The Emergence of the New Localism

Several voices challenge this trivialization of local economies and local politics and the consequent marginalization of those continuing to live in urban areas. Jane Jacobs (1984), of course, was an early, eloquent advocate of viewing city economies as the backbone of national wealth. Boldly labeling national economies as "grab bags" of very different local economies, she emphasized the diversity and versatility—one might say "flexibility"— of localities as production environments and as markets. She framed a city's innovative capacity in terms of its import substitution potential, characterizing "explosive episodes" and chain reactions of import replacing as the heart of local economic adaptation. From her perspective, cities are resilient and adaptive; their import replacement efforts create, in many cases, rich, dense, complex city regions that are the appropriate focus of study. Jacobs's import substitution perspective must now be considered on a global scale, but her emphasis on cities as the locus of national wealth provides an important starting point.

A more recent argument on localism simply points out that globalization and economic restructuring processes are neither universal nor monolithic (Logan and Swanstrom, 1990). Communities vary in their experiences with these processes; even those facing similar difficulties make different choices about how to respond to these changes. Although variations in responses are not compelling evidence of real local autonomy (Sassen, 1991), they do suggest that the grounds for political choice are broader and deeper than initially assumed. Furthermore, they indicate that these choices are essentially political, not determined by larger economic forces (Stone, 1989; Pagano and Bowman, 1995).

A parallel argument regarding national responses to local restructuring processes points out the ideological, rather than technical or functional, nature of those national policy responses (Barnekov, Boyle, and Rich, 1989). The interpretation of globalization and restructuring processes is a political process of problem definition; as such, the causes identified by policy makers drive the solutions chosen (Clarke and Gaile, 1997). For both the Reagan and Bush administrations in the 1980s, globalization trends were constructed as a market process in which any public intervention in support of people or places would lead to suboptimal economic outcomes. Yet critics of this policy stance point out that the implicit understanding of economic processes is simplistic and vestigial (Reich, 1991; Kuttner, 1997);

as a result, national policies based on these assumptions are likely to be misspecified and outdated, with daunting consequences for localities.

Those pursuing a more nuanced understanding of global change point to the emergence of regional economies as an important element of the new order. In this view, citistates (Pierce, Johnson, and Hall, 1993) or metropolitan economies (Barnes and Ledebur, 1991, 1998; Cisneros, 1995; Kresl and Gappert, 1995; Savitch et al., 1993) are the foundation of national economic well-being. Suburbs cannot prosper without viable urban cores (Rusk, 1993; Savitch et al., 1993). And far from being the drags on national competitiveness portrayed in the early 1980s, metropolitan areas, with their clusters of firms and specialized labor forces, are seen as the engine of international productivity in the 1990s and beyond. From this perspective, globalization trends are manifested as regional processes (Budd, 1994; Pierce et al., 1993) in which urban regions come to play a critical economic role (Parker, 1995; Swanstrom, 1996; Harrison, Kelley, and Gant, 1996).

Localities as the New Arenas for Global Competition

We want to take this argument further. In this book we pull together the different strands of thought disputing the conventional wisdom on cities—that they are obsolete relics of an earlier era—and sketch the new geography of the twenty-first century. This new geography is rooted in a seeming paradox: globalization may mean that regions and localities become more important decision arenas. Our work begins with this potential paradox and builds on the argument that the work of cities in a global era is grounded in the work of globalization (Sassen, 1996).

The Work of Nations and the Work of Cities

To some, it will appear incongruous to speak of the new work of cities in an age of global economic change. The scope and magnitude of changes in production systems and investment patterns seems to challenge the very notion of sovereign nation-states and collective self-interests. In *The Work of Nations: Preparing Ourselves for 21st Century Capitalism*, Robert Reich (1991) argues that this new globalism, coupled with increasing disparities in wealth and power, has inextricably altered the work of nations. We argue here that Reich's argument transcends scale: globalization also changes the work of cities in the twenty-first century. Rather than an epoch characterized by the "end of geography" (O'Brien, 1992)—in which localities become less important as investment and location decisions move to a global scale—we contend that city roles and functions are changing dramatically and taking on greater importance. Most important, we provide evidence in this volume that many city officials are adapting to these new roles in ways unanticipated by scholars, analysts, and policy makers. Rather than an end of geography, we are facing a transformative era in which we need to redefine the links among local, national, and global economies.

Two aspects of Reich's approach prompted us to rethink our own work on local economic development: Reich's emphasis on human capital investment as a critical element in value-added production processes and international competitiveness, and the opportunity to integrate the local scale as a stronger element in his globalization argument. Building on Reich's arguments, we delineate the ways in which the emergence of a global web alters the work of cities. Cities now are critical locales for processes in which value is added by investments in human capital rather than in traditional fixed production factors. Reich also argues that the "global web" of the new world economic order transcends the traditional nation-based relationships that previously determined the operation of national economies. And clearly, there has been a transcendence of scale upward. Economic transactions that in the past were normally confined within a nation's borders now typically flow freely around the globe. Yet this transcendence upward also has dramatic implications for a move down the geographic scale. How nations interact with the global economy influences how cities interact with both the national *and* the global economy.

Defining the Work of Cities

The work of cities has changed dramatically. As Sassen points out, globalization is more than an abstract concept: it exists as "concrete economic complexes situated in specific places" (1996, 630). As such, it is constituted and enabled by an array of local *practices* rather than broad, unspecified sweeps of technological and economic changes. These local practices are economic, political, and social. They include the myriad activities directly and indirectly linking local economies to global economic networks; this obviously encompasses local firms exporting internationally but also those firms and workers supplying necessary materials and skills to enterprises engaged more directly in global markets. This necessarily pushes the analytic focus beyond global cities to encompass the many types of places in which "the work of globalization gets done" (Sassen, 1996, 630). But this economic viewpoint is not sufficient; it slights the political and social practices in which these economic activities are embedded. As Michael Peter Smith notes, there is a tendency to view "the global context of urban life" as "some objective structure existing 'out there'" rather than as a socially constructed process (1992, 503). That is, local citizens and leaders engage in struggles over how to understand globalization trends, how to respond to them, and who the winners and losers will be in a global era. The resulting array of local definitions and solutions gives witness to the many different ways communities choose to view the work of cities (Clarke and Gaile, 1997). By bringing localities into the globalization argument, we therefore necessarily bring in the issues of volition and choice on the part of local officials. Far from being impotent and irrelevant, localities are the political arenas for the new work of cities—negotiating local citizenship and national competitiveness in the global economy.

Six Propositions

Drawing on Robert Reich's framework, our perspective is based on six propositions about the local policy context that contest much of the conventional understanding of cities. These six propositions frame the following chapters.

1. A new geography of value-added production processes underlies the work of cities.

In the past, value-added production was based on locations where factor costs were most favorable; urban geography reflected these patterns of factor cost production processes. As Reich (1991) points out, new economic processes add value—and wealth—primarily through human capital investments. The economic geography of American cities in the coming century will be based increasingly on the distribution and factor costs of human capital.

Economic restructuring and globalization processes remain contested issues. They must also be recognized as distinct trends. Both, however, contribute to a new geography of value-added production processes. Although there is continued debate about how different new economic activities are from industrial production processes, there is some consensus that new production activities are emerging in which value is added through the production process in very different ways.

These views have been shaped by an influential argument that flexible accumulation processes are superseding the "Fordist" modes of production (Amin, 1994; Piore and Sabel, 1984; Scott, 1992; Jessop, 1993). In these new modes, monetary flows are globalized, the international division of labor accelerates wage competition and pressures national and local wage rates, and the edifice of the welfare state begins to crumble under fiscal crisis and declining tax base (Peck and Jones, 1994). The flexibility of these new processes in response to shifting demands is the key contrast with other historical periods: flexible production demands flexible labor working in nonstandard work regimes, fluid inventories, production configurations alterable for new products, and ready access to a pool of design and engineering technicians and subcontractors (Scott, 1992; Pollard and Storper, 1996). The sources of value added, and profitability shifts from internal economies of the firm, gained through more efficient use of the factors of production, as in the high-volume industrial model, to production economies, gained from minimizing transaction and linkage costs among firms, suppliers, outsourcers, innovators and so on (Scott, 1992). This new flexibility in the use of capital and labor increases profitability for firms but also contributes to the decoupling of historic relationships between economic growth and changes in employment and poverty rates (Tobin, 1994). That is, increases in income and productivity are no longer associated with decline in poverty and unemployment rates.

The job anxiety emanating from flexible production is heightened by globalization trends. Technological breakthroughs allow finance capital and information to move quickly across the globe; deregulation permits these flows to be relatively free and costless. The globalization of the economy stems from these capacities to overcome distance; indeed, to some they suggest "the death of distance" as a salient factor in investment decisions ("The Death of Distance," 1995). As a result, many manufacturing enterprises decentralize their operations by shifting routine production tasks to low-wage areas and maintaining management and control functions in world cities (Friedmann and Wolff, 1982; Knox and Taylor, 1995). This new international division of labor means jobs are lost in the manufacturing heartland; new jobs coming in tend to be at lower skill levels and garner lower wages. Despite the emphasis on economic transition and transformation, many workers remain caught in the surf of the last, receding wave of economic change.

Human capital is the linchpin in this globalization picture. The growth of service sector activities, the decline of manufacturing production, the advent of knowledge-based industries, and the importance of information technology distinguish the contemporary period as one building on human capital resources. This is not to argue that technology and physical assets are insignificant, but to emphasize, as Reich (1991) puts it, that wealth and the potential for future gain are no longer best measured by fixed assets and stock, such as plant and equipment, but by accumulated knowledge and experience—human capital. *Human capital*, the analytic and information skills critical to the capacity to innovate, becomes a key element of profitability and wealth creation.[2] Specialized knowledge and skills able to contribute to high-value production processes are critical; these high-value processes target special customers through unique enterprises and specialized knowledge that are not easily duplicated (Reich, 1991).

The shift from industrial giantism to an economy based on service and knowledge-based industries featuring flexible production and high value-added processes presents both problems and prospects for the economic development of cities. The increasing importance of human capital contributes to the duality so prominent in many communities—the bright prospects for the fortunate fifth, as Reich puts it, and the potential immiseration of the remaining four-fifths of the citizenry. We bring into focus the prospects for coping with these aspects of the "fourth wave" in chapter 7.

2. Economic and geographic changes encourage parallel shifts in state relations.

Relations among different levels of state authority will shift significant development decisions from national arenas to supranational scales and local/regional scales.

As spatial and economic dynamics undergo transformation, parallel changes in the state are likely. Drawing direct parallels from economic changes to new institutional configurations is unrealistic, but anticipating the interaction of political and economic changes is prudent (Stoker, 1995; Harding, 1994; Painter, 1995). In particular, we consider the prospects for the "hollowing out" of the state—shifting economic development decisions to supranational and subnational levels (Jessop, 1993; Peck and Tickell, 1994). Despite a historical tradition of localism, trends toward state devolution are particularly troublesome for American cities as they work under the constraints imposed by the political logic of federalism and the economic imperatives of global capitalism.

For many communities, the growing dependence on a volatile, interdependent global economy portends a future of chronic fiscal instability. As the rate of capital mobility accelerates and the global competition for investment tightens, local communities become more vulnerable to external decisions that influence their economic well-being. In particular, the complexity and rapidity of economic change threaten the stability of local revenue sources. This revenue imperative—the effort to increase the stability and lower the vulnerability of the local revenue base—is prompting many local officials to consider new economic development strategies. In part this is due also to state devolution, including the withdrawal of national programmatic aid and the indifference of many state legislatures to urban concerns (Weir, 1996). Given continuing pressures to control spending and reduce the national deficit, increases in federal spending on local economic development programs are unlikely, regardless of the makeup of incoming administrations. Decisions on local development increasingly are designed and carried out within local arenas.

3. Local political arenas are expanding as localities take on more entrepreneurial economic roles and broader political responsibilities.

As localities become the new economic and political arenas for negotiating economic development processes and social tensions, they will take on more entrepreneurial economic roles and broader political responsibilities.

As cities struggled to adapt to economic changes and volatile political pressures in the 1970s, many began to reconsider the role of locational strategies in light of globalization and post-Fordist processes. Although the structural features of the American economic and political system ensure that locational incentives will always be part of the local repertoire, many local officials are adding strategies targeted to aspects of these new economic growth processes. Many cities began to reframe their economic roles and policies in terms of facilitating the climate for growth rather than providing locational incentives to subsidize individual firms. This meant establishing an institutional infrastructure generative of future growth. At the heart of these institutional shifts is an interest in finding local institutional arrangements that bridge market and democratic values. In Eisinger's (1988) terms, through these entrepreneurial initiatives, local officials are attempting to shape markets and climates through demand-side policies rather than relying on supply-side policies to assist specific firms. Thus American cities continue a historical tradition of local economic intervention, but the magnitude and mode of intervention are changing dramatically in response to a changing worldview at the local level.

4. Localities choose contextually specific paths in responding to globalization.

These problems and policies are contextually specific. Localities will choose different paths, in part because their constitutional, economic, and social features vary, but also in response to political configurations at the local level.

There is no "silver bullet" promising successful local adaptation to a global era. Cities vary on so many salient dimensions—from the fiscal powers granted them by their state legislatures, their economic bases, their social structures and social capital, and their environmental features to their share of the metropolitan area—that it is unrealistic to search for the one best solution. Yet these static dimensions and conditions are not sufficient explanations for local variations in policy choices. The mobilization of different interests and organizations with competing definitions of local economic development problems is crucial. This mobilization is not merely a matter of interests and resources: we see new ideas and institutions as shaping local political dynamics by changing how people think about local development and by giving some voices more weight than others (Clarke and Gaile, 1997).

At issue is not only the effectiveness of these new arrangements in addressing problems but their compatibility with other local interests and institutional relations. The emerging focus on competitiveness and innovation in economic processes, for example, frames policy solutions and institutional arrangements in terms of performance measures rather than expenditure programs meeting other values and serving other interests (Mayer, 1994).

5. A fourth wave of local policy initiatives will center on linking localities to global webs and investing in human capital.
The theoretical framework informing our empirical work leads us to anticipate a fourth wave of local policy initiatives investing in human capital initiatives and linking local economies to global markets through trade and telecommunications strategies.

The waves of local policy change over time surfacing in our analyses reflect efforts to adapt to these economic changes. They mirror the contemporary understandings of economic growth processes and the competing interpretations of new trends. For a brief period in the 1970s, national programs championed particular interpretations of growth trends that appeared plausible and accommodated national political dynamics. Cities learned certain entrepreneurial skills during this federal period; in the absence of this national role, few have returned to risk-averse positions, although most have scaled back local development efforts. Many continue selected use of entrepreneurial strategies for coping with the changing nature of economic competition and increased capital mobility. As currently adapted by most cities, however, this entrepreneurial orientation overlooks the importance of human capital development and information technologies (Parker, 1995). If local policy waves continue to be prodded by adjustments to economic and technological change, we anticipate the next wave of local economic development policy change—the fourth wave, by our count—will direct greater attention to the integration of human capital and economic development concerns and to the information infrastructure necessary to link local economies with the global web.

6. Inattention to the erosion of citizenship and decline in social capital will undermine local development efforts.

Reinventing government is an insufficient policy goal; reinventing local citizenship in a global era is a necessary element in policy frameworks at the national, state, and local levels.

The sectoral shifts to a service and information-based economy promote new economic growth, but they also generate growing inequalities. In some ways, the inequalities stemming from these economic changes are more invidious and difficult to confront than racial or gender discrimination, because they appear to reflect a meritocratic distribution of rewards (Bluestone, 1995). By valuing and rewarding education and training, these new sectors act as "the inequality express" (Bluestone, 1995): they privilege those individuals with the proper credentials and distribute earnings in line with formal education. As the gap between the earnings of the more and less educated grows, inequalities escalate. Even college education is becoming less of a buffer against joblessness and stagnant incomes (Uchitelle, 1994); disparities increasingly are tied to differences in the growth of earnings for different occupational groups, distinguished by specialized skills (Mincy, 1994b).

Thus skills alone—investing solely in human capital programs—are not sufficient to restore the economic and social well-being necessary for meaningful citizenship. Reconnecting citizens with jobs, with information channels, and with each other is a crucial and elusive task. Although Reich (1991) champions human capital investment, he also recognizes that shoring up social capital is essential to the success of these economic efforts. In Reich's argument, we are no longer "we": globalization has launched separate boats in which some workers are sailing smoothly but most—four-fifths, in Reich's estimate—are in rough waters or already sinking.

We think there is more to this argument. These trends toward greater income inequalities and the secession of the rich are especially strong in American cities. While federal aid to cities has declined precipitously since the Carter administration, transfer payments to individuals have increased dramatically. Yet social polarization and segregation continue to grow, and our sense of citizenship erodes as we feel less in common with one another. Thus human capital investment is a necessary but not sufficient local response to globalization. Enhancing the prospects for social capital—the associational ties and norms binding people together—is a precondition for reconstructing local citizenship and ensuring smoother sailing in American cities.

The Plan of This Volume

This new worldview is more familiar at the local level than at the national level, even as it is still debated within scholarly circles. In this book, we examine these propositions about the work of cities with statistical analyses of the actual policy choices cities make and through interviews with those most directly experiencing globalization and economic restructuring processes—local officials and activists in American cities. We tell their story in terms of how larger globalization and federalism trends reconfigure the problems cities face and the choices officials make about their local economies.

Overall, we find evidence that, in the absence of national resources, many cities continue to use specific entrepreneurial skills learned in earlier national programs, that distressed cities are now more likely to innovate and try these experimental strategies, and that policy specialist networks are facilitating this shift in a city's worldview. Furthermore, we present preliminary evidence that the next wave of local policy choices entails crafting local responses to globalization that integrate rather than isolate citizens. As Reich's (1991) argument reminds us, the problems now facing cities are more than economic: globalization trends are recasting local citizenship as well as local economies. We reach these conclusions by taking up the six propositions in turn, in chapters 1 through 8.

In chapter 1, we consider the proposition that a new geography of value-added production processes underlies the work of cities. We use Robert Reich's (1991) *The Work of Nations* to sketch the critical points in the transformation of the United States to a postindustrial economy situated in a global web. This is a familiar story to many. Reich, however, places particular emphasis on how new production processes and changing employment structures contribute to a new geography of human capital. We recast his story to draw out the interactions of these national economic and political changes and local policy initiatives. The era of economic nationalism, for example, supported the growth of "national champion" corporations in the American economy during the twentieth century, backed by government policies, and encouraged communities to seek such champions to bolster their local economies. As these national champions faltered in the face of international economic challenges, the national economy was transformed by changing production processes and new forms of global competition. A new political landscape emerged as well, featuring state devolution and new and unfamiliar economic and political roles for cities.

Reich's account is not the only story about this period, but he is one of the few to weave together the economic trends, political dynamics, and policy implications.[3] His work provides an effective organizational frame for our work; it presents a window for understanding why cities made the choices they did throughout the postwar period. Although Reich does not dwell on the local implications of his national analyses, his emphasis on the shift to high value-added production processes and on the importance of human capital investment persuades us that these issues are at the core of local development in a global economy. In chapter 2, we examine shifting state relations and trends toward state devolution by delineating the geographic, economic, and political settings in which American cities function. Our belief is that the problems facing American cities are not limited to older cities but involve all cities' capacities for adaptation and policy change. American cities work and adapt under the constraints imposed by federalism and global capitalism. Because these structural constraints take different forms at different historical moments, we describe three policy settings that shaped the choices available to cities: the smokestack-chasing era, the federal partnership era, and a more entrepreneurial, nonfederal era.

Chapter 3 presents an empirical study of the proposition that localities increasingly are political arenas for negotiating economic development and social tensions. In order to explore the emergence of local entrepreneurial policy choices in the face of economic and political restructuring processes, we draw on our study of large (more than 100,000 population in 1975) American cities' development policy choices during the federal partnership era and the recent era of dwindling federal resources. Our analyses track the policy shifts theorized and debated by other authors: we find three distinct waves of policy use since the 1970s and evidence of the emergence of a fourth policy wave. These local development choices increasingly are cast beyond the familiar questions of mobilizing land and capital to encompass broader concerns. In the course of the analyses reported in chapters 3 and 4, we consider a range of arguments about why and how cities learn these new approaches: whether new entrepreneurial orientations were learned in past national program experience; whether cities merely mimic their competitors' policy choices; whether innovation is more likely in conditions of stress or in times of slack resources; and whether innovation is diffused through networks of policy specialists. Overall, neither spatial nor temporal diffusion arguments account for these waves of different policy use. There is no significant evidence that cities adopt policies in response to choices made by neighboring cities. Nor is entrepreneurial use of federal resources significantly related to current entrepreneurial strategy choices. Thus policy learning is not necessarily contingent on a city's previous policy experience or on spatial competition. This suggests the need for a more detailed analysis of the conditions under which cities now choose various strategies.

In chapter 4 we go on to test the proposition that localities choose contextually specific paths in transforming their local economies. The local context shapes strategy choices as well as institutional design choices. Our analyses indicate that local slack resources were associated with entrepreneurial use of national resources during the federal partnership era. However, there is a distinct shift in the postfederal period to use of entrepreneurial policies by cities facing significant employment stress and fiscal and social problems. Thus in the federal period, better-off cities were more innovative, whereas now need appears to be more determinative. Furthermore, political conditions shape these choices: they are most likely in cities with strong mayoral leadership. And policy networks, particularly participation in training programs such as those sponsored by the National Development Council in the 1980s, distinguish those cities choosing entrepreneurial strategies from other cities.

Most research on subnational economic development policy effectiveness is inconclusive. In our empirical analyses we employ standard statistical techniques coupled with spatial statistical analyses to explore the policy effectiveness issue. The spatial statistical techniques filter out the heavy regional "noise" hampering other studies; our analyses yield some modest positive results. We establish a positive (though weak) statistically significant relationship between the use of entrepreneurial policies and favorable outcomes such as employment growth, the addition of fast-growing industries, and lower government taxes and expenditures. Further, we find specific entrepreneurial strategies associated with positive job growth and business formation indicators.

Numbers alone are seldom compelling or convincing. We continue the exploration of local context in chapters 5 and 6 by using comparative case studies to illustrate another significant local choice: the institutional framework used to make local development decisions. In the course of our study, we visited several cities; here we present four—Cleveland, Tacoma, Syracuse, and Jacksonville—that shared a history of federal program participation but responded differently when making choices in the absence of federal resources. In these cases, we focus on the ways in which these cities restructured the institutional context for local economic development policy making in the absence of national guidelines. We see these context-structuring processes as the heart of local transformation and adaptation processes: they shape who the players are, what values will be maximized, what the rules of the game are, and, consequently, what the agenda priorities and preferred strategies will be. What emerges from these comparisons is a mosaic of distinctive policy paths. This highlights the absence of any "silver bullet" approach to city transformation and underscores the political aspects of developing contextually specific initiatives.

In chapter 7 we consider the likely features of the fourth wave—the future work of cities. Our discussions with local officials over the past seven years—and Reich's template—persuade us that global-local links and human capital-oriented policies are the essential components of the next (fourth) wave of urban development policy initiatives. This next wave builds on two issues: How do cities rethink their position in response to globalization trends and make choices that better incorporate them into the global web? And how can they respond to the growing economic importance of human capital? We introduce and analyze the concept of *unmet human capital potential* as a way of looking at what will be forgone in local economies if human capital investments are not pursued. We construct human capital "report cards" for American cities to assess the gaps that we call unmet human capital potential. Given the national stalemate on the human capital issue, America's cities face a daunting policy task. Yet our follow-up survey, conducted in 1996, indicates that most cities are launched on the fourth wave; in particular, they are developing trade and telecommunication strategies to link their communities with the global web and, in many cases, they are experimenting with human capital investment initiatives.

We conclude in chapter 8 with the proposition that inattention to the erosion of citizenship and decline in social capital will ultimately undermine any local development efforts. We question whether "reinventing government" along the lines of the corporate model is appropriate or sufficient. The corporate model of a "businesslike city" does not encourage citizenship, has little in the way of a normative component, and may well be inappropriate for local governments trying to satisfy multiple objectives. Clearly, we hope to push the political debate beyond "reinventing government" to reconstructing citizenship. We reject the political calculations marginalizing many urban citizens—that they have little to contribute to a global economy and even less stake in participating in political processes. Rather than seeing the poor and unskilled as a cost, we argue that those fully understanding the economic and geographic changes of the twenty-first century will see these groups as presenting questions of unmet potential. Local citizenship in a global era presumes that citizens will have the social and economic means to participate in a viable, responsive local government. In the absence of a fuller understanding of the new work of cities in the twenty-first century, local citizenship will continue to deteriorate, and narrow efforts at local economic development will be misguided.

These themes of a new geography of production, shifting state power, new local political roles, context-specific development paths, rising concerns with telecommunications and human capital, and eroding citizenship inform the following chapters. We address them in a number of different ways, ranging from statistical analyses to interviews to historical narratives. The emerging picture of the new work of cities foregrounds the importance of seeing the unmet human capital potential in local citizens and the necessity of encouraging the social capital that will make investments in human capital effective in both economic and citizenship terms.

1

Transcending Scale

Nationalism, Globalism, Localism

*A new geography of value-added production
processes underlies the work of cities.*

In this chapter we trace the emergence of a new geography of value-added production processes by drawing on Robert Reich's framework in *The Work of Nations* (1991). Reich's narrative presents an economic and political history of the last half century as the United States transformed from an industrial giant to a postindustrial economy situated in a global web. In a sense, the telling and retelling of this transformational story has become a marker of the millennium (see Drucker, 1994; Krugman, 1995; Porter, 1990).

To Reich, this story is one of new production processes and changing employment structures that contribute to a new geography of human capital. In the past, value-added production was based on locations where factor costs were most favorable; urban geography reflected these patterns of factor cost production processes. As Reich (1991) points out, new economic processes add value—and wealth—through human capital investments. In his account, the economic geography of the coming century will be based increasingly on the distribution of human capital.

We rely here on Reich, rather than on other relevant and insightful authors, in part because he extends his analysis to incorporate consideration of policy alternatives. Yet his analyses and policy prescriptions are primarily situated at the national level and leave out matters of local choice. Thus we recast his story to draw out the interactions of national economic changes, local policy contexts, and local policy initiatives. This requires greater attention to interpretations of the local political implications of globalization trends and to the economic and political constraints limiting local initiatives in American cities.

The Era of Economic Nationalism

Until the late nineteenth century, the national economy was a loosely knit web of local economies. The notion that the nation's citizens shared a common economic fate took hold slowly, but by the end of the century a true national economy had evolved as a national transportation system developed (through heavy national and state subsidies) and a national capital market was created. Industrial innovations rapidly diffused throughout the nation, resulting in a transformation of the economy into one characterized by high-volume industrial production processes. In the early twentieth century, industries responded to overproduction problems by reducing domestic competition through consolidations into large nationally based corporations.

In Reich's (1991) narrative from *The Work of Nations*, this emerging era of economic nationalism saw giant corporations determining the success of the national economy and the well-being of American citizens. American national government was reluctant to regulate industry and markets despite the national concern regarding the evils of monopoly. Even with the passage of the Sherman Antitrust Act of 1890, corporations continued to grow through mergers into giants that effectively allowed them to control prices. Their control and competitive advantage were further facilitated by the scale economies that their sheer size engendered. Debates over the rise of giant corporations replaced earlier tariff debates, but the rebuttal was the same for both—they were necessary to stem foreign competition and they were seen as efficient firms and providers of substantial employment. Yet a nagging concern remained: the corporate giants were viewed as economic renegades, relatively free from political control and lacking public accountability.

According to Reich, by the time of the New Deal, some notion of accountability on the part of large corporations was growing. In return, the government continued policies of protectionism, but assisted in passing favorable laws to facilitate labor bargaining. As the existence and persistence of giant corporations became entrenched, "gradually, the top executives of America's largest corporations would come to view themselves as 'corporate statesmen,' responsible for balancing the claims of stock holders, employees, and the American public. Surprisingly, the American public would come to share this view" (Reich, 1991, 42).

By the middle of the twentieth century, Reich claims, the nation's core corporations had matured into "national champions." The debates about the evils of giant corporations had been stilled by their service to the country in World War II and by the economic success that permeated the post-war era. The American business community heralded this prosperity in a spirited public relations campaign that extolled the wonders of the free market system (and quashed inclinations to return to wartime controls or state interference) and the virtues of mass consumption. The national champions, the largest corporations, were the purveyors of the products of mass production. They dominated the nation's economy, accounting for half of the national output and the lion's share of assets and profits. The giants of these large corporations sported economic growth figures that rivaled those of some European nations. Banded together as roughly twenty-five industries, they set norms on wages, prices, and methods of production. Thousands of individual corporations served the giants, and, in turn, hundreds of thousands of smaller firms provided specialized goods and services. The giant corporations perceived their prosperity as determining that of the nation. "As steel goes, so goes the nation" was a representative attitude.

According to Reich, the general prosperity of the United States in the 1950s led the government to strike a "national bargain" with its giant corporations in an effort to maintain the status quo. This further underscored the acceptance of the legitimacy and performance of the "national champion" corporations. The government would employ a "hands-off" policy on industry, with only minimal regulations in such areas as safety, health, and the environment, and would not attempt to influence corporate decision making through planning or to enforce antitrust legislation.

The government would, however, assume some responsibility for continued corporate profitability by helping to smooth out business cycles and by encouraging the economy through low-interest loans. Corporations would keep their end of the bargain by continuing to produce a large volume of goods at high enough prices to ensure substantial revenues that would allow both reinvestment in new capital goods and some distribution of the largesse to middle-class voters. Further, the government would support a good educational system to train the labor pool for the corporations. In providing for the national defense, the government would grant research and development funds and contracts to American corporations for that cause. The cause of defense was broadly writ; it included the National Defense Education Act and the National Highway Defense Act, both programs having substantially greater civilian than military impacts. Finally, the government would encourage the global expansion of American capitalism. By 1960, large American corporations were more actively seeking international markets, and the United States was playing a lead role in global economic development through its hegemonic influence on the World Bank, the International Monetary Fund (IMF), and the General Agreement on Tariffs and Trade (GATT) process. The large scale and technological superiority of American industry fostered the global diffusion of American capitalism.

Localism in an Era of National Champions

Local economic development initiatives must be seen in this historic context. Given our decentralized federal structure, a community's collective standard of living depends on the health of the local economy. Cities, like nations, compete for economic investment, but cities are not in a legal position to impose tariffs and other protective restrictions. Thus industries and households migrate freely among American cities. To compensate for their weak controls over their own economies, and to counteract potential employment and economic opportunity loss, cities often subsidize industries to attract them to or retain them in their localities. This subsidy-based "smokestack chasing" among urban competitors justifies local tax breaks for firms in terms of the overall benefits to the community from more jobs and net tax revenues. Thus the sacrifice of forgone tax revenues—as well as environmental degradation and other opportunity costs—is portrayed as being in the overall self-interest of local citizens.

These structural conditions mean that employment, revenue, taxes, and multiplier effects generated by large corporations give them a highly privileged position in American cities, especially those cities that are dominated by single industries. Not surprisingly, city development policies in the 1950s mirrored the country's attitude toward these "national champions." The prevailing regional growth theory was that of "economic base," which argued that a city's economy was determined by what it "exported" out of the local economy (Tiebout, 1962). These "basic industries" provided for the import of revenue into the local economy, which in turn was used to support the myriad (nonbasic) firms that operated solely within the local economy. The implication for city officials was evident—attract and retain basic industries, that is, the large national champion corporations.

In cities, the "corporate statesman" role was paralleled by a "corporate civic leader" role. Chambers of commerce, under the guiding hands of top executives from large corporations, strongly influenced local governance. Campaign contributions to corporate-friendly officials consolidated corporate influence on civic affairs. Many cities operated as "growth machines" (Logan and Molotch, 1987), reflecting the correspondence in the corporation's need for city support and the city's needs for tax revenues and jobs generated by the firm. The corporations had heavy investments in plants that were fixed in location. They also required infrastructural support (ports, roads, water supplies), which often provided external economies to the city. They required large skilled and unskilled labor forces, which depended on the city for housing, education, recreation, and other services. And because of their sheer size and economic impact, their corporate images became linked with the cities they dominated: Pittsburgh and steel, Akron and rubber, Toledo and glass, and, most notably, Detroit the Motor City (Motown).

But cities were affected in varying ways by the postwar "national bargain." On the one hand, many cities benefited from postwar national investments in defense and education. Those cities where world-class universities grew and prospered remain beneficiaries of one of the most important assets in today's global economy. The postwar investments in defense, however, were more geographically diverse and spatially biased against the traditional industrial heartland. The diffusion of the defense industry into the South and West during World War II (for strategic reasons) resulted in these areas' receiving great benefits from government contracts during the Cold War arms race. Along with the continued diffusion of industries from the northern and central regions to the southern and western areas, and the increased birthrate of new firms in those regions, these investments spurred the emergence of the Sunbelt region as the postindustrial center of the American economy.

The Snowbelt-Sunbelt migrations (Abbott, 1987; Weinstein and Firestine, 1978) of the 1970s and 1980s signaled a demographic upheaval: Americans became the most mobile populace in any peaceful advanced industrial nation. People and firms headed for the growing cities in California, Florida, Arizona, and Texas, among others. With the traditional urban demographics of natural population increase and rural-urban migration generally inconsequential by the second half of the century, this mobility manifested itself almost completely as urban-urban migration. In this near zero-sum game, one city's gain was another's loss. The losers were the main homes of the national champions. Cleveland and St. Louis, among others, lost more than half their peak population by the 1990s. Government-sponsored attempts to foster the internationalization of American capitalism also affected cities differentially. Ocean port cities, centers of trade and capital markets, and cities with busy international airports prospered disproportionately to more landlocked (freshwater port) industrial cities in the heartland, while other landlocked cities outside the industrial heartland that were well served by transportation prospered.

The changes *within* American cities were no less dramatic. The National Highway Defense Act had a major impact on American cities. The greater access and mobility the highway system provided radically changed the face of urban America. Intercity transportation was greatly facilitated, generating a marked increase in the mobility of American people and products. The new freeways allowed people employed in central cities to trade off "space for place" and move to the relative safety and spaciousness of the suburbs, where schools and parks were better and crime less a concern. The declining tax base in the central cities led to a precipitous fiscal spiral that accentuated the city-suburb differences. Wealthy suburban neighborhoods saw improved schools, recreation, and community services, while the central cities saw a general decline in these community assets. As David Harvey points out: "It is intriguing to note that since the 1930s the United States has experienced the most sustained rate of economic growth (capital accumulation), the greatest growth in the white-collar sector, and the most rapid rate of suburbanization of all the advanced capitalist nations. These phenomena are not unconnected" (1989, 122).

Reich (1991) and others note, however, that while a majority of the populace shared in the heady postwar consumerism of the growing middle class, the very poor remained nearly invisible, especially people of color. Women shared in the growing prosperity indirectly, mostly depending on their marital status, and if directly, only peripherally because of lower wages. In the cities, this persistent poverty was exacerbated by economic and racial segregation. As the middle class deserted central cities for the suburbs, segregation contributed to the ghettoization of the poor black population (Morrill, 1965; Massey and Denton, 1993). In many industrial cities, this constituted hypersegregation of racial and ethnic groups: these groups were physically, socially, economically, and politically isolated from the majority community (Massey and Denton, 1993). This isolation made them particularly vulnerable to the economic shocks attendant to the decline of economic nationalism in the 1970s.

The Decline of the National Champions

As Reich relates, by the 1970s the methods of high-volume production of standardized goods had diffused to other countries, often through multinational corporations with American roots. These foreign firms and multinational subsidiaries were staffed by production workers earning lower wages and benefits than American workers (Dunning, 1993). They could sell their wares on the global market at highly competitive prices. Further, transport and communication costs were declining rapidly as products themselves became more portable with the usage of transistors and computer chips.

Of equal consequence was the fact that American national champion giant corporations could no longer set prices in the face of foreign competition. According to Reich, the initial response to this trend was a strong return to protectionism. By 1980, one-third of the standard goods in the United States by value were protected (1991, 71). Foreign governments were asked to exert "voluntary" trade restraint, knowing that if they declined they would be embargoed by quotas. This strategy failed. Protection actually hurt related industries; for instance, automakers were forced to purchase more expensive American steel, thereby eroding their competitive advantage with foreign competitors. A second response entailed cutting costs of high-volume production through wage cuts and the "rationalization" of operations. America's giant corporations closed inefficient factories, laid off workers, and set up factories abroad to take advantage of cheap labor. These policies also failed to save the hegemonic position of the national champion corporations, because the giants had left the world of imperfect competition and entered a strongly competitive market. By definition, competition strips away excess profits. The familiar corporate prosperity through profit surplus had evaporated.

The third strategy was financial dexterity. Initial attempts at simple conglomerate formation failed to yield new economies of scale, and most acquired assets were sold off with little or no gain. Then the Reagan administration's deregulatory zeal assisted a wave of financial restructuring as corporate executives utilized the tax advantages hidden in hostile takeovers and leveraged buyouts. This did not change the production system, however, and, as Reich notes, the corporate headquarters boardroom turned out to be an awkward locale for playing the stock market. American core corporation profits continued to decline.

These efforts to save the national champions had differential impacts on cities. Whereas protectionism had some locational component depending on industry, the strategies of "rationalization" and "financial dexterity" had especially strong locational impacts. The resulting layoff of workers and the closing of factories crippled local economies and disrupted the local political order. The Youngstown, Ohio, steel mill closings are poignantly documented by Buss and Redburn (1983). The decline of the "corporate civic leader" is clearly portrayed in the 1989 movie *Roger & Me*, which details the travails of Flint, Michigan, and the civic unaccountability of corporate executives.

Financial restructuring was accompanied by locational dexterity.

Many corporations were no longer run by long-standing "civic leaders" with local ties, but instead by managers of conglomerate firms located elsewhere. These changes left many cities unsure of their "economic base." Investments and jobs became more mobile and volatile, often leaving industrial cities with substantially reduced tax revenues and greatly increased social burdens. The national champion economic strategies pursued by many cities seemed increasingly anachronistic. In this new era, cities seemed in even less control of their economic destiny than in the age of national champions.

The national champion strategy to revitalize the large American corporation as a means of shoring up economic nationalism is, according to Reich, no longer viable. He claims that American corporations no longer exist in any meaningful way and that any policy aimed at their revitalization is based on vestigial thoughts. Reich argues that the American standard of living now depends less on American corporations or a "national economy" than it does on the worldwide demand for the skills and insights the American *people* possess. *Human capital* is the basis for wealth in the new economy. Whereas Reich centers his argument on the national policy implications of the decline of national champions, we argue that the work of cities is changing as well as cities take on new economic and political roles in the global web.

The Global Web

Reich maintains that the heart of today's economy is a "global web" of decentralized units continuously contracting with a wide array of similarly diffuse working groups all over the world: "The threads of the global web are computers, facsimile machines, satellites, high resolution monitors, and modems—all of them linking designers, engineers, contractors, licensees and dealers worldwide" (1991, 111). This transformation from a hierarchical economy based on national champions to one interwoven in a global web is momentous. It is also singularly local. We trace these local implications below in discussing three key features of the contemporary economy:

1. The shift from high-volume to high value-added production processes
2. The integral role of human capital in the changing nature of international economic competition
3. The hollowing-out processes underlying the new localism and the new geography of human capital

High Value-Added Production Processes

The shift from *high-volume* to *high value-added* production entails a con-comitant market shift. High value-added production responds to special-ized customers. Thus high value-added business is unique and not easily duplicated, because the business strategies involved require highly special-ized knowledge. The global web features a high value-added production system in which products are international composites and few have na-tional identities. Indeed, international trade is often in intellectual services rather than durable products. Much of this occurs within complex global corporate structures (indeed, in 1990 half of U.S. international trade was within global corporations). These corporations are flexible and multi-national (Christopherson, 1989). Although they still characterize them-selves as "loyal citizens," their capital investments in specific nations and cities are more fluid and less intense than in the era of national champions.

If, as Reich argues, this new global web no longer survives and thrives based on economies of scale, this would confirm the "end of geography" thesis. The centralized locations necessary to achieve economies of scale now seem less meaningful; indeed, globalization trends and hypermobile capital appear to neutralize locations. The traditional location-based link-ages and multiplier effects are certainly less obvious than in the past. But certain externalities that could broadly be classed as urbanization economies remain salient. This is true not only for world cities (Knox and Taylor, 1995), but for nearly every city if we recognize that "the work of glob-alization" takes place through the practices of multiple formal and informal enterprises at the local level (Sassen, 1996).

The Integral Role of Human Capital

Along with Porter (1990), Marshall and Tucker (1992), and Dertouzos, Lester, and Solow (1989), Reich (1991) interprets the diffusion of high-volume production processes globally as shifting attention to the role of human capital investment as a critical element in high value-added pro-duction processes nationally. *Human capital,* the analytic and information skills critical to the capacity to innovate and diffuse useful ideas, becomes a key element of profitability and wealth creation. In the new global competi-tion, America's new national champion is no longer found among its corpo-rations; it is the nation's stock of human capital. The policy issue becomes when and by whom value is added; the implications are that value is added most significantly where human capital is effectively used to identify, solve, and broker problems.[1]

Symbolic Analysts and the Skills Revolution

These human capital issues become especially significant when we consider the intersect of the skills revolution and the international division of labor. The domestic implications of the unfolding of the skills revolution have merited serious attention (Lasswell, 1965; Harrison, Kelley, and Gant, 1996). The local impacts are especially pronounced.

Reich (1991) argues that three basic categories of work are emerging: routine production services, in-person services, and symbolic-analytic services. These categories are difficult to match with previous classificatory schemes (Sass, 1990). Basic education skills may suffice for the repetitive tasks performed by routine production service workers earning hourly wages. In 1990, about one-quarter of jobs in the United States fell into this category, but that percentage is declining as routine production jobs move overseas. In-person service workers also tend to engage in simple and repetitive tasks, but the distinction is that they work with their clientele on a person-to-person basis; they, too, are usually paid by the hour. In 1990, this group accounted for 30 percent of American jobs, and that percentage is increasing. Finally, the broad category of workers Reich dubs "symbolic analysts" account for no more than 15–20 percent of American jobs, yet Reich sees these workers as the primary source of value-added because they contribute to key aspects of the global economy. These workers manipulate symbols and wield analytic tools to allocate resources more efficiently, to move financial assets, and to yield new inventions or applications.[2] Although these symbolic analysts may, as Reich claims, contribute the greatest amount of value added to the economy, their contribution should not be taken out of context: along with routine production workers and in-person service workers, they constitute the "concrete economic complexes" in which "the work of globalization gets done" (Sassen, 1996, 630).

These analysts play valued roles in the economy of the global web: problem identifier, problem solver, and strategic broker.[3] Strategic brokers link both problem identifiers and solvers to work together and help market the products of this collaboration. Profits flow from the success of this customized linkage. Locationally, this customized linkage *may* be global, involving skilled human capital from various international locales. But also, by the very fact that it requires close, frequent, and informal contact among the various links, it may find optimal locations in particular local environments.

Thus, in the Schumpeterian tradition, Reich (1991) locates value in the capacity to continue to innovate; this shifts the focus from product to

process. In Reich's account, those now adding value in production processes are dramatically different from those in the era of economic nationalism.
Different types of workers are valued now; these changes in employment
structure and the spatial distribution of these workers have implications for
both the national well-being and various city fortunes.

A Localized Geography of Human Capital

As a consequence of the changes discussed above, there is a distinctive and
localized new geography of human capital in the United States. Reich
claims:

> In the United States as in no other nation, symbolic analysts are
> concentrated in specialized geographic pockets where they live,
> work and learn with other symbolic analysts devoted to a common
> kind of problem-solving, -identifying and brokering. The cities and
> regions around which they have clustered, and the specialties with
> which these places are identified, are valued around the world.
> (1991, 234)

Thus the most important value-added processes in the global economy are inherently *localized*. Specific places have an agglomeration of
shared learning that locates this amalgam of knowledge in a way that is far
less portable than the mobility of a single idea. Despite the ease provided
by telecommunications and transport advances, there is often no substi-
tute for face-to-face interaction (Kanter, 1995). The more complex the
problems, the more strategic brokerage is needed, and the more the level
and rapidity of interaction become important. The more the level and rapidity of interaction become important, the more the ability to engage in
face-to-face interaction remains critical. The more critical the need for
face-to-face interaction, the greater the need for a constrained geography—that is, localism. As Reich notes, "In this highly efficient but informal
system, talents and abilities continuously shift to wherever they can add
most value" (1991, 237).

These agglomeration economies are familiar in classical industrial location theory (Webber, 1984; Harrington and Warf, 1995); they are now
being recognized as features of human capital investment and aspects of
competitive locational advantage. There is not, however, a simple or guaranteed strategy to spur development of clusters of high-skilled firms. Such
zones have evolved in a complex manner over time (Leslie, 1990; Saxenian,
1994) and are difficult to replicate. Nor is there any guarantee that these
clusters will persist, although Reich notes America's zones have been re-

silient over time. Most significantly, such strategies do not necessarily account for the well-being of the 80 percent of the populace employed in more vulnerable occupations. There is a dark side to this local dynamic. Reich's three boats analogy hints at the dilemma.

The Three Boats

With globalization and the loss of a distinct national economy comes a differentiation in the economic fates of citizens whose destinies are no longer linked together. As Reich puts it: "No longer are Americans rising or falling together, as if in one large national boat. We are, increasingly, in different, smaller boats" (1991, 173). Indeed, since 1973 polarization in income distribution in the United States has increased (Harrison et al., 1996; Bluestone and Harrison, 1982; Danziger, Sandefur, and Weinberg, 1994). Although these inequalities were accelerated by the Reagan-Bush administrations' regressive tax and social policies, and broader demographic factors, employment changes attendant to globalization also played a major role. Half of the people (and two-thirds of the children) living below the poverty line now are in households in which at least one member has a job (Reich, 1991). These trends toward greater income inequality and more working poor in the United States stem from the emergence of a global meritocracy based on an international division of labor. The lack of political will to redress these trends makes the American experience more dismal (e.g., Levine, 1995).

Reich's (1991) analogy of three different boats—one sinking rapidly, one sinking slowly, and the third rising steadily— illustrates this situation. The routine production workers' boat is sinking rapidly in the United States. Although these workers were paid relatively well when protected in the "national bargain" era of the 1950s, they are rapidly losing out to a global pool of lower-wage labor. With declining transportation and communication costs came declining profit margins on high-volume production. Jobs are "exported" to locales where wages are lower than in the United States. Union bargaining power has weakened with the evolution of the global web (e.g., approximately a half million workers are employed in *maquiladoras* across the Mexican border). In fact, routine production jobs (and lower- and middle-management jobs as well) are disappearing most rapidly in the traditional union industries of steel, automaking, and rubber (Reich, 1991, 213). This rapid decline has particular impacts on the male labor force concentrated in traditional blue-collar occupations ("Tomorrow's Second Sex," 1996).

In Reich's scenario, workers in the in-person service boat are sinking slowly and unevenly. Their pay is generally slightly higher than minimum wage; this is not a family wage, so more in-person service employment in the economy generates more working poor. These workers typically have few benefits associated with their employment. Because their work requires direct contact with their clientele, they are shielded from direct foreign competition, but, as Reich notes, they are vulnerable to job loss through automation: automatic teller machines, self-service gas stations, and even cable television.

In contrast, the symbolic analysts' boat is rising. Rapid technological advances in communications and transportation expand the market for their services. As the demand for symbolic analysts rises, their compensation demands also increase. The increased wages and consumption needs of symbolic analysts open up a variety of linked markets for in-person services as well as valorization of neighborhoods where these analysts and service providers cluster (Sassen, 1996).

The Secession of the Rich

This polarization of economic fortunes feeds spatial segregation. Their wealth and mobility allow the better-off symbolic analysts to secede from the other four-fifths of the nation. This secession is of little consequence at the national level, where the tax base reflects income rather than residency. But the symbolic analysts' contribution to greater national wealth is paralleled by their threat to local communities. City economies may benefit from the presence of symbolic analyst clusters, both directly and through multiplier effects of these clusters. But if these economic clusters, and those engaged in symbolic analyst tasks, withdraw into suburban or edge-city enclaves (Garreau, 1991) while still taking advantage of city amenities, the net local gain is problematic.

When the wealthy spatially segregate themselves within cities and in exclusive suburbs and exurbs, they can replicate high-quality public services through private means. There are more private security guards in the United States today, for example, than there are public police officers (Cunningham and Taylor, 1985). As a consequence, many cities have developed a split character—"dual" cities (Mollenkopf and Castells, 1991) or "divided cities" (Fainstein, Gordon, and Harloe, 1992)—wherein the streets are given over to a lower-class public and the wealthy reside and work in security buildings that are isolated from the public by walkways, enclosed shops and garages, and the use of security devices. To date, there has been little challenge to this secession:

The four-fifths of the population whose economic future is growing more precarious has not vociferously contested the disengage-
ment of the one-fifth whose economic future is becoming ever
brighter. The widening divergence in their incomes, the growing
difference in their working conditions, the regressive shift of their
tax burden, the difference in the quality of primary and secondary
education available to their children, the growing disparity in their
access to higher education, the increasing difference in recreational facilities, roads, security, and other local amenities available to
them—no part of this broad trend toward inequality has generated
overt resentment from the majority of citizens. (Reich, 1991, 282)

This growing spatial and social polarization creates a paradox: the
new geography of value-added production portends the growing importance of symbolic analysts, yet the spatial clustering of these groups can exacerbate income inequalities and segregation from the majority of workers
who fit into more vulnerable occupational categories. As Reich notes,
"Ironically, as the rest of the nation grows more economically dependent
than ever on the fortunate fifth, the fortunate fifth is becoming less dependent on them" (1991, 250).

Governmental collusion with this secession trend underscores the
pattern of American apartheid highlighted by Massey and Denton (1993).
The secession of the rich is enabled by political choices at the national,
state, and local levels. The role of federal highway programs and housing
policies in facilitating class- and race-biased suburbanization patterns is
well-known. Federal urban policies have favored investment in amenities
such as hotels, conference centers and research parks benefiting the well
skilled rather than the unskilled. Privatization of telecommunications and
the airways continues to focus investment in well-off areas.

At the same time, the secession of the rich undermines support of
local public programs. Local property tax revenues from corporations fell
from a level of 45 percent in 1957 to 16 percent in 1987 (Advisory Commission on Intergovernmental Relations, various years); local budgets increasingly are supported by sales taxes and user fees, which are more elastic but
tend to be more regressive. Central-city dwellers often have substantially
higher tax burdens than do their neighbors who have isolated themselves
in the suburbs, and their taxes buy them substantially lower-quality services (Ladd and Yinger, 1986). In the United States, local communities are
left to wrestle with a degree of social polarization and spatial segregation
not tolerated in other societies. As long as national and state governments
avoid facing the consequences of policies adopted to favor their broader

constituencies, many central cities will continue to suffer. This rending of the urban social fabric and economic base makes community and citizenship problematic issues.

The Rationale for a New Localism

The emergent global web has an important spatial dynamic. As sketched here, the dynamic centers on a new geography of value-added processes, building on localized stocks and agglomerations of human capital. These changes in scale, production structure, and value-added processes encourage a new localism, with cities taking on new economic and political roles and functions (Cooke, 1989; Goetz and Clarke, 1993; Persky and Wiewel, 1994; Preteceille, 1990). Adaptive roles may include, for example, taking on strategic broker roles in a local setting, promoting global-local trade ties, and encouraging the in-person service sector that supports symbolic analyst clusters. Globalization is a two-way street: not only are local fortunes shaped by global forces, but localities are actively engaged in constituting global practices and processes. Local officials do more than "mediate" global pressures; they make strategic choices about resistance, accommodation, and adaptation to these forces (Beauregard, 1995, 244). Broker roles also may encompass providing the public amenities that complement symbolic analyst functions and consumption preferences, such as convention centers, research parks, international airports, universities (Jaffe, 1989), and convenient access to leisure activities. Reich argues:

> So important are these public amenities, in particular the university and the airport, that their presence would stimulate some collective symbolic analytic effort even on parched desert or frozen tundra. A world-class university and an international airport combine the basic rudiments of global symbolic analysis—brains and quick access to the rest of the world. (1991, 238–39)

Rather than merely inferring localism or deducing local practices from economic processes, we begin by assessing why "place" or locality may be more or less important in light of these trends and consider the likely direction of local political response. For American cities in particular, this apparent new localism plays out within a series of structural constraints on local fiscal and social initiatives.

The End of Geography?

There is general agreement that the global context for local politics is characterized by an international division of labor, the hypermobility of finance capital, the substitution of capital for labor, and the growth of the service sector (Organization for Economic Cooperation and Development, 1983). Two different interpretations of the implications of these trends for local politics stand out: one positing the declining importance of localities, the other presenting the new localism argument in the context of the changing nature of competition and state devolution.

The initial interpretation of the impacts of globalization on localities was rather dismal. It truly signaled "the end of geography" (O'Brien, 1992): place becomes less important as financial market transactions occur independent of location. This is one of the more influential interpretations of global economic restructuring, a perspective depicting local actors with little room to maneuver. In this view, the hypermobility of capital pits community against community, nation against nation, in competition for private investment. This competition limits the abilities of nation-states and localities to carry out autonomous economic and social policies. From this viewpoint, globalization and technological change, in association with new flexible production processes and facilitated by the hypermobility of capital, spell the decline of local autonomy (Gottdiener, 1988; Clarke and Kirby, 1990). If places are becoming less important and the process of local decision making counts for little, local political analysis seems moot (Fuchs and Cox, 1991).

The Hollowing Out of the State?

Critics point out that restructuring and globalization are not the monolithic, universalizing processes often portrayed; rather, they are partial, incomplete, spatially uneven, and layered with other production processes (Logan and Swanstrom, 1990; King, 1990). But the nearly exclusive focus on hypermobile capital and changing production processes means important spatial and social changes tend to be merely "read off" or inferred from economic changes (Peck and Jones, 1994). Furthermore, the prevalence of the "geological metaphor" (Beauregard, 1995, 245) demarcating global, national, and local scales as distinctive vertical layers restricts theorizing about local responses to global change. To accommodate these new spatial and political dynamics, it is necessary to loosen the assumption that the work of globalization takes place at a national or supranational level (Kresl and Gappert, 1995).[4] Similarly, it is useful to acknowledge the interdependence of actors and practices operating at different scales and, indeed, socially constructing scale through their actions (Beauregard, 1995, 243).

Although there has been scant attention to, or agreement on, the attendant changes in institutional structures and strategies (Peck and Jones,

1994), recent accounts of the changing bases of competition and profitability and the geographic reconstitution of the state lay the groundwork for anticipation of diverse local roles. Alan Scott (1992), for example, argues that flexible accumulation means the sources of profitability shift from internal economies of the firm, gained through more efficient use of the factors of production, to production economies gained from minimizing transaction and linkage costs among firms, suppliers, innovators, and so on. The institutional implications point to an *opportunistic state* (Fuchs and Cox, 1991): local officials' economic development role is to sustain a local climate in which firms' transaction costs are minimized and premature closure on policy choices is avoided (Scott, 1992).

In contrast with the firm-specific subsidies of the era of economic nationalism, these orientations involve more activist public roles in structuring and positioning local economies. The focus of local efforts is the creation of conditions for successful enterprise, whether envisioned as Silicon Valley enclaves, "Marshallian industrial districts," or other differentiated niches. Relative to the managerialist state of the industrial period, the opportunistic state is more likely to follow market opportunities than any coherent public agenda.

Reich's view corresponds to Scott's contention that profits are derived from linkages and networks among production units and enterprise structures. But Reich's (1991) attention to the role of human capital investment suggests a different local response: here a *value-added* state role takes precedence. The spatial implication of this *value-added* emphasis is that cities will prosper depending on the strength of their human capital, particularly the extent to which their local employment structures feature symbolic analysts and related service workers versus routine production workers. Local efforts to support high value-added production processes and invest in human capital are likely.

But polarization of wages and job instability fosters anxiety and discontent. At the local level, it encourages tax and expenditure limitations that cripple the ability of local governments to function, much less invest in human capital development or meet the needs of those unable to make sufficient wages or find jobs. The local tax base is also undermined by suburbanization and other means of secession. This is prompting interest in strategies aimed at functionally reconstituting cities as if they were without suburbs (Rusk, 1993). Recent efforts to establish metropolitan and regional networks to recapture the wealth produced by urban agglomerations signal an attempt to functionally reintegrate the fortunate fifth.

Although suggestive, these approaches lack geographic precision and institutional direction. Jessop (1993) takes us further by noting the spatial implications of a shift from the familiar Fordist factor-driven competition to a Schumpeterian notion of innovation- and investment-driven competition in a global era. In contrast to the nation-state orientation of the Fordist era, he sees economic and technological changes contributing to a "hollowing out" of the state, in which supranational and local scales become more significant than the national scale. The process resembles the hollowed-out corporations with transnational headquarters in one country and operations elsewhere implicit in Reich's metaphor of the global web. But here the process is one of hollowing out of the nation-state as the locus of economic and political power is shifting *upward* to supranational institutions, *outward* to transnational networks of cities, and *downward* to subnational scales. Not that the nation-state withers away, but important economic and political functions shift to other scales. National context remains important (Ettlinger, 1994), but the national government becomes an enabler rather than a regulator ("New Economics of Growth," 1996). This hollowing-out process will differ according to political economic settings but presents a spatial and political parallel of post-Fordist processes.

From this perspective, the local economic policy niche emerges from the inadequacies of national government in dealing with these new economic processes. Decentralization and devolution occur at this historical moment precisely because of the inability of the central state to pursue sufficiently differentiated and sensitive programs needed by investors; as a consequence, there is a devolution of policy responsibilities to local policy arenas (Mayer, 1994). *Enabling* local roles stem from the need for cooperation of business and local governments at local and regional scales in activities that contribute to international economic competitiveness.

This accounts for the darker side of concern to Reich. This Schumpeterian perspective implies that at the national level, strategic macroeconomic policy orientations will emphasize promotion of innovation and structural competitiveness and the economies of scope Scott (1992) describes. Cities pursuing human capital development strategies may create what Jessop (1993) characterizes as a workfare state if their human capital orientation is framed in terms of labor flexibility and business needs. Welfare policies become workfare policies, and the social programs of the welfare state, including education and job training, become subordinated to competitive needs (see King, 1995). Notably, the public discourse of planning is displaced by a rhetoric of entrepreneurial agendas and public-private partnerships across policy arenas (de Neufville and Barton, 1987). Whether these entrepreneurial and workfare orientations prevail at the local level is perhaps contingent on local political configurations and state policy roles. For American cities, historical, political, and economic dynamics press local officials toward such entrepreneurial and workfare options.

All in all, Jessop's (1993) perspective provides a locus and direction to the new localism argument. In the era of national champions, for example, local corporate elites and factor-driven competition encouraged the "smokestack-chasing" and "arms race" economic development policies that shaped many localities' agendas. With globalization, the influence of alliances of land-based elites and public officials in local growth machines that historically shaped local development choices is eroding (Dicken, 1994; Goetz, 1994). Innovation- and investment-driven competition requires policies that accentuate differences among localities, or, as Hanson (1993) puts it, greater product differentiation. The importance of variations in production environments across localities and policy efforts to differentiate these settings provides a further economic rationale for local initiatives (Ettlinger, 1994).

What to Do? The Policy Implications of the New Localism

The arguments cited above provide compelling grounds for anticipating more local activism in a global era, but few clues as to the types of choices localities will make. Given the lack of consensus on which local attributes are most significant in a global era, local policy makers gain little guidance from scholarly theories. Reich claims that local production environments are distinguished by their human capital features, Scott emphasizes institutional flexibility, and Jessop warns of potential workfare states and the undemocratic practices of an opportunistic state.

Nor is there much direction from national policy makers. Previous administrations acted on interpretations of restructuring and globalization in ways that trivialized the roles of cities in the national economy (Barnekov, Boyle, and Rich, 1989). Through the 1980s they advocated the need for enhanced national competitiveness in an international economy and viewed any spatially targeted policies as hindering efficient locational investment decisions.[5] With the exception of recent emphases on "regionalism" (Swanstrom, 1996), no new articulation of a national policy for cities is evident.

In the absence of national policies or resources, and given the context of decentralized federalism and interjurisdictional competition for investment, the new localism picture in the United States is especially complex. From the city's perspective, the new terrain bears little resemblance to the era of economic nationalism and national champions. Well aware of competing ideas about globalization and restructuring, local officials recognize that new local roles are possible but remain uncertain about the consequences of different local paths. Local economic development strategies that work actively to support innovation, global-local links, and human capital are necessarily different from the smokestack-chasing schemes of the past. Even available information bases no longer fit the task.[6] Furthermore, the locus of new economic activity is not necessarily congruent with decision makers' political boundaries. This intensifies the need for cooperation across governmental levels as well as between public and private actors. Hollowing-out processes are as likely to engender conflict and tension over policy initiatives as cooperation between localities and other levels of government. To the extent that social polarization and spatial segregation accompany these changes (and we have argued they do in most American cities), local officials must make choices that recognize these diverse elements of the new local context.

Conclusions

Although there are many intriguing accounts of the responses of individual communities to restructuring and globalization pressures,[7] we lack a sense of the larger picture. Individual case studies are essential for an understanding of processes and relationships, but they can tell us little about the broader patterns of local policy responses. And many of these anecdotal studies are limited to familiar, well-studied cities. We do not yet grasp how globalization is experienced in Tacoma, Cedar Rapids, or Huntsville. Nor do we know how representative the understandings of local responses gleaned from more well-studied cities are for other communities.

To gain this more complete picture of local economic transformations, we build on the conceptual frameworks described above but turn our attention to matters of agency and volition. That is, we are interested in finding out what policy makers do when faced with the trends and dilemmas described so elegantly and persuasively by Reich and other scholars. The following chapters present our understanding of those larger patterns of local policy choices. We make no claims to a theory of local adaptive behavior in response to a global economy, but we argue that any such theory would need to take account of the theoretical and conceptual arguments presented here and the empirical relationships raised by our analyses.

2

The Changing Work of Cities

*Economic and geographic changes encourage
parallel shifts in state relations.*

From an era of dynamic central cities that were homes to the national economic champions, we have entered an era characterized by multilocational production processes, high value-added activities, a new international division of labor, and the growing significance of human capital resources. Here we consider the proposition that these broad economic transformations are accompanied by equally sweeping geographic shifts and some devolution of state authority across scales. To assess this new political context for local policy making, we consider evidence of hollowing-out processes, or state devolution trends, in which state authority is shifting from the national arena to subnational scales.

Overall, national policies lag the new global realities: through the 1980s, they failed to recognize the new economic roles cities play in a global era and the contribution of cities to a competitive national economy. Even worse, the political dynamics of American federalism and vestigial notions about economic growth processes encourage continuation of cost-reduction strategies that are increasingly irrelevant to the new work of cities.

Our critique centers on the extent to which national policies recognize the new geography of production, the increased importance of local human capital and social capital resources in national economic competitiveness, and the need to restructure local citizenship. From this perspective, the Clinton administration promotes a hybrid urban policy: it is grounded in prosaic cost-reduction orientations, but advances some initiatives to strengthen local institutional infrastructure, foster regional and metropolitan collaboration, encourage urban entrepreneurial climates, devolve decision making, and support human capital investment.

In this chapter we set out the geographic backdrop, the decentralized federal system, and the national political context in which local transformational efforts take place. It is a mistake to assume that these transformative dilemmas are restricted to older industrial cities. Our fieldwork and survey data indicate that many different types of cities are struggling to adapt to a context of changing production processes, global markets, and new human capital issues. In this chapter we chronicle the structural constraints limiting this adaptation and the eroding national support for and guidance of local initiatives.

Where Value Was Added: The Geography of Traditional Capital

Cleveland, Ohio, ironically, once sported the slogan "The Best Location in the Nation." This assertion was based on an assessment of metropolitan locations featuring minimum surface transportation costs relative to national markets in an industrial era (Harris, 1954). However, the industrial locational advantages that were critical to urban growth in the nineteenth century and the first half of the twentieth century are less economically relevant today.

Each of the twenty largest cities in the United States in 1950 was a port on either an ocean or an inland river. Today, the top twenty list includes Dallas, Denver, Indianapolis, Phoenix, and San Antonio—inland cities whose economies are not based on heavy industry. The geographic change in the national urban economy and labor force in the last half of the twentieth century has been remarkable. No other country has faced such dynamism in a territory not engaged in war. Charting the spatial progress of this change allows us to reflect on the economic and demographic structural changes that precipitated the near demise of America's "best locations."

The concentration in the United States of high value-added industry in 1958 was in a "triangle" roughly defined by Chicago, Boston, and Baltimore. In this period, this "manufacturing belt" accounted for more than 80 percent of the manufacture of special dies and tools, industrial controls, industrial patterns, safes and vaults, cutlery, pharmaceutical preparations, machine tool accessories, electron tubes, and pressed and blown glass, among other products, for which the value added as percentage of output was more than 70 percent (Pred, 1965, 116). Today, not only has the locus of high value-added changed, but so has the sectoral mix of industries (and more so services) that contribute to the overall value added to the economy.

Yet it is important to recognize that these historical patterns of industrial concentration were linked to more diffuse networks of specialized activities, presaging the current pattern of diverse geographic specialization that surfaces in our discussion of the "fourth wave" in chapter 7. Although manufacturing was undoubtedly spatially clustered at midcentury, other specialized sectors of the economy (then perceived as less important) were distributed over a much wider geographic space. Early classifications of city economies by Harris (1943) and Nelson (1955) showed this clearly. Harris (1943) demonstrated graphically that cities that specialized in retail, wholesale, resort, or educational activities were located outside the manufacturing belt. In Nelson's (1955) classification, the most highly specialized nonmanufacturing cities were San Francisco-Oakland, Atlanta, Minneapolis-St. Paul, and Dallas (finance, insurance, real estate); Miami (personal service); and San Diego and Washington (public service). All the most highly specialized cities were engaged in economic activity other than manufacturing, and all were outside the manufacturing belt.

By the 1980s, the "deindustrialization of America" was well under way (Bluestone and Harrison, 1982), and calls for the reindustrialization of America were strong (Abernathy, Clark, and Kantrow, 1983; Cohen and Zysman, 1987). Reich's (1991) reassessment of American comparative advantage in the global economy leads him to argue that bids to "reindustrialize" are wrongly targeted: the days of America's industrial giantism are being replaced by a new form of global competition. This is clearly reflected in the U.S. economy of today. For the United States in 1991, 68.6 percent of gross domestic product was attributable to services, compared with only 29.3 percent for industry, even though much of the high value-added sector of the economy (computers, telecommunications) still falls into the industrial category (World Resources Institute, 1994, 257). As human capital replaces the machinery, boilers, and smelters that were at the top of yesterday's economic heap, cities are facing massive adjustments.

This half century's economic dynamism has been accompanied by a parallel geographic dynamic. Yesterday's acclaimed manufacturing belt, which was the backbone of the national economy, is today's Rust Belt—the site of plant closures and population emigration. In many minds these old industrial cities have been written off as obsolete, like the industries they once championed. Now that there is no rubber made in Akron and little steel made in Pittsburgh, have these cities lost their raison d'être? Is there a life cycle to cities, especially those that have been industrially specialized, that implies a necessary acceptance of their eventual demise? This question is of interest to those living in the older cities themselves, but also to those in new specialist cities such as Portland, Oregon, with its advanced semiconductors cluster; Minneapolis, with its specialized medical devices and instruments sector; the Denver-Boulder area, with its telecommunications and biotechnology sector; and Little Rock and Fayetteville, with their investments in molecular biology and biotechnology (Reich, 1991, 234–35).

Rather than decline and obsolescence, we foresee a transformative process in which cities continually adapt to new political contexts and new production demands. Firms seek production environments appropriate to new production processes, technological needs, and market networks; this search increasingly is conducted on a global rather than a national scale. As firms seek the best locational fit for their investment needs, cities and regions have become the arena for global competition.[1] This turn of events means the decision context for city officials now is broader than local or national boundaries. These changing politics of scale are exemplified by the formalization of regional markets such as the North American Free Trade Zone. In this global marketplace, firms compete through technology and export capacity; the issue is whether cities can adjust to this turbulent environment and capture these new sources and forms of growth and wealth.

The Political Setting for American Localism

Although the American political tradition is one of decentralized and fragmented authority, indeed of localism, trends seeming to support new local economic and political roles may turn out to limit the options available to American communities. This paradoxical situation stems from the structural constraints in which American communities operate.

Structural Constraints on Local Policy Initiatives

Local policies are shaped and bounded by the decentralized political and fiscal political structures in which American cities are embedded. Many of the economic and political constraints imposed on localities by these structures are elegantly articulated as "city limits" by Paul Peterson (1981). Peterson's model of local policy choice portrays economic forces as determining subnational policies due to the decentralized American federal structure. In contrast to cities in many other advanced industrialized countries, American cities are relatively free from central oversight by national legislation and regulation (Gurr and King, 1987; Goldsmith, 1990). But in return for this historical tradition of local autonomy, they are more fiscally dependent for revenues on private investment in their local and regional economies. As a result, local governments often are more conservative and risk averse than the national government. With limited public authority and dependence on state enabling legislation for their fiscal powers, local governments seek a delicate fiscal balance of revenue, debt, and user fees to support their operations (Sbragia, 1996).

These circumstances create a calculation all too familiar to local officials. Peterson claims that business and residents will be attracted to places with the most favorable ratio of taxes paid to services received. Developmental policies supporting local economic activity enhance that ratio, and so it is "in the interest" of a polity to enact them because the resulting benefits are gained by all citizens. These developmental policies seem a constant imperative because each city is in competition with other cities; there is the anticipated threat that both residents and firms can exit whenever they perceive the benefit/tax ratio to be no longer favorable. Therefore, in Peterson's view, cities will have a unitary interest in creating economic activity that employs residents, generates tax revenues, and contributes to attractive locational sites for capital and households.

From this perspective, only limited policy choices are possible if cities are seeking primarily to maximize their economic position in a web of interjurisdictional—and now global—competition. In choosing local economic development policy strategies, local officials seek to promote investment, and hence aggregate development, in a particular location. In market economies (Lindblom, 1977, 173) governments cannot command business to invest; they must induce investment. Theoretically, a modest stimulus on the part of government can be of consequence to a local economy if the new public and private expenditures set in motion a multiplier effect—by creating new jobs or retaining existing ones, diversifying the local economy, and ultimately increasing the income and well-being of the populace. Hopefully, the incentives provided by the city stimulate new private investment that would otherwise not have been made in that location *but for* the inducements.

However, in reality, city officials face a prisoner's dilemma: each community is competing with others for private investments, but each is uncertain about what other deals are being offered; in the absence of sufficient information, there is a tendency to offer unnecessarily generous incentives to ensure that investors choose one's community (King, 1990). The bidding dynamic resembles an arms race in which incentives escalate as they are bid up and matched across states and communities (Hanson, 1993). As in the classic Ricardian rent model, cities act as bidders and the surplus profits are captured by the owners of the desired good—the businesses themselves (see Alonso, 1960). This dependency on private investment for local public revenues encourages every locality to make suboptimal choices—too high a subsidy is offered because the community does not really know the marginal costs of business affected by incentives (Jones and Bachelor, 1986). Given this uncertainty, and the political gains from "winning" the investment competition (Wolman, 1988), state and local governments tend to oversubsidize business investment. As a consequence of this "arms race" dynamic, and the perceived political and economic costs of not bidding, subnational economies are weaker than they would be otherwise (Wolman, 1988).

Not only does this competitiveness and uncertainty bias local agendas toward economic development policies and oversubsidization of businesses, it actively discourages local efforts to help those in need. In the deductive logic of Peterson's model, redistributional policies distort local fiscal ratios by directing services and benefits to those paying few taxes. The logic of interjurisdictional competition and necessary sensitivity to cost-benefit ratios implies that redistribution of local funds to social needs is not in a city's interest, given the burden such transfers place on the productive members of the community for the benefit of unproductive members. Furthermore, there are perceived opportunity costs in redistributing funds; local redistributional policies may make cities into welfare magnets (Peterson and Rom, 1990) and discourage future private investment. The implication is that, at best, only cities and states with growing economies can afford policies targeted at those in need or at those on the margins of the labor market (but see Goetz, 1994; Wong, 1988). More likely, the menu of local choices will shrink further in the face of greater global competition, with increasing emphasis on entrepreneurial economic development and the subordination of social policies.

Limits to the City Limits Model

Despite the elegance and logic of the city limits model, there is substantial empirical evidence that these are not determinative conditions constraining local policy choices (Goetz, 1990; Miranda and Rosdil, 1995; Elkins, 1995; Beauregard, 1995; Judd and Ready, 1986). Because local officials face a dual dilemma of satisfying economic interests and citizen demands (Friedland, Piven, and Alford, 1978), political mobilization in support of alternative policies—or benefit/cost ratios—can generate more diverse policy choices than the city limits model would suggest. Local political features and conditions, therefore, may counter some of the seeming imperatives created by the decentralized American federal structure. But in the absence of viable mechanisms such as coherent party structures or stable social change coalitions, local demands for redistribution are not easily translated into redistributive policies.

Similarly, the city limits model assumes that policy choices stem from the self-interest of officials predominantly concerned with reelection chances and tax-based budgets. But as we detail in chapters 5 and 6, increasingly local politics are characterized by nonelected public, private, and nonprofit actors as well as decision organizations and partnership arrangements that bridge public and private sectors and extralocal scales. The incentives shaping their policy choices are not as obvious as those assumed in the city limits model.

More intrinsic challenges to the city limits model, however, come from the very acontextual features that give it so much analytic power. Its analytic virtues are countered by an ahistorical bent. As the nature of economic competition changes, it is necessary to reconsider the extent to which Peterson's public choice model assumes local development policies centered on factor-cost competition. The logic of competition presumed by Peterson's model may be historically specific: it characterizes a period—the era of national champions and industrial production— in which growth occurred and wealth was gained primarily through the minimization of factor costs. Economic location theory suggests that, other things being equal, firms will seek those locations where the combined costs of land, labor, capital, energy, and transportation are minimal (Webber, 1984).

The historical predominance of "smokestack-chasing" locational incentive strategies mirrors this model of economic growth emphasizing the importance of factor costs—basically, the costs of land, labor, and capital— in production processes. Cities promoted policies to reduce those costs, acknowledging the threatened loss of investment to competing localities if incentives proved insufficient (Ambrosius and Welch, 1988). Thus, for the city seeking a competitive advantage over other cities, the logic is to create an advantageous price structure for "production factors," thereby creating a comparative locational advantage.

But as production processes shift from high-volume production to high value-added production processes, the nature of competition has changed, and with it the calculations facing local officials. As a result, communities may seek to differentiate themselves and their production environments, rather than become more like their competitors. Although some cities will still try to emulate competitors' urban success stories, the cities they are seeking to emulate are now performing within a global economy.[2] The traditional focus on the effects of interjurisdictional competition, therefore, must be complemented with greater attention to the global context shaping local economic development policy choices.

Nevertheless, given the widespread evidence of locational strategies, many cities continue to cope with changes in their environments by applying decision rules and programmatic solutions that worked in the past. In that sense, city development responses may be path dependent: they "lock in" the protected interests of certain sectors of the business community as well as solution sets linked to factor costs.[3] This limits the city's ability over time to adjust to changing constituencies and to address emergent problems unrelated to factor cost issues. Local institutions continue to reflect this past legacy of interests and economic growth models, particularly those articulated by past national programs. The constraints on cities' adaptive behavior, therefore, stem from the structural features of federalism privileging economic priorities, but also from the context of national-local relations.

The National Context of Local Policy Choices

The national context for local policy choices is beset by lags in adjusting policy assumptions about economic growth and scale to these new circumstances. These lags are reinforced by the weakening coalitional base for urban initiatives. As a consequence, the relations of national and local governments over the past decades have been marked by declining support and, we would argue, misspecified policies. More extensive analyses tracing the evolution of past federal-local programmatic links are available elsewhere (Barnekov, Boyle, and Rich, 1989; Bartik, 1994; Rich, 1993b). Here we sketch selected features of the recent national role in cities as a foundation for understanding the choices local officials make as state devolution trends reinforce the decline in national support.

The Era of Federal Partnership

American cities' relative dependence on private investment contributes to their long-standing record of economic development activities (Sbragia, 1996). Historically, this local activity centered on providing locational incentives. When economic competition centered on Fordist production processes, these growth models and factor cost strategies appeared to be appropriate bases for local strategies. National postwar programs for local areas also incorporated these growth models and provided additional incentives for local officials to focus on locational approaches. The national Urban Renewal and Model Cities programs of the 1950s and 1960s, for example, subsidized land clearance and redevelopment in selected cities in hopes of attracting private investors to blighted areas. The Great Society programs of the 1960s attempted to bring poor people into the economic mainstream by subsidizing the costs of improving deteriorating neighborhoods and the labor market skills of their residents.

The period from roughly the mid-1970s through the mid-1980s encompasses extensive, active national involvement in supporting place-based cost-reduction urban redevelopment schemes. By 1978, a new generation of federal programs supporting local economic development was in place and actively used. These programs consistently encouraged cities to focus on their economic roles, to assess their economic development needs, and to work with private investors on revitalization projects. The Urban Development Action Grant (UDAG) program started in 1978, the Economic Development Administration (EDA) Title II and IX programs encouraged local economic development efforts, and by 1984 the Community Development Block Grant (CDBG) program allowed use of local CDBG funds for extensive economic development activities, including loans and grants to for-profit entities.

In hindsight, this period was the height of national support for local economic development efforts. National policies centered on place-based cost-reduction strategies proved especially attractive in a decentralized federal system and territorially organized political structure. In Lemann's (1994) skeptical account, place-based policies persist because they are attractive to place-based politicians, to foundations interested in feasible, localized community development schemes, to business groups seeking support for small businesses, to grassroots groups craving a prominent community role, and to White House staff needing cheaper and higher-impact programs than those proposed by national agencies.

Along with these political factors, we contend that the continuing national policy emphasis on cost-reduction strategies reflects vestigial assumptions about growth processes. Both cost-reduction and place-based strategies slight new production arrangements and overlook the effects of globalization and regionalization trends on local communities. These communities no longer operate in closed economies or national investment circuits in which cost reduction is an effective option. Furthermore, the interdependence of local economies means that regional markets increasingly influence local well-being. Although it is a matter of continued debate, many argue that the wealth of suburbs is increasingly tied to the vitality of central-city areas (Barnes and Ledebur, 1991; Savitch and Vogel, 1996). Any belated national recognition of these new realities, however, was scuttled with the Republican capture of the White House and the ascendance of New Federalism in the 1980s.

Rationalizing Retrenchment

In the 1980s, the New Federalism approach to urban problems embodied two concerns: (1) a belief that national funds for local development encourage inefficient locational decisions and, consequently, a suboptimal national economy; and (2) a concern that national funds distort local agendas. By reducing these funds, the national government would reduce the potential for suboptimal investment decisions and let city agendas correspond more closely to local preferences. State programs were expected to take up the program slack where necessary; nonprofit organizations and private sector organizations were seen as more appropriate local development partners than federal agencies.

The expectation, therefore, was not necessarily that there would be either more or less local economic development effort. Perhaps those believing that an active public role in development is inappropriate may have hoped that fewer national resources would diminish local interest in economic development. But, overall, local efforts were expected to be more aligned with local needs and priorities. This match of local policy efforts and local priorities would be reflected in the public share in development costs as well; local officials investing state or local resources could be expected to be more prudent in both the amount invested and the level of risk accepted. And under these conditions of greater prudence, market feasibility would be a major factor in the choice of development projects. Indeed, it would be incumbent on local officials to work closely with persons and organizations in the private sector on development projects. The aims characterizing many previous national programs might be pursued if congruent with local views, but obviously would no longer be a necessary condition for public investment. Together, these expectations suggested that the withdrawal of national resources would lead to potential changes in local economic development approaches.

By the 1980s, therefore, officials were rethinking the national role in local development efforts. Although much of this debate stemmed from ideological preferences for minimal government intervention in market processes, there were serious concerns about the inefficiencies of locational strategies and the pervasive political pressures to spread national program benefits to a wide range of communities rather than to those most in need. These efficiency and effectiveness matters invite a range of solutions, but they became cloaked in the rhetoric of globalization and international competition in the early 1980s. This rhetoric, along with outdated economic assumptions and partial understandings of globalization trends, allowed national officials to justify cuts in many urban programs as a means of improving the economic competitiveness of the national economy.

The Political Logic for Devolving Economic Development Roles

During the 1980s the national policy interpretations of globalization trends suggested the declining importance of location and spatial relations. During the Reagan and Bush administrations, this undermined any rationale for a national urban policy. Both Reagan and Bush emphasized economic recovery programs with a "de facto urban policy" encouraging market-driven spatial restructuring processes (Warren, 1990).

Beyond ideology, the effects of demographic shifts reinforced this position. Suburban and rural constituents now elect a majority of the House of Representatives; even if all representatives from urban districts voted as a bloc, they could not pass urban legislation in Congress (Cook, 1997). Not surprisingly, this reality now dominates both electoral and governing strategies at the national level. Furthermore, these demographic and political dynamics are replicated at the state level. As Weir (1996) argues, the organizational and political power of urban areas in state politics declined as political parties waned and state legislatures became more professional, specialized, and fragmented. Cities' ability to "deliver" votes at the state legislature became less salient as electorally active constituencies suburbanized; policy making by logrolling politics gave way to the influence of special interests and direct democracy provisions. Devolution of authority and policy responsibility from the national to the state level, therefore, is rarely good news for cities. These demographic and political changes suggest a creeping indifference to cities in both national and state politics.

Recent presidential campaigns have featured little attention to urban issues by either Democrats or Republicans. For both Reagan and Bush, the enterprise zone concept popularized in Britain (Green, 1991) constituted the sole urban initiative of their presidential campaigns. The enterprise zone strategy emphasized reliance on tax incentives and regulatory relief, rather than federal grants and revenue sharing, as a means to revitalize distressed urban areas. In a climate of fiscal austerity and government retrenchment, it promised Reagan and Bush policy makers a relatively cost-less, hands-off means of dealing with urban decline.[4] Despite the numerous enterprise zone bills introduced during the 102nd Congress, the free market urban initiative remained moribund. Bush's zone proposal was packaged with an array of other tax increases in the Tax Fairness and Economic Growth Act of 1992 and was vetoed by the president in March 1992. The civil disturbances in Los Angeles in 1992 prompted the resurrection of Bush's zone legislation and the addition of the Weed and Seed Implementation Act directing federal grants to distressed communities for criminal justice and economic development projects. Again, the zone legislation was included in other legislation increasing tax revenues; mindful of the loss of support following his earlier reversal on tax increases, the president pocket vetoed the entire package.

Clinton Redux

These electoral and governance lessons were not lost on Bill Clinton in his first presidential campaign. Clinton also included enterprise zones in his campaign platform, but downplayed urban concerns in favor of broader "wedge issues." Clinton's efforts to construct an electoral coalition that would recapture three key constituencies—Reagan Democrats, suburbanites, and young voters—entailed his repositioning himself on the cultural, moral, and racial wedge issues that appeared especially salient to white, suburban taxpayers (Edsall, 1992). This included a rhetoric of welfare reform emphasizing the need to limit so-called welfare dependency and the claim to represent those "who work hard and play by the rules" (Edsall, 1992). This cut across class and race to create a discourse emphasizing the emerging cleavage between those perceived as "productive" and those seen as "nonproductive" members of society; to many voters, this cleavage resonated with racial distinctions as well. Nevertheless, Clinton's core electorate in 1992 included disproportionate support from African Americans (82 percent), Hispanics (62 percent), African American women (86 percent, compared with 41 percent of white women), the unemployed (56 percent), low-income families (59 percent), and those who felt their family financial situations were worse since the last election (61 percent) ("Portrait of the Electorate," 1992). Although these figures are not broken down by residence, arguably these are disproportionately urban voters. Clinton's difficulties in translating his electoral coalition into a governing coalition were exacerbated by the shift in congressional power to representatives from suburban and rural districts with fiscally conservative agendas (Drier, 1995).

Clinton's Hybrid National Urban Policy

Given this political climate, the Clinton administration's delays in releasing a national urban policy report are telling, but not surprising. When transmitted to Congress in August 1995, the report's theme of empowerment emphasized four principles: linking families to work, leveraging private investment in urban communities, designing strategies locally, and "traditional values—hard work, family, responsibility" seen as essential to inner-city revival (U.S. Department of Housing and Urban Development, 1995).

Although the Clinton administration advocated more funds for the urban programs that survived the Reagan cuts, its orientation and strategies to date appear to reprise old themes rather than signal fundamental rethinking of the federal role in urban development.

In some respects the Clinton approach appears to follow the path of least resistance marked out by the Reagan-Bush administrations: reliance on privatization and market forces to restore local and regional economies (see Rich, 1993a). Clinton's major urban initiative is similar to Bush's 1992 empowerment zone proposal: zones get tax incentives and special priority for federal funding. Programmatically, the administration is committed to a two-tiered Community Empowerment Zone and Enterprise Community program passed by Congress in May 1993. The Community Empowerment Zone program and the parallel program for enterprise communities are spatially targeted programs designed to encourage job creation in distressed areas through the use of subsidies to reduce the costs of economic activities. These cost-reduction strategies may lower firms' operating costs but do not necessarily improve their productivity or enhance net employment linkages (Wolman et al., 1992).

In Clinton's version (authorized in December 1994), six empowerment zones (EZs) were created—in Atlanta, Baltimore, Chicago, Detroit, New York, and Philadelphia/Camden—along with two supplemental empowerment zones in Cleveland and Los Angeles City/County. The six empowerment zones will receive up to $100 million in federal funds (primarily Title XX Social Service Block Grants) and tax incentives (wage tax credits, expensing deductions) per zone; Cleveland will receive $87 million in Economic Development Initiative Grants as well as Enterprise Community designation, and Los Angeles City/County will receive $125 million in Economic Development Initiative Grants. Sixty-five Enterprise Communities meeting poverty and distress criteria, two-thirds of them in urban areas, will receive $3 million in Title XX Social Service Block Grant funds plus expanded state and local tax-exempt bond financing privileges.[5]

Some of these inefficiencies are remedied through program design features that encourage a "bottom-up strategy" of national support for local initiatives and organizations. The multi-agency, challenge grant process for EZ designation selected localities with community-based strategies combining government, private, nonprofit, and community sectors in order to enhance local linkages. Detroit exemplifies this approach: leading businesses including General Motors Corporation, Ford Motor Company, and Chrysler Corporation, pledged to create 3,275 jobs and invest nearly $1.8 billion in the zone area; banks promised to increase overall annual lending in the zone by $17 million; utilities promised to expand services; accounting and law firms agreed to discount their services for businesses and nonprofit organizations in the zone; local universities agreed to focus resources there; and local media planned to highlight the new programs (Pierce, 1995). All local proposals had to include strategic plans coordinating economic development, physical infrastructure, and human service plans in the nominated area. In contrast to previous administrations' zone proposals, national support for community policing, employment and training programs, and educational reform is promised. Education and job training elements are emphasized: communities could not receive federal aid unless they demonstrated that such help would increase the earning opportunities and incomes of people in the areas (Hambleton, 1994, 17). Finally, each strategic plan identified the state, local, and private resource commitments available to the designated area. In Baltimore, this amounted to eight dollars in local commitments for every one dollar in federal funds (Pierce, 1995).

In terms of funding levels, national roles, and implementation strategies, the Clinton administration's empowerment zones do diverge from previous proposals.[6] The Clinton empowerment zones are more comprehensive and better funded than the enterprise zone programs regularly forwarded by the Reagan and Bush administrations. They recognize the multiple disadvantages in distressed areas that must be addressed as preconditions of economic development, as well as the need to increase economic opportunities for urban residents.[7] There is a deliberate and conscious effort to emphasize initiatives that reconnect citizens and jobs, citizens and information, citizens and community organizations. In contrast to the hands-off mentality of the 1980s, the Clinton administration speaks of covenants and compacts of "reciprocal responsibilities" (Stanfield, 1993, 1345). This includes a national policy role closer to "facilitator and supporter" of local efforts than to director and fixer (Stanfield, 1993, 1344).

Beyond Empowerment Zones: Facilitating the Work of Cities

Clinton's familiar urban initiatives are sketched out, however, on a broader canvas that tentatively recognizes the human and social capital issues associated with the work of cities in a global era. Embedded in the Clinton administration's hybrid policy approach are definitions of urban problems that center on the weak institutional infrastructure in cities, emergent scales of regionalism and city-suburban collaboration, the role of urban entrepreneurialism, devolution of economic development decision making, and human capital investment.

Strengthening Local Institutional Infrastructure

Institutional reforms are one of the more distinctive features of the Clinton urban policy approach, although these, too, draw on policy legacies from Reagan, Bush, and their predecessors. Nevertheless, the Clinton administration's emphasis on developing an institutional infrastructure stands out (Cisneros, 1995). Some proposed neighborhood and nonprofit organization initiatives shift the scale of policy formulation down to the neighborhood level and move the decision-making site to nonbureaucratic organizations. They are so modestly funded, however, that they must be seen as experimental at best.[8] Although the major contours of the Clinton urban agenda are prosaic cost-reduction strategies, these institutional reform elements hint at efforts to move beyond the assumptions of past urban policies. They draw on the community organizing of the 1960s and the private sector involvement of the 1980s, but also the asset-based ethos of the 1990s (Kretzmann and McKnight, 1993) that emphasizes the associational strengths, rather than weaknesses and pathologies, of communities in need.

Encouraging Metropolitan and Regional Cooperation

Another emergent theme centers on the grounds for anticipating greater regionalism and city-suburb collaboration. These themes became prominent as the Clinton team staked out a focus for urban policy in the early 1990s (Kaplan, 1995; Swanstrom, 1996). The empirical argument builds on the contention that regional economies are the building blocks for national economic well-being, the spatial correlates of new production systems, and the appropriate focus of national economic and spatial policy (Barnes and Ledebur, 1998; Sabel, 1994; Savitch et al., 1993). In particular, large income disparities between a central city and its suburbs appear to weaken the regional economy and create locational disincentives throughout the metropolitan area (Stanfield, 1996; Savitch et al., 1993; but see Wolman et al., 1992). Pragmatically, a regional focus provides a means for reuniting urban and suburban political constituencies in support of policies targeting metropolitan development.

Enhancing Local Entrepreneurial Climates

To many, *public entrepreneurialism* seems an oxymoron: the risk-taking business actors who spot new opportunities for making profits and challenge the status quo and the rules of the game seem remote from the constrained risk-aversive politicians seen as dominating local government. Yet some national programs, notably the Urban Development Action Grants, supported entrepreneurial activities by local officials; that is, they encouraged systematic, strategic behaviors by public officials in the pursuit of greater public revenues and also supported strategies to overcome the bureaucratic, incrementalist rules of the game (often created by past national programs) limiting local development roles. This required sensitivity to the decision rules in both the public and private sectors and richly developed organizational networks. The UDAG program represented the peak of federally sponsored urban entrepreneurialism; no subsequent national programs have encouraged the risk-taking, revenue-generating practices undertaken by local governments in UDAG public-private partnerships. In the context of retrenchment and state devolution, even critics of the UDAG program now find merit in drawing on UDAG design elements that might provide some local public voice in corporate investment decisions (Fainstein and Fainstein, 1995).

The urban entrepreneurialism now espoused by the Clinton administration is more limited. It emphasizes proactive local governments and development of local strategic visions based on identifying and building on an area's comparative advantage in a globalizing economy (Cisneros, 1995). It argues for helping local entrepreneurs but does not advocate entrepreneurial behavior on the part of local officials. But, as our study shows, local governments continue to apply earlier entrepreneurial lessons to their own initiatives. In a sense, local government officials retain a broader commitment to urban entrepreneurialism than does the national government.

Devolving Resource Decision Making

The entrepreneurial emphasis on performance rather than process, however, is reinforced in the "performance partnership" directives emanating from the U.S. Office of Management and Budget (OMB) in 1995. At this point, these performance partnership arrangements have been stalled in congressional deliberations. But eventual implementation of these directives for devolution of decision making may have greater long-term impacts on cities than the empowerment zone legislation.[9] Using the "reinventing government" rhetoric, OMB defines the problems with the current national-local grant system as too many funding categories and regulations, too much paperwork, a misdirected emphasis on remediating rather than preventing problems, and no clear focus on measurable outcomes. "The system stifles initiative and squanders resources without achieving sufficient results" (Rivlin, 1995). OMB's performance partnership concept reframes the funding of existing programs in terms of performance criteria. It also promises to integrate flexibility and accountability in ways not possible in block grants and categorical programs; it does so by "exchanging funding restrictions for a new incentive-based focus on performance and outcomes" (Rivlin, 1995). Rather than the focus on process prevalent in most grant programs, the funding decisions would shift to outcomes and outputs as measures of success; communities would gain more flexibility in how to address their problems but would be held accountable for the results of their choices.[10] The intent is for federal funds to be allocated, at least in part, on the basis of actual performance that is exceptional or highly improved.[11]

Promoting Human Capital Investment

The Clinton administration has had little success in persuading Congress to support its human capital initiatives in the face of the budget deficit issue. By the mid-1990s, the administration managed to push through a $.90 increase in the minimum wage to $5.15 an hour and ensured continuance of the Earned Income Tax Credit, which provides low-wage earners with a tax refund. To complement these wage initiatives, they also implemented a school-to-work apprenticeship program, extended low-interest loans to workers seeking additional training, created America's Job Bank on the Internet, and set up one-stop job centers in more than twenty states, combining unemployment compensation services with counseling and training. Efforts to consolidate the sixty-year legacy of federal employment and training programs into "skills grants" given directly to individuals, as in the GI Bill, have yet to succeed.

The trend toward replacing place-based funding with transfer payments to individuals, particularly the nonurban middle-class and elderly, continues unabated. In 1996, Clinton proposed that 61 percent (1960, 35 percent) of federal aid to states and local governments go directly to individuals, 16 percent (1960, 47 percent) to capital grants to state and local governments, and 22 percent (1960, 17 percent) to other state and local grants ("Long Term Shifts," 1996). To some, this is the key to future national urban policy. Given the shifts in political climate and constituencies, some prominent urbanists argue that future urban legislation must focus on people-oriented concerns that will bring together urban, suburban, and rural representatives rather than on place-oriented policies targeted at cities (Nathan, 1992; Kaplan, 1995).

Conclusion

The broad sweep of economic restructuring and globalization marking the past two decades is mirrored by equally sweeping political changes. The structural constraints on cities imposed by federalism and capitalism remain. These city limits ensure that local officials will continue their efforts to stabilize and enhance cities' revenue bases through economic development strategies. But the nature and design of these local strategies increasingly reflect the realities of global competition and the weakening of national guidelines.

The national policy context augments the new localism foreshadowed by economic trends. In particular, after a brief postwar period of national support for cities, a pattern devolving responsibilities for urban development to the states and cities began to emerge. Surviving national policies for cities—and rare national initiatives such as empowerment zone legislation—continue to be informed by outmoded ideas of growth and competition processes. The Clinton administration's hybrid urban policies have introduced some recognition of the new realities facing local policy makers. In many ways these lags and lurches in policy are not surprising. National aid to localities occurs in an ambivalent and complex national political setting. By turning away from cities and their workforce in the 1980s and pursuing devolution strategies, however, national policy makers thrust local officials into economic and political uncertainty. With cuts in national programs, cities were cast out on their own.

Rather than continuing with deductive analyses of the constraints limiting city choices, we now turn to our empirical studies of what local officials have done in response to this national retrenchment and how they are coping with global economic changes. We take up this context-specific approach in the following chapters, beginning in chapter 3 with a comparison of the choices local officials made when national program support and guidelines were in effect with the choices they made as cities were left more on their own. Although such a comparison implies an expectation of important differences in local choices, it also allows us to pinpoint the ways in which national program history has shaped local orientations. By moving ahead to the contemporary era, we also can trace the shifts in local strategies as officials encounter the realities of globalization, state devolution, and technological changes.

3

The Era of Entrepreneurial Cities

Local political arenas are expanding as localities take on more entrepreneurial economic roles and broader political responsibilities.

In American cities, local officials face continuing imperatives to pursue local economic development activities, but with problematic authority and resources. Local economic health is shaped by national and international investment decisions over which local officials have little control. These external constraints and opportunities are likely to persist. Simultaneously, local officials face fiscal pressures and competing demands for local resources. On the one hand, they have a real stake in sustaining and enhancing local economic development processes because of their dependence on private investment for public revenues. On the other hand, they need to satisfy citizen demands for services as well as jobs. They literally cannot afford *not* to do so, in fiscal and political terms. For these reasons, the local search for new policy approaches is ongoing.

The policy objectives, then, are to work out local economic development strategies that will increase revenue stability, decrease vulnerability to external "shocks," provide good jobs to local citizens, and increase the overall satisfaction of city residents. These strategies must be sensitive to both economic uncertainties and political constraints and cognizant of the limited effects of previous strategies designed to increase local employment and income. Because they increasingly rely on local resources, local officials have strong incentives to find the most efficient uses of their funds for development purposes.

Here we provide an overview of the changing orientations of local development policy choices over time, linking policy characteristics to their particular historical and political contexts (for other classifications of economic development policy orientations, see Sternberg, 1987; Hanson and Berkman, 1991; Lowery and Gray, 1990; Leicht and Jenkins, 1994). We chronicle the development of these policy choices through the federal era, detail policy shifts in response to the national withdrawal from cities, examine the different waves of policy use in the postfederal era, and identify clusters of development policies used by cities.[1] Four overlapping waves of policy initiatives stand out:

> **First wave:** locational strategies (historical)
> **Second wave:** transitional entrepreneurial strategies (mid-1970s to mid-1980s)
> **Third wave:** Postfederal entrepreneurial strategies (late 1980s through 1990s)
> **Fourth wave:** globalization and human capital (mid- to late 1990s)

We trace the first three waves by defining the distinctive characteristics of policy orientations predominant during these periods. The entrepreneurial strategies documented in this chapter are transitional strategies, moving away from the industrially oriented locational strategies. If the changing work of cities unfolds in the ways scholars anticipate, this activist entrepreneurial approach should ease the move toward local strategies aimed at human capital development and global-local links. Our recent studies detect the emergence of this fourth wave: more initiatives that incorporate human capital concerns and infrastructure development appropriate for a global economy (see chapter 7).

It is important to note the overlapping nature of the waves of policy innovation. This is not a process of policy displacement but of layering of different approaches. Once adopted, strategies build constituencies around the benefits they provide, so policy termination is difficult and infrequent. With each successive wave, policies from previous waves are usually retained while new initiatives are explored for their fit with changing circumstances. Thus while the tool kit of policies expands, over time its composition may alter to reflect different emphases in approaches. Cities gain knowledge about many economic development approaches through participation in national programs and in specialized policy networks. After a brief discussion of the broad issues involved in data collection and methodology, we compare below local strategy choice during the period of active federal programs and later in the absence of federal resources.

The Historical Context of Local Policy Choices

Keeping in mind the structural imperatives and broad policy objectives present in every American city, the menu of possible local policy initiatives is shaped by knowledge of policy options and the nature of competition and production processes at any historical moment. These policy options reflect local officials' understanding of contemporary growth processes as well as the influences and incentives proffered by national policy makers as they steer local choices.

First-Wave Strategies: Locational Incentives

As noted in chapter 2, locational incentives are designed to reduce the costs of production factors in a community relative to other locations in order to attract business relocations or expansions. For the city seeking a competitive advantage over other cities, the logic is to create an advantageous price structure for "production factors," thereby creating a comparative locational advantage. Eisinger (1988) labels these policies as supply-side approaches aimed at subsidizing production costs.[2]

A reliance on the taxing and regulatory authority of local governments is integral to locational strategies. Low-interest financing—frequently offered in the form of industrial revenue bonds, tax credits, abatements, deferments, and exemptions—subsidized industrial job training, and assistance with site selection and preparation are common locational policy tools (Fosler, 1988b, 312). The rubric of locational strategies also includes the notion of creating a "positive business climate." The aim is to project an image of a probusiness atmosphere. This deliberately vague concept usually includes low taxes and regulatory policies designed to keep production costs low, such as relaxed environmental legislation and right-to-work laws (Plaut and Pluta, 1983, 99). Overall, the defining characteristic of locational policies is the effort to produce lower costs for business relative to other cities. The local policy role entails calculating the city's comparative advantage and bidding for businesses; the public role remains subordinate to private sector decisions (Eisinger, 1988; Fosler, 1988a).

The reassessment of local development policies under way in many American communities is prompted in part by changing economic conditions. It is also buttressed, however, by a conviction that previous approaches to local economic development, particularly locational incentives, cannot be justified on grounds of effectiveness or efficiency (e.g., Lugar, 1985; Blair and Premus, 1987). Business attraction and retention strategies are criticized, for example, because no net national economic growth occurs, the firm itself garners the great bulk of the profit (according to rent models), and the profit to a firm located in the city may well "leak" to a multinational corporate conglomerate. The use of subsidies, tax incentives, and tax abatements also raises substitution issues regarding the use of public funds—would this investment have occurred anyway?

Second-Wave Strategies: Transitional Entrepreneurial Incentives

Although revenue imperatives and interjurisdictional competition for investment ensure that locational incentives will remain in local repertoires, the trends and changing economic conditions we have discussed encourage consideration of a distinctive policy orientation reflecting more market-based, or "entrepreneurial" (e.g., Eisinger, 1988; Harvey, 1989), economic development strategies. According to Eisinger, entrepreneurial policies shift the intent of the inducements from locational incentives to fostering "those indigenous capacities to serve new or expanding demands by providing resources that permit direct penetration or capture of a particular market or that permit a risky but potentially productive undertaking that would not have gone forward without government support" (1988, 230).

Like locational economic development policies, entrepreneurial economic development policies have roots in a theoretical understanding about the process of economic development. Conventional economic development strategies were based on the premise that the market had failed and therefore required direct public intervention in support of private business activities. Market-based strategies argue that market failure (e.g., unemployment) or market underdevelopment (e.g., low-wage or part-time jobs) can be redressed through the market system itself. Market-based public policy relies less on direct grants and more on leveraging with public funds and authority to minimize market imperfections in labor and capital markets (often due to information gaps) and to encourage market expansion in a locality.

Reducing market imperfections and encouraging market expansion are not new economic development strategies. What distinguishes market-based economic development strategies from more traditional approaches is the focus on facilitating value-creating processes by private investors and the investment and risk-taking role adopted by local officials (Vaughn and Pollard, 1986). Variously labeled "generative development," "enterprise development," and "entrepreneurial" strategies, these new approaches center on policies that support the creation of new economic activities by the private sector (Committee for Economic Development, 1986, 20). Their wealth-creating approach entails removing barriers to the creation and expansion of smaller firms and increasing the rate of enterprise development within the community. This is seen as enhancing the adaptiveness and flexibility of local economies and thus hedging against external "shocks." Some analysts dispute the emphasis on small firms per se (Vaughn and Pollard, 1986), but there is general agreement that an emphasis on removing barriers to the formation of new enterprises is an essential policy objective.

The federal lineage of many local entrepreneurial strategies is not well-known and rarely acknowledged. Although the advent of these market-oriented, entrepreneurial approaches onto state and local agendas is often traced to the period during and after the recession of the early 1980s (Clarke and Saiz, 1995; Lowery and Gray, 1990), their roots go deeper. Many market-oriented tools and financing techniques were introduced to local officials by involvement in federal economic development programs. Not every national program was amenable to entrepreneurial use. A few, however, are notable for providing local officials with flexible and relatively discretionary resources to respond to economic problems and opportunities in their jurisdictions. The programs permitting cities to use market-based strategies include the Economic Development Administration's Title II (Business Development Loans) and Title IX (Special Economic Development and Adjustment Assistance) programs; the Department of Housing and Urban Development's Community Development Block Grant program after 1978, when economic development became an eligible activity; and HUD's Urban Development Action Grant program.

The incentives and resources in these programs provide the distinctive characteristics of the second wave: cities often continued to pursue cost-reduction strategies, but they expanded their concerns to encompass new growth processes and gained experience in more entrepreneurial public roles. Originally, none of these programs envisioned local officials as entrepreneurs or direct participants in local economic development. In general, program funds most often were aimed at providing public services or facilities to encourage community development or at providing loans and grants to businesses either directly or through intermediary organizations. And in our interviews, local officials indicated that cities are not entrepreneurs across programs: cities may use one program conventionally and another in a more entrepreneurial fashion. This flexibility may reflect program differences and changes in program design over time but also is likely a response to local program constituencies and expectations.

Beginning in the mid-1970s, EDA Title II and Title IX laid the groundwork for local entrepreneurial efforts by encouraging the establishment of revolving loan funds and a wide range of local economic development activities. Given that many cities at this point did not have the legal capacity to make loans to either for-profit or nonprofit organizations, EDA's requirement that funds be used to make loans fostered the formation of quasi-public organizations and local development corporations to receive funds "passed through" by local government. By 1979, the Carter administration proposed to reshape EDA programs to emphasize business development in distressed areas through more locational incentives and increased credit availability. Although these ambitious plans were not realized, both Title II and Title IX offered cities, public corporations, and nonprofit organizations substantial, flexible economic development assistance. Most cities continued to use their EDA funds for planning, public works, and public facility provision efforts. Some cities, however, used these funds in more market-oriented ways, by setting up revolving loan funds, investing in industrial parks, or entering into joint ventures for rehabilitation or commercial revitalization.

The Community Development Block Grant program amendments of 1984 included two important features: (1) they allowed cities to use CDBG funds for an extensive range of special economic development purposes, and (2) they allowed cities to direct funds to private for-profit entities where "necessary and appropriate." Even economic development projects not explicitly listed as eligible, such as new housing construction, might be undertaken if sponsored by neighborhood-based nonprofit organizations, small business investment companies, or local development corporations. The program allocations vary widely each year at the city level (see Rich, 1993b). But by FY 1988, economic development spending accounted for 13 percent of CDBG program spending (U.S. Department of Housing and Urban Development, 1989, 14). Nearly half of that amount went into loans and grants to businesses, revolving loan funds, joint federal-private projects, and investment in activities generating program income; the rest was spent on conventional infrastructure improvements.

Urban Development Action Grants, the most market-oriented approach, started out in 1978 with local officials acting as contractual partners but functioning primarily as financial conduits for federal project funds. Over time, cities began to use UDAG funds in more entrepreneurial ways: instead of making grants or unrestricted loans to private sector partners, cities began to use UDAG funds as public investment capital. That is, cities used UDAG funds for equity participation in projects or committed funds in exchange for net cash-flow participation in project returns. They increasingly used loan repayments and program income to capitalize revolving loan funds or as venture capital for local projects. By FY 1988, more than 66 percent of UDAG projects included equity participation providing future income streams (U.S. Department of Housing and Urban Development, 1989, 56). Cities, usually friends of business, had now become partners in both the planning and the profits.

Although these national programs inspired local entrepreneurial initiatives, cuts in program funds for local economic development began during the Carter administration and accelerated under the Reagan administration's New Federalism approach. During the 1980s, decreases in national program resources were accompanied by periodic efforts to eliminate or consolidate several community development programs. The volatility of federal resources, as well as absolute cuts in the level of resources, persuaded many local officials to turn to other sources of support for local economic development activities.

Third-Wave Strategies: Postfederal Entrepreneurial Incentives

In a growing number of American cities, local policy choices in this nonfederal period are characterized by market-based, "entrepreneurial" economic development strategies.[3] The complex, market-based local policy initiatives of the postfederal generation are less visible and less easily characterized than are nationally designed programs for local economic development. These initiatives are not embodied in specific programs or agencies, but rather in particular policy tools or strategies used by local officials to encourage entrepreneurial processes. These strategies encompass a number of different policy instruments, but they share certain features that distinguish them from previous policy approaches. Below is a list of features that characterize market-based, entrepreneurial strategies (Clarke and Gaile, 1989b):

Purpose: They tend to stimulate new enterprise rather than stabilize or protect (Dubnick and Bardes, 1983).

Focus: They tend to focus on using government authority to shape market structure and opportunity rather than to influence the functions of individual businesses (Sternberg, 1987, 152).

Criteria: They tend to use market criteria, such as maximizing rates of return, rather than political criteria in setting priorities for allocation and investment of public funds.

Finance: They tend to leverage public and private funds rather than rely solely on one or the other.

Public roles: They tend to rely on joint public-private ventures for implementation of economic development projects rather than on bureaucratic approaches.

Administrative ease: They tend to be easier to administer because they often are managed through quasi-public agencies rather than line agencies.

Decision processes: They tend to involve negotiated decisions on a case-by-case basis rather than juridical, standardized decision processes.

Linkages: They tend to establish contractual, contingent relations with those affected rather than linkages based on rights or entitlement.

Risk: They tend to tolerate risk and uncertainty regarding investment outcomes rather than operating on risk-aversive principles.

It is important to reiterate that cities adopt market-based policies selectively and differentially. Cities initiating these policies also use a variety of policies that are non-market based. Cities tend to compromise between the neoliberal market paradigm and the traditional liberal "service provision" and "safety net" paradigms. The market cannot effectively replace government in certain sectors of public interest, and the government is underappreciated for what it has accomplished in the public interest (Kuttner, 1997). Nonetheless, the market works effectively in certain areas of enterprise; cities are adopting strategies that coordinate with private sector interests to foster both public and private goals.

Constructing Policy Indices

To trace these waves of policy responses through time requires comparable measures. Detecting changes in policy orientations raises daunting measurement issues. For one thing, these changes cannot be measured in terms of dollars and cents and are not easily quantifiable in any terms. As Figure 3.1 shows, state and local spending over the past decades has been primarily on economic development, with little redistributive spending at the local level. It thus appears as if the public choice arguments made by Peterson and others are correct: interjurisdictional competition for private investment skews subnational agendas toward developmental goals.

But we agree with Reich, Jessop (1993), and others (e.g., Scott, 1992)

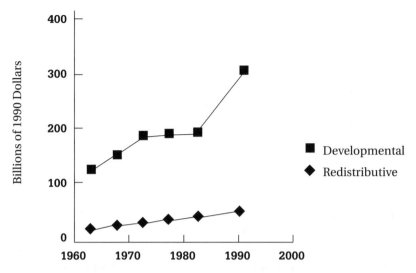

Figure 3.1. Local spending 1962–90 (based on data in Peterson, 1995)

who argue that new economic development roles at the local level may be the most significant responses to globalization. These would not necessarily be reflected by expenditure levels, but in programmatic orientations and strategic policy choices. In these new roles, the goals and mode of policy intervention are distinctive: in the context of globalization, local economic development moves away from the traditional place wars of the industrial era and toward a more facilitating, entrepreneurial approach to encouraging growth processes, structuring markets, and linking local and global economies.

Although the notion of an "entrepreneurial" local government may seem oxymoronic to some, such a government reflects the attributes we have described, embedded in a range of programmatic policy options emphasizing demand-side strategies that foster new market and growth opportunities, in contrast to traditional locational incentive strategies that subsidize firms (Eisinger, 1988; see also Bingham, Hill, and White, 1990). Our aim is to use these dimensions to categorize local policy tools as more or less entrepreneurial; these indices must be able to detect entrepreneurial attributes under two distinctive resource conditions—when cities are using federal resources and when they are using nonfederal resources. Thus we begin our search for the roots of entrepreneurial orientations in the national programs that brought many local governments into the economic development arena.

Data Collection

The core analysis centers on cities' choices under three resource conditions: when federal program funds were plentiful, as federal program funds began to dwindle, and current conditions. In addition to levels of activity, in the first two periods we focus on whether cities used federal funds in relatively entrepreneurial ways and whether they chose relatively entrepreneurial nonfederal strategies since 1980. We look at the current period for indications of both change and inertia and to try to understand the degree to which policy shifts are reactive or proactive.

The baseline population for the study includes all American cities (178) with populations above 100,000 in 1975. The study period for policy implementation—beginning in 1978—includes the peak period of national support for local economic development in the late 1970s; the programs analyzed were the major sources of federal funding for local economic development activities during this period. In the 1980s, federal resources tapered off and local officials could pursue local economic development activities only by drawing on other resources. We developed our data on local choices in four ways: we gathered program data on city use of EDA, CDBG, and UDAG funds; made field visits to cities active in these federal programs; conducted a national survey in 1989 of local development officials; and conducted a follow-up survey in 1996 of these officials to determine changes that have occurred in policy orientation.

The Federal Era

The data on local use of federal resources include all cities above the population threshold that received EDA, CDBG, and/or UDAG federal program funds for local economic development from 1978 to 1988. Program information was collected on the level of local program activity—the dollars spent—and, where possible, the nature of city fiscal roles. Measures of entrepreneurial choices using federal resources are based on how cities used these specific program funds.

Classifying Local Use of Federal Program Funds

City use of EDA Title II and IX funds was characterized as entrepreneurial on the basis of information in annual reports and management information provided by EDA staff. Entrepreneurial activities for projects from 1978 through 1981 included establishment of revolving loan funds, joint enterprises for rehabilitation, public enterprises, joint venture industrial parks, and other activities meeting the basic criteria set out above.

City use of CDBG funds was characterized as entrepreneurial on the basis of the relative allocation of CDBG funds in FY 1988 for economic development activities. This is a less satisfactory measure because it reflects local program reallocations rather than actual entrepreneurial usage, as in the above measures. Creation of comparable measures for local CDBG use is possible only if one individually codes each CDBG annual report archived at HUD for each community. The percentage measure used here is an indirect measure of cities' relative willingness to commit significant shares of CDBG funds to economic development purposes rather than more traditional purposes. The larger the reallocation, the more likely it is that the city is engaged in extensive economic development projects allowed by 1978 eligibility and the 1984 amendments.[4]

City use of UDAG funds from 1978 to 1981 was classified as more entrepreneurial if UDAG project grant agreements showed UDAG funds would be used for revolving loan funds, venture capital, net cash-flow participation, interest subsidies, equity pools, use of program income for other economic development projects, or other revenue-generating strategies rather than for a basic grant or loan to the developer (see Clarke and Rich, 1985). Data from all UDAG project grants were then aggregated by city.[5]

The Postfederal Era

In a series of field visits in 1989 to a sample of cities with distinctive federal program participation profiles, we carried out unstructured open-ended interviews with local officials. On these field visits, we developed instruments to collect comparable information systematically from the 178 cities identified (the total population of cities above the population size criterion). In each city, two government officials responsible for economic development were identified and asked to provide this information in a mail survey. Of the 178 cities in this population, usable responses were gathered from 101 cities.[6]

In our 1989 mail survey, we asked whether respondents had ever used each of forty-seven economic development strategies (see Appendix B) practiced by some local governments (see also Urban Institute et al., 1983; Bowman, 1987, for other national surveys; see Blakely, 1989, for a review of local strategies). The mail inquiries focused on (1) the use of economic development strategies that do not require federal resources, (2) the timing of strategy adoption, and (3) the assessment of strategy effectiveness. The forty-seven strategies included tools such as revolving loan funds, venture capital, net cash-flow participation, interest subsidies, equity pools, use of program income for other economic development projects, and other revenue-generating strategies that were present in some federal programs; most tools listed, however, were identified by local officials during the field interviews.[7]

Classifying Postfederal Entrepreneurial Strategies

Many policy choices in the 1980s, a period of reduced federal program funds, built on the strategies developed during the federal era. Our interest here was in sorting out market-based strategies first used by a city since 1980. We assumed this tapped entrepreneurial strategies adopted in the absence of federal funds supporting this approach. The indicators of postfederal entrepreneurialism include whether a city first used revolving loan funds, venture capital, net cash-flow participation, interest subsidies, equity participation, equity pools established by private-public consortia, or program income for economic development purposes in 1980 or later.

Current Orientations

To update the analyses, in 1996 we resurveyed the cities that responded in 1989. We specifically focused on policy changes since 1989, including current and proposed strategy use, the evolution of new strategies, and policy responsiveness to human capital and globalization trends. We continued to use the postfederal index of entrepreneurial strategies to track the use of such policies. The responses confirm our expectation of an emergent fourth wave of policy innovation, which we describe in more detail in chapter 7.

Methodological Issues

The purpose of the empirical analyses in the next two chapters is to rate cities according to the levels of their entrepreneurial policy use and then to determine the characteristics of those cities that use entrepreneurial policies. Further, the analyses represent an attempt to determine whether these policies, in sum or in part, can be considered effective (a topic we take up in the next chapter). These data also help establish a chronology of, or the existence of waves in, policy choice.

We began our analyses well aware of the significant methodological problems that have plagued many studies of urban economic development activities (Bartik, 1991). Two implicit assumptions mar many studies. In many cases, depending on the conceptualization of local economic development activities, there is an assumption that communities claiming they use certain programs use them in a persistent and continuous fashion. The lack of a temporal variable neglects the reality that the use of particular approaches may be temporary or sporadic, and is not always continuous. Furthermore, simple measures of the level of activity have limited utility; they fail to differentiate among different types of policies and, in weighing all policies equally, misstate policy achievements (Hanson and Berkman, 1991). In contrast to indices distinguishing among policies by dollars spent (Hanson, 1993; Hansen, 1989), we are interested in the aspects of local policies that signal the entrepreneurial orientations anticipated by the new localism models.[8]

We have attempted to improve on earlier analyses by constructing policy indices able to measure important variations in the nature of local economic development policy orientations over time. This entailed an accounting of the incidence of various market-based strategies when cities were using federal and nonfederal resources. The cities could then be compared according to an additive score reflecting their use of market-based policy activity at different time points. By developing comparable indices of market-based strategies at the first two time periods, we were able to rate cities empirically as more or less entrepreneurial based on their use of federal and nonfederal resources. Guided by these concerns, we constructed a set of entrepreneurial policy indices, which we detail later in this chapter.

An equally serious methodological flaw in most studies involves researchers' dealing with continuous space through the use of nominal variables to represent regions simplistically.[9] Given the significant regional socioeconomic patterns and dynamics that exist in the United States today, we concluded it was imperative to control explicitly for spatial patterns in all variables through use of trend surface analysis techniques (see Appendix A).[10]

Moving toward Entrepreneurial Policy Strategies

The Federal Roots of Entrepreneurial Activity

It is important to recognize that few cities took an active aggressive role in economic development before federal funds became available for this purpose. Although American cities have a historical, structural interest in economic development, the lack of resources and public authority (Sbragia, 1996) often dictated a passive and sporadic public role. Indeed, most cities were relatively inactive in local economic development projects before the 1970s. Of the more than one hundred large cities studied and surveyed here, 40 percent described themselves as somewhat active in local economic development projects before 1978, and 42 percent claimed to be not very active or never active during this period. Only 17 percent saw themselves as very active before 1978. The influx of national funds (and the increasing volatility of the economy) in the 1970s engendered new local roles and more consistent activism.

By the mid-1980s, federal program funds were the most important revenue sources for local economic development efforts. Of all the revenue sources for local economic development cited as important in our survey of 174 local officials on pre-1984 activities, 49 percent involved federal program funds. CDBG funds received the most mentions (20 percent), although UDAG (10 percent) and EDA (10 percent) funds were also important (this survey is fully described in the next chapter). Even during this period, local general funds were drawn on: they were 16 percent of the sources mentioned. Local economic development activity in the late 1970s and 1980s, therefore, was significantly subsidized by federal funds.

These funds not only supported more local development activity, they influenced the types of strategies cities chose to use. Table 3.1 ranks those cities characterized as using federal funds entrepreneurially by level of activity.[11]

Table 3.1

Cities using federal funds entrepreneurially

Moderately Active	Very active	Most active
Hollywood, Florida	Chicago	Hartford
St. Petersburg	Louisville	Minneapolis
Tampa	Lansing	
Atlanta	St. Paul	
Indianapolis	Albany	
Springfield, Massachusetts	Buffalo	
Worcester	New York	
Jackson	Tulsa	
St. Louis	Knoxville	
Syracuse		
Portland, Oregon		
Providence		
Fort Worth		
Hampton		
Madison		

Source: Based on an overall index of entrepreneurial federal fund use combining federal indices (reported in Table 3.3).

Making Entrepreneurial Use of Federal Resources

Communities used entrepreneurial strategies differently to match their local needs, even when using the same federal resources. Philadelphia, for example, committed $30 million of CDBG funds as a 2.5 percent construction loan (packaged together with a UDAG) to support construction of a $43 million hotel at the University City Science Center, a nonprofit research park owned by local colleges and universities, including the University of Pennsylvania. Located near one of the poorest neighborhoods in West Philadelphia, the center will share in the net cash flow of the project (Scism, 1990). An American Bar Association survey found that 27 percent of the UDAG projects surveyed included such "kickers," or provisions for sharing a percentage of cash-flow participation after the developer receives a specified rate of return on the investment (Hessel, 1988).

In Flint, Michigan, the city sponsored a group of minority entrepreneurs as equity partners in the city's UDAG for construction of a Hyatt Hotel; the net cash flow from the project was to be used for minority economic development. An American Bar Association survey of 775 UDAG projects in the mid-1980s found that 29 percent reported city equity participation, although this varied significantly across cities, as did the beneficiaries of these arrangements (Hessel, 1988). With more than fifty UDAG projects since 1979, Chicago generated millions of dollars in loan repayments and returns on the city's equity participation in projects. Both repayments of the loan principal and interest are considered as program income. Repayments of UDAG loans made by the city to private investors can be used only on CDBG-eligible projects; this recycles the funds back to development and housing projects benefiting low-income neighborhoods, as the city sees fit. Program income also includes any income generated by the city's position as an equity partner in a project, sharing the risks but also the potential profits of investment; this program income is not restricted and neighborhood organizations often propose it target affordable housing and local development corporations.

Revolving loan funds were created by cities such as Denver, Fort Wayne, and Dayton with EDA funds or capitalized with CDBG funds. With this initial capital, cities were able to make loans, often at below market rates, to firms unable to find conventional financing. Depending on the city, these loans could be targeted to particular types of firms, lenders, or areas. Repayment of the principal, interest, and administrative fees replenished the city's funds for further loans.

These are not always successful ventures. $10 million in industrial revenue bonds and another $7 million in loans went into development of Toledo's $18.5 million Portside Festival Marketplace, a 56,000-square-foot, two-story retail mall developed by James W. Rouse's Enterprise Development Company. But Portside opened in 1984, just as Toledo's economy began to suffer employment losses from corporate downsizing and mergers. Instead of stimulating downtown investment as hoped, the mall was plagued by high vacancy rates and, after a series of developer turnovers, a city takeover was proposed (Stoffel, 1990).

Responding to the Retrenchment of Federal Resources

What actually happened at the local level as federal development funds began to decline? City officials tell a complex story. The most obvious change is a tremendous increase in public-private cooperation during the 1980s. Nearly two-thirds of the cities studied in 1989 reported public-private cooperation on economic development as very active or extremely active. For 75 percent of the cities, this is a substantial increase in public-private activity compared with five years previously.

Resource Constraints

Cities see the lack of resources, constricting state laws, land availability, federal restrictions, and loss of federal funds as major constraints on present local economic development efforts. In our first survey of local development officials, 237 total problems were noted. The lack of resources stands out: lack of funds, tight budgets, and lack of staff were mentioned most frequently (24 percent) as major problems. State laws restricting local fiscal powers and fiscal authority are also perceived as serious barriers, making up over 9 percent of problems mentioned. Fragmented public voice is also a problem; 9 percent of the problems cited involved the lack of political consensus and leadership and the absence of focus for economic development efforts. Many cities are limited by land availability problems; these issues constituted more than 7 percent of all problems mentioned. Aging infrastructure and the lack of amenities or perceived image problems limit some cities (7 percent of mentions). Finally, federal restrictions on (1) program eligibility, (2) fund uses, and (3) environmental effects, as well as the loss of federal funds, are seen as constraints in 6 percent of the mentions, but rank behind lack of resources, state laws, and land availability issues.[12]

Local responses to the loss of federal program funds take three forms: shifting to reliance on local general funds (25 percent), reallocating CDBG funds to economic development purposes (18 percent), and utilizing revenues or program income from successful redevelopment projects (7 percent). The first two suggest reallocation of funds across functional areas; in the absence of federal funds previously used to assist local economic development efforts, cities turn to general funds or CDBG funds. Cities increasingly devote CDBG funds to economic development: the median share of local CDBG funds allocated to economic development in FY 1988 (10 percent) is double the median reported by these cities five years previously. Increased reliance on tax increment financing and program income from previous redevelopment projects point to efforts to make economic development a self-financing local enterprise.

State Programs

With the exception of state enterprise zones, traditional state programs for job training, infrastructure improvement, and financing were seen as most useful in the first survey. State enterprise zone programs were mentioned more often (17 percent) than any other state program. Although other innovative programs such as business incubator and high-tech programs were noted (5 percent), they were not regarded as being as useful as conventional programs (infrastructure assistance (11 percent), revolving loan funds (10 percent), linked deposit schemes (10 percent), job training programs (8 percent), and marketing and promotion efforts (7 percent), including international trade promotion. The diffuse endorsement of state programs and the 9 percent specific mentions that state programs are not useful signify that state governments have yet to fill the gap left by the removal of federal funds.

New Local Roles

In most cities, mayors have taken the lead in promoting economic development. Economic development line agencies reporting to the mayor, city manager, or city council have primary responsibility for economic development policies in most cities. Thus the design of economic development policy rests with elected officials or those appointed by them. More than 50 percent of cities surveyed place lead responsibility in economic development line agencies, separate from community development or planning agencies. Many of those citing the importance of the mayor's office mention that deputy mayors have special responsibilities in this area.

In contrast, economic development line agencies often share implementation responsibilities with special authorities or citywide development corporations. Cities often turn to these quasi-public organizations, especially special authorities such as redevelopment agencies and port authorities, to carry out economic development projects. Many of these organizations have special financing authority or resources not available to line agencies; furthermore, they are able to bring expertise and resources from the private sector that are especially germane to economic development projects.

Policy Shifts

Local officials report that the policy shifts prompted by cuts in federal economic development programs led to changes in local objectives, smaller projects, more diverse projects, and smaller public shares of development costs, but not to changes in sectoral, spatial, or minority targeting efforts in most cities. Nearly 40 percent of the cities responding to the first survey report that federal cuts resulted in more diverse economic development objectives. In many instances, these objectives included more housing and social programs. About one-third (29 percent) of the cities see these cuts as negative, leading to restricted, narrower local objectives. Most cities are involved in smaller projects (55 percent), and many report that local projects are more diverse (38 percent), often because the choices are market driven. Public shares of development costs have decreased in many cities (46 percent). Targeting efforts appear to be unchanged in most cities, although the proportions of cities claiming to do more minority (17 percent) and low-income (20 percent) targeting are similar to the proportions claiming to do less (15 percent and 21 percent, respectively).

In comparison to five years previously, cities characterize their current policies as oriented more toward risk taking, job growth, downtown development, job creation, local concerns, market feasibility, and aiding local firms; they see the city's role as a public developer engaged in contractual relations rather than entitlement obligations. This profile of policy orientations signifies that cities are rethinking traditional strategies in favor of orientations emphasizing job creation and new, locally based growth. This accommodates more risk taking by local officials, who are likely to see themselves more as public developers than as regulators of development. Accordingly, local officials are likely to view their relationships with groups more in contractual terms than as entitlement obligations; they are also likely to take market feasibility rather than social criteria into account in making development decisions.

Policy Choices in the Postfederal Era

We also asked officials more directly about specific local strategy choices. Of those cities responding to our request for information, at least 50 percent reported using twenty-five core strategies. Of those twenty-five, seven were first used after 1980 by at least half the cities. Table 3.2 shows that various planning, management, and marketing strategies are prominent. Land acquisition and building demolition and infrastructure improvement to support development are other standard local development tools used by many cities. These strategies, based on traditional local land use controls and fiscal authority, are complemented by approaches based on federal initiatives. Revenue bonds, general obligation bonds, historical tax credits, and use of program income reflect past federal initiatives; with the exception of program income, these local strategies depend on federal tax code provisions that encourage local investment.[13] In the 1980s there were serious efforts to eliminate or modify these provisions. Historical tax credits were reduced and restrictions were placed on the amount and uses of revenue bonds. In the case of program income resulting from previous investment of public capital, the federal government challenged cities' claims on these revenue streams and attempted to recover program income from projects initially capitalized by federal funds. Eventually, the federal government lost in court, and cities were allowed to keep and reinvest these revenues.

Indirect legacies of federal programs are also evident in current strategies. Federal programs spread, or diffused, more widely the use of revolving loan funds, local development corporations, enterprise zones, strategic planning, below-market-rate loans, and community development corporations. Thus today's local economic development strategies are partially shaped by federal efforts, past and present. Some of the local strategies used most frequently since 1980, however, reflect state influences rather than federal funds or fiscal regulations. The state-influenced strategies include tax increment financing, trade missions abroad, and more metropolitan and regional cooperation.

The strategies reported as least used by more than 75 percent of the cities responding are those that would interfere with private investor decision making or compete with private investment capital. Five strategies sharing this distinction are mechanisms allowing cities to pool public and private capital or to influence the use of private investment funds. These "never used" strategies include using pension funds for economic development (95 percent), using equity pools with private-public consortia (87 percent), linking deposits (87 percent), issuing zero-coupon bonds (86 percent), and coordinating venture capital funds (82 percent). As the recent Orange County, California, debacle suggests, this may be with good reason; these tools demand a high tolerance for risk. Many cities cannot invest pension funds for economic development purposes because state personnel systems control these funds. And few cities have the technical capacity or private sector cooperation to undertake highly sophisticated financing strategies. However, the results of the follow-up survey, which we discuss in chapter 7, suggest continued consideration of these initiatives.

Table 3.2

Most used: Economic development strategies ever used by 50 percent or more of cities responding

Economic Development Strategy	% use
Comprehensive planning	93%
Capital improvement budgeting	91
Marketing and promotion	86
Land acquisition and building demolition	80
Infrastructure as in-kind development contribution	83
Revenue bonds	79
Strategic planning	74
Revolving loan fund	73
Streamlining permits	73
Selling land	69
Industrial parks	68
Below-market-rate loans	67
General obligation bonds	65
Local development corporations	63
Annexation	62
Historical tax credits	60
More metro and regional cooperation	58
Tax increment financing	56
Industrial development authorities	55
Enterprise zones	55
Using program income for economic development	55
Special assessment districts	54
Community development corporations	52
Land leases	52
Trade missions abroad	50

Note: Strategies shown in italics are those that a majority of cities first used after 1980.

Comparing Policy Choices When Using Federal and Nonfederal Resources

Is there any relationship between cities using federal funds entrepreneurially and cities making entrepreneurial choices now? Constructing policy indices allows us to compare the strategies employed by cities when using federal and nonfederal resources (see Table 3.3). Based on the entrepreneurial policy features identified above, we developed two aggregate measures of more entrepreneurial development policies. These additive indices are used to derive standardized policy scores that help sort out local strategies according to their entrepreneurial nature (Clarke and Gaile, 1989b, 1992).

The relationships between market-based strategy usage in the federal and postfederal eras are less linked than we had anticipated. Overall, we find the use of market-based strategies over time (COMBINDX) is modestly associated with the level of participation in federal economic development programs. However, there is no statistically significant relationship between overall use of federal funds for market-based strategies and present use of market-based local economic development strategies.

Counter to our expectations, we find that UDAG entrepreneurial use indices (Fiscal Entrepreneur, Social Entrepreneur) are not significantly associated with new (NEWINDEX) or overall (COMBINDX) entrepreneurial use; with one exception, there is no evidence that past entrepreneurial use of federal money in these cities shapes present entrepreneurial strategies. Current use of a specific tool promoted in UDAG projects—net cash-flow participation—is directly related to past use of this tool, but there are no other clear relationships between past and current strategy choices.

There is, however, evidence that the past ability to generate relatively high amounts of private investment with UDAG funds is associated with present entrepreneurial strategies.[14] Past private investment in UDAG projects, on a per capita basis, is positively associated with recent entrepreneurial policy adoptions (NEWINDEX). Thus successful deal making on past federal projects, reflected in relatively high levels of private investment rather than use of specific financing mechanisms, seems most important in shaping current usage.

Learning through Federal Program Participation

Why the lack of a stronger relationship between past federal fund use and postfederal use? The most obvious explanation is that these are different cities: Were those currently using entrepreneurial strategies eligible for or active in past federal economic development programs? Yes! More than two-thirds of those cities scoring high on the nonfederal market-based New Index were also active in the UDAG program, particularly after the introduction of "pocket of poverty" eligibility criteria. Thus the lack of relationship is not a function of comparing different sets of cities.

Table 3.3

The policy variables: Measures of local market-based strategies when using federal and nonfederal resources

Federal program resources

Index of Federal Economic Development Program Participation (Total Fed $ Per Cap): Total federal dollars per capita from CDBG, UDAG, and EDA programs during 1978–84 (trend surface residual data used).

Index of Use of UDAG Funds (Fiscal Entrepreneur): Whether city used UDAG funds for revolving loan funds, venture capital, net cash-flow participation, interest subsidies, equity pools, or other revenue-generating efforts in projects, 1978–84.

Index of Use of UDAG Funds (Social Entrepreneur): Whether city used UDAG funds for revolving loan funds, venture capital, net cash-flow participation, interest subsidies, equity pools, or other revenue-generating efforts and also imposed social conditions on the private partner, such as low-income housing set-asides, day-care center provision, and other noneconomic requirements, 1978–84.

Index of Use of EDA Title II and IX Funds: Whether city used EDA Title II and Title IX funds for revolving loan funds, interest subsidies, joint ventures, or other revenue-generating efforts, 1978–81.

Index of Use of CDBG Funds: The percentage allocation of CDBG funds for economic development purposes in FY 1988 and 1983 and the change in percentage allocation over time (1988 minus 1983).

Nonfederal resources

Index of Current Level of Activity Using Nonfederal Resources (CURRENT): Whether city is currently using any of 47 economic development strategies relying on nonfederal resources.

Combined policy indices

Index of Market-Based Strategies Ever Used by City (COMBINDX): Whether city ever used revolving loan funds, venture capital, net cash-flow participation, interest subsidies, equity participation, equity

Table 3.3 *(continued)*

pools established by private-public consortia, or program income for economic development purposes.

Index of Market-Based Strategies First Used by City since 1980 (NEWINDEX): Whether city first used revolving loan funds, venture capital, net cash-flow participation, interest subsidies, equity participation, equity pools established by private-public consortia, or program income for economic development purposes in 1980 or later.

Note: Variable names appear in parentheses. Except where it is clearly stated that an index is based on dollars spent or percentage use, these indices are additive, such that a yes answer on an item in the list is valued as a one.

Another argument is that local officials adapt their risk-aversive behavior to the source of revenues. Those willing to risk federal dollars on more entrepreneurial strategies such as net cash-flow participation are less likely to do so when using their own revenues. This explanation would be more strongly supported if we found a negative relationship (versus the absence of a relationship) between market-based use of federal resources and present strategies; nevertheless, the lack of a strong positive relationship suggests some backing off from entrepreneurial strategies when local dollars are at risk.

It is also possible that this lack of relationship signifies the diffusion of entrepreneurial approaches beyond cities active in earlier federal programs. As the analyses in the next chapter will show, different types of cities used entrepreneurial strategies in these two periods. In the nonfederal period, more economically and socially disadvantaged cities adopted entrepreneurial strategies.

Learning through Policy Competition

A policy history perspective of learning through policy competition is essentially a temporal argument: the experiences and strategies learned at one point in time are transferred or carried over to another. Those that did not learn specific skills in an earlier period are less likely to display them in a later period. Further, there is a distinct inertial tendency plus a tendency to be reactive versus proactive, which suggests that policy lags are likely. Although there is some evidence for the importance of participation in federal development programs, the policy history argument is not sufficient to explain current patterns.

The spatial competition perspective on policy learning is more intrinsically persuasive. Given the interjurisdictional competition for investment driving local economic development policy choices, it is reasonable to expect cities to mimic the policy choices of neighboring or competing or successful cities in order to maintain their competitive advantages with those cities. Although this "learning" often has the desultory suboptimal consequences we describe in chapter 2, it is a plausible explanation for why cities would choose a particular strategy. Our findings, however, do not support the emulation-of-neighbors hypothesis: there are no statistically significant relationships between geographic location and policy adoption.[15]

Given the near universal acceptance of the adage that cities are locked into a "bidding war" with other localities, this nonfinding merits further attention. We suspect that the aphorism of urban competition needs to be redefined in a global era. Although it is possible that all city officials wish to engage in this cutthroat competition, their opportunities to do so are highly variable. Many are constrained by state prohibitions limiting their policy options, by the absence of state enabling legislation allowing less traditional strategies, by high ratios of tax-exempt property, by sufficiently weak tax bases, by stalemated local political factions, by lack of institutional capacity, and by other local features that preclude their merely mimicking the policy choices made in other communities. Furthermore, globalization alters the types of locational incentives that make sense.

The nature of the policies themselves also may alter the grounds for policy competition. The diffusion of smokestack-chasing locational incentives appears to have been through spatial policy competition patterns, because communities were seeking to minimize the differences between their localities and neighboring ones in the eyes of investors. This encouraged emulation of other cities' cost-reduction strategies and homogenization of place. But entrepreneurial strategies presume differentiation of place, the need to create a niche by shaping local markets and establishing the uniqueness of a particular locale. They may also anticipate globalization and human capital enhancement arguments. This demand-side market-shaping approach, rather than a supply-side cost-reduction strategy (Eisinger, 1988), is inherently less supportive of policy emulation because strict emulation defeats the purpose of differentiation. Thus we would not expect to see entrepreneurial policies diffused by emulation and policy competition to the same extent as locational incentives.

Our spatial statistical analyses of potential diffusion processes revealed no evidence of such processes. We believe that trend surface analysis, used in this testing, provides a more precise means of measuring the effects of geographic relationships than do the dummy variables frequently used in analyses of policy diffusion. Thus our counterintuitive nonfinding may reflect better measurement of the impact of relative location. It allows us to argue that the policy arena is a national one. Although policies may indeed diffuse and emulation still plays a major role in cities, the evidence suggests they do so on a national basis and that regional differences in entrepreneurial policy selection are essentially nonexistent.[16]

Ranking City Entrepreneurial Policy Use

Responding cities indicate varying levels of use of these entrepreneurial strategies. Table 3.4 ranks the cities responding to the survey based on their overall levels of entrepreneurial strategy use activity (COMBINDX). Asterisks in the table indicate cities where the majority of entrepreneurial strategy use began after 1980.

Table 3.4

Cities that responded ranked on overall entrepreneurial policy activity

Very Active	Active	Somewhat Active	Inactive
Birmingham*	Akron*	Ann Arbor*	Albany
Chesapeake*	Albany	Aurora*	Beaumont
Chicago	Atlanta	Austin*	Cedar Rapids
Hartford	Buffalo	Bakersfield	Colorado Springs
Lincoln*	Charlotte*	Boise City*	Durham
Louisville	Chattanooga	Canton*	Fremont
Milwaukee*	Garden Grove*	Cleveland*	Fullerton
Minneapolis	Hammond*	Corpus Christi*	Houston
Oklahoma City	Hampton*	Dallas*	Independence
Rockford*	Jacksonville*	Davenport*	Livonia
St. Paul	Lansing	Denver*	Mesa
St. Petersburg*	Lexington*	El Paso	Norfolk
Savannah*	Los Angeles*	Eugene	Roanoke
Tacoma*	New York	Evansville	Salt Lake City
	Orlando*	Flint*	Seattle
	Oxnard*	Fort Worth	Stamford
	Peoria*	Grand Rapids*	Sunnyvale
	Portland, Oregon*	Greensboro*	Tempe
	Raleigh*	Hollywood, Florida	Topeka

Table 3.4 *(continued)*

Very Active	Active	Somewhat Active	Inactive
	Rochester	Huntsville*	Waco
	St. Louis	Indianapolis	Youngstown
	San Diego*	Irving*	
	Spokane*	Jersey City*	
	Springfield, Alabama	Kansas City, Missouri	
	Tampa	Las Vegas*	
	Waterbury*	Little Rock*	
	Winston-Salem*	Lubbock*	
		Miami	
		Newport News*	
		Pittsburgh	
		Portsmouth*	
		Santa Ana	
		Springfield, Illinois*	
		Stockton*	
		Syracuse*	
		Tulsa*	
		Wichita	
		Worcester	

*Cities where the majority of entrepreneurial activity reported began after 1980 (NEWINDEX).
Source: Based on scores on COMBINDX

Waves of Policy Innovation

As the work of cities changes, the policy responses change both reactively and proactively. The data show three waves of policy adoptions in which cities move toward the roles of risk takers and development partners, similar to the roles Jessop (1993) and others (Norton, 1995) theorize. The first wave of policy adoptions—those reported as first used before 1980 by at least 30 percent of the cities responding—still rely heavily on cities' abilities to regulate and facilitate development through land use controls, public services, and provision of infrastructure (Table 3.5). There are only limited, traditional financial tools entailing debt or cheap loans and scant evidence of higher-risk strategies.

Table 3.5

Waves of economic development strategies

The first wave: Locational orientation

Economic development strategy	% used before 1980
Comprehensive planning	84
Capital improvement budgeting	77
Revenue bonds	69
Land acquisition and building demolition	67
Infrastructure as in-kind development contribution	64
Selling land	59
General obligation bonds	59
Industrial parks	57
Annexation	53
Marketing and promotion	47
Strategic planning	46
Industrial development authorities	40
Local development corporations	38
Special assessment districts	37
Land leases	37
Land banks	34
Below-market-rate loans	33
Enterprise funds for public services	33
Historical tax credits	31

The second wave: Transitional entrepreneurial orientation

Economic development strategy	% used after 1980
Streamlining	59
Enterprise zones	52
Revolving loan funds	45
Business incubators	40
Trade missions abroad	39
Marketing and promotion[a]	39
More metro and regional cooperation	36
Below-market-rate loans[a]	34
Use program income for economic development	33
Tax increment financing	32

Table 3.5 *(continued)*

Anticipating the third wave: Postfederal entrepreneurial orientation

Economic development strategy	% under study in 1989
Business incubators[b]	21%
More metro and regional cooperation[b]	14
Tax increment financing[b]	12
Special assessment districts[b]	11
Foreign trade zones	10
Strategic planning[b]	10
Land banks[b]	10
Export and promotion	10
Equity participation	10
Taxable bonds	9
Streamlining[b]	7
Tax abatements—targeted at new business	7
Equity pools: private-public consortia	7
Tax abatements—targeted at selected sectors	6
Enterprise zones[b]	6
Enterprise funds for public services[b]	5
Venture capital funds	5
Local development corporations[b]	5
Linked deposits	5

[a]Also reported in the first wave.
[b]Also reported in the first or second wave.

In the transitional entrepreneurial second wave, city policies are characterized by a stronger investment and entrepreneurial approach (Table 3.5). The use of revolving loan funds, below-market-rate loans, and program income from successful projects reflects a public finance role. Furthermore, both enterprise zones and tax increment financing districts let cities reorganize their local economic bases to direct future revenues through allocation procedures outside the usual budgetary processes. In this sense, revenues come into the city on the basis of public investment decisions, rather than on the basis of tax policies or federal programs; future resources may be allocated with little public notice or accountability. Finally, attention to markets and business start-ups—two hallmarks of entrepreneurial approaches—also characterizes strategies using nonfederal resources.

The third wave features postfederal entrepreneurial strategies, which predominate in the many programs reported by local officials in 1989 as "under study" (Table 3.5). The importance of business incubators as a recent (Table 3.5) and current (see chapter 7) strategy underscores the salience of approaches encouraging new business start-ups, and perhaps enabling human capital, rather than conventional "smokestack chasing." There is also a clear interest in reorganization of the local tax and resource base. In particular, many cities are carving their local tax bases into foreign trade zones (responsive to the globalization trend), special assessment districts, tax increment financing districts, and enterprise zones. In each instance, these spatial arrangements tend to reduce the revenue base allocated by normal budgetary processes; tax revenues from these arrangements often are dedicated to debt service and further areal redevelopment rather than deposited into the general fund. The interest in greater metropolitan and regional cooperation on development issues suggests that cities may find economic teamwork more palatable than political consolidation. Finally, local officials are adopting a more business-oriented approach toward use of local assets; land use control strategies under study emphasize the flexible management of land rather than permanent transfers or sales in which land passes from public to private control. Similarly, there is a growing inclination to view public capital in terms of its investment potential, with the greater public risk taking that implies.

Our 1996 follow-up survey of cities confirms the entrepreneurial policy movement (the third wave) predicted from the 1989 survey. Table 3.6 illustrates the growing adoption of entrepreneurial policies by cities responding to the 1996 survey. These strategies, foreshadowed in Table 3.5 based on the 1989 survey, have now become established practice in many cities and will likely remain in use, even as a new "fourth wave" of strategies featuring globalization and human capital is added to the strategy tool kit of local economic development practitioners.

Different Policy Paths

Finally, we present another way of looking at these patterns of local choices. Although the statistical analyses used here are standard approaches for analyzing policy choices, a more contextual way of analyzing these policy strategies is through cluster analysis of bundles of policies. Here the emphasis is not on the linear relationship of policy options, policy history, location, or specific city characteristics, but on how cities bundle policy choices together. This approach allows us to uncover the complexity and diversity of policy portfolios constructed in cities (Miranda and Rosdil,

Table 3.6

Use of third-wave strategies in the 1990s

Economic development strategy	% first used since 1989	% use 1996
Streamlining licensing and permits	22.6	83.2
More metro and regional cooperation	46.0	74.9
Strategic planning	30.4	73.3
Local development corporations	20.0	71.5
Special assessment districts	22.2	67.7
Enterprise zones	20.4	63.6
Tax increment financing	26.3	62.6
Tax abatements—targeted at new businesses	33.9	56.9
Equity participation	35.9	56.3
Tax abatements—targeted at selected sectors	26.3	55.8
Land banks	14.3	55.4
Business incubators	18.5	45.1
Taxable bonds	21.1	41.9
Export production promotion	24.0	41.1
Foreign trade zones	12.7	37.3
Equity pools: public-private consortia	25.5	33.2
Venture capital funds	27.8	33.2
Enterprise funds for public services	7.3	32.7
Linked deposits	11.1	16.7

1995). The cluster procedure sorts the cases—here, the strategies—into groupings most like each other and most different from all others. Cluster analysis is a classificatory rather than explanatory device; it illustrates the different economic development policy paths cities choose, as the cities characterize them rather than as imposed by the analyst.[17] The results are portrayed as packages of development strategies with patterns of joint use. We see them as depicting different development policy paths. The cluster analysis highlights four clusters of policy choices:

Low-Use cluster: capital oriented, investment related, state regulated

Territorial cluster: uses spatial redefinition and local authority

Classic cluster: core conventional and widely used entrepreneurial strategies

Organizational cluster: organizational innovations that foster new investment

The Low-Use cluster includes twenty-three strategies, twenty-one of which were not used by the majority of the cities in the survey. Although many cities did use them, the profile reflects policies used by less than a majority: equity pools, zero-coupon bonds, export production promotion, sale-leasebacks, loan guarantees, general tax abatements, foreign trade zones, enterprise zones, use of pension funds for development purposes, venture capital funds, cash-flow participation, donation of land, interest subsidy, land lease, trade missions abroad, sectorally targeted tax abatements, loan deposits, taxable bonds, export promotion, procurement assistance, tax abatements targeted for new business, land banking, and earmarking of tax revenues.

Many of these are capital-oriented strategies, and several are investment-related strategies; many cities may be deterred from using these tools because of the absence of state enabling legislation or more risk-aversive stances when own funds are at stake. We characterized five of these strategies as entrepreneurial, as described above: equity pools, venture capital funds, interest subsidies, export promotion, and cash-flow participation. Two strategies used by a majority of cities fall into this Low-Use cluster: enterprise zones and land lease programs. Most states created state enterprise zone legislation in the 1980s in anticipation of a federal program; these programs vary widely in their eligibility criteria and development features. Although cities must apply for participation in the enterprise zone program, the zones depend on state initiative.

The Territorial cluster includes annexation, metropolitan and regional cooperation, tax increment financing, and special assessment districts. These entail territorial or spatial redefinitions for development purposes; they indicate efforts to capture new investment at different scales. In contrast to the investment orientation and capital-intensive nature of many of the strategies in the Low-Use cluster, the Territorial cluster exemplifies employment of local land use authority for development purposes. Another strategy, use of public enterprise funds for public services, is included in this cluster; this is often used by cities in states with conservative local fiscal authority because it creates independent financing capacity for fee-based services. Although a majority of cities do not use these funds, cities choosing territorial strategies are more likely to also use these funds.

The Classic cluster includes the core strategies used by the greatest number of cities; many conventional economic development options, such as infrastructure development and industry parks, are in this cluster, but it also includes relatively entrepreneurial strategies, such as revolving loan funds and generation of program income from development projects. The strategies in this cluster are industrial development authorities, infrastructure as in-kind investments, capital improvement budgeting, historic tax credits, selling land, use of program income, industrial parks, land acquisition, comprehensive planning, revenue bonds, strategic planning, marketing and promotion, below-market-rate loans, general obligation bonds, revolving loan funds, and streamlining. Of these sixteen strategies, six are investment oriented, five are land oriented, four are capital oriented, and one—industrial development authorities—is organizational.

This eclectic menu suggests the direction of local policy in the absence of federal resources, given that most of these tools are contingent on state authority or dependent on local capacity. The two more entrepreneurial choices very likely were capitalized in earlier federal or state programs; localities are now reallocating these funds for their own agendas.

The Organization cluster could be merged with the Classic cluster in terms of use patterns, but it is distinct enough to stand on its own. It includes three strategies: business incubators, community development corporations, and local development corporations. In each instance, localities are choosing organizational innovations that foster new investment; these are often at the neighborhood level and often targeted at small businesses (Vidal, 1992).

Conclusions

Overall, our findings indicate that many American cities did not respond to cuts in federal economic development funds by adopting more risk-aversive stances. Indeed, cities increasingly are using entrepreneurial strategies that entail some risk of their own revenues and substantial opportunity costs. A number of subtle shifts in policy orientation mark this entrepreneurial orientation: ascendance of market feasibility criteria over social criteria, resurgence of the downtown as the locus for redevelopment, reliance on nonprofit organizations rather than government agencies for implementation, and redefinition of city responsibilities as a public developer.

Neither policy history nor policy competition appears to explain these choices. A history of extensive participation in federal local development programs is not associated with current entrepreneurial policy choices, nor is previous entrepreneurial policy experience associated with current use of entrepreneurial policy approaches. Furthermore, we find little support for the argument that cities choose policy strategies in response to the choices of their neighboring or competitive cities. These policy choices appear to be more context specific; understanding these patterns requires more attention to city economic and political characteristics.

4

Context and Policy Effectiveness

*Localities choose contextually specific paths
in responding to globalization.*

Our fourth proposition is that there is no "silver bullet" for cities seeking to enhance their economic well-being, largely because of their contextual differences. As the policy clusters reveal, different policy paths are possible. Local officials choose diverse paths, in part because their constitutional, economic, and human capital situations vary, but also in response to political configurations at the local level.

Some American cities fare better than others in meeting the challenges of a changing economic and political setting, even though they face similar constraints. As we demonstrated in the preceding chapter, the emerging pattern of policy responses seems substantively different from the historical pattern of locational incentives. But our findings have led us to reject arguments that these choices reflect temporal or regional spatial diffusion patterns. That is, current entrepreneurial orientations are not more likely to be selected in cities that have histories of entrepreneurial use of past federal resources. Nor is there evidence that cities merely mimic their nearby competitors' policy choices, as the spatial diffusion model suggests.

Instead, local context matters. To understand these policy patterns more clearly, we examined the city features associated with the different paths chosen. In particular, we are interested in whether innovation or policy change is linked to local conditions of stress or to the availability of slack resources (Rogers, 1983). Similarly, we need to move beyond models of temporal and spatial diffusion to explore the role of networks of policy specialists in bringing new ideas to cities (Lowery and Gray, 1990). The analyses presented here show that cities employing entrepreneurial policies in the postfederal era differ from the cities using similar policies when backed by federal funds. We find evidence that better-off cities were more likely to use federal resources in entrepreneurial ways, but that, in the absence of federal resources, distressed cities are more likely to choose entrepreneurial approaches. Although a federal policy history of using entrepreneurial tools is not linked to current entrepreneurial choices, there is evidence that the Urban Development Action Grant program taught cities some specific entrepreneurial skills. Finally, we find that participation in policy specialist networks, encouraged by programs such as those established by the National Development Council, is related to local policy choices.

With understandable caution, we ask whether there is any evidence that these different strategies are effective: Do they influence the performance of the local economy in desired ways? Although we provide some evidence that these entrepreneurial strategies are linked to vibrant local economies, we do not pretend to demonstrate causal relationships of policy effectiveness. We do believe, however, that cities using these strategies are signaling an understanding of new growth processes and positioning themselves in the shifting economic order of globalization.

Comparative Analyses of Cities Using Entrepreneurial Policies

In chapter 3, we used data on local policy choices to describe cities' use of market-based approaches when using different types of resources—federal or nonfederal. In this chapter, we ask three important questions: Do different types of cities choose market-based strategies? Does it matter whether they are using federal resources or relying on their own resources? Is there evidence that the policies are effective?

This analysis of the city characteristics associated with policy choices is an exploratory effort. There is little guidance from previous analyses of local economic development efforts, as most tend to focus on *levels of policy activity* rather than the types of approaches adopted. There is general agreement that more fiscally stressed cities are more likely to engage in economic development activity generally. And there is some evidence that more distressed cities pursue distinctive strategies that are relatively high risk (Rubin and Rubin, 1987). But there have been few empirical analyses of city characteristics associated with market-based, or entrepreneurial, policy choices. Clarke and Rich (1985) have found a significant relationship between a city's past federal program experience and entrepreneurial use of UDAG funds, but it is not clear that this relationship continues in a period of federal retrenchment. Goetz (1990, 1994) has examined the conditions under which cities adopt Type II development strategies, local efforts to balance the needs of mobile capital with community needs by requiring private developers to provide services or public benefits in exchange for public aid.[1] Testing a range of alternative explanations for adoption of Type II policies, Goetz found an unexpected relationship with economic and fiscal stress. Could it be that more distressed cities are more likely to adopt Type II policies? In a 1990 study, David Elkins (1995) confirmed this finding for certain types of Type II policies, but found fiscal health to be associated with most Type II adoptions. He also found strong mayoral power and high African American representation to be associated with adoption of Type II policies. At a minimum, these studies indicate that contextual effects on policy choices are not straightforward and that local political configurations are especially salient.

In the absence of compelling theoretical arguments about the types of cities most likely to use entrepreneurial strategies, we organize this exploratory analysis around a series of null hypotheses.[2] Basically, this logical structure posits the absence of any significant relationships between, in this case, city socioeconomic or political features and city policy choices in the federal and nonfederal periods.[3] It is then up to the researchers to reject these presumed "nonrelationships" through the use of analytic methods testing for any relationship; finding evidence of a relationship lends support to the alternative hypotheses—that there *are* links between city characteristics and policy choices.[4]

Characteristics of Cities Using Federal Resources for Market-Based Strategies

In the federal period, the work of cities was in transition from the primary use of locational incentives to the adoption of strategies more geared to market dynamics. Concerns with human capital and globalization trends were nascent. National program funds, however, constituted "side payments" to cities, encouraging or permitting experimentation with new techniques at relatively little risk to local resources. Which cities took up this opportunity? Because our ability to trace links between city characteristics and entrepreneurial use of federal program funds is limited by the different types of program data available, our analytic strategy varies for each program considered.

UDAG Resources

UDAG program data from 1978 to 1984 are used for this analysis because project-level data on local usage are the most comprehensive and detailed. They allow construction of two distinctive policy indices (also described in chapter 3): a Fiscal Entrepreneur Index and a Social Entrepreneur Index.

Briefly, the Fiscal Entrepreneur Index measures whether local projects used UDAG funds for revolving loan funds, venture capital, net cash-flow participation, interest subsidies, equity pools, or other revenue-generating efforts. The Social Entrepreneur Index indicates whether social conditions are imposed on the private partner, such as low-income housing set-asides, day-care center provision, and other noneconomic requirements. Were certain types of cities more likely to score highly as UDAG fiscal entrepreneurs or UDAG social entrepreneurs?

It appears so. There are significant relationships between specific city social and economic characteristics and use of market-based strategies with federal UDAG resources.[5] In the UDAG program, cities using federal UDAG funds entrepreneurially—as measured by the Fiscal Entrepreneur and Social Entrepreneur Indices—tended to be cities with above-average incomes, above-average housing values, above-average educational achievement, and below-average social problems of teenage pregnancy and poverty. Recall that UDAG funds were allocated to cities deemed eligible according to a distress index; of these distressed cities, those with more affluent, less disadvantaged populations chose to use their UDAG funds in more fiscally entrepreneurial ways and imposed greater conditions on investors benefiting from use of city UDAG funds. This corresponds to an argument that such cities can "afford" to take risks (Elkins, 1995) and to negotiate with developers, although there are notable examples of less well-off cities taking similar stances (Rich, 1993a, 1993b; Goetz, 1990, 1994). Although attitudinal data are not available, it may be that local officials in affluent communities face citizen pressures that demand more conditions be put on developers. There is also anecdotal evidence that early UDAG entrepreneurs were encouraged by HUD regional offices to strike better, tighter deals with their private partners in order to legitimate the "efficiency" of this use of public funds. All in all, we are confident that cities using UDAG funds in entrepreneurial ways tend to differ from other cities.

EDA Resources

EDA Title II and Title IX programs provided another source of funds that cities could use with some discretion. EDA staff provided us with Title II and Title IX fund use information for projects from 1978 through 1981.[6] Again we ask whether there are important differences in city features between those using EDA funds entrepreneurially and those not using them entrepreneurially. Again we find modest patterns between city economic and social characteristics and policy choices using federal EDA resources. But the EDA pattern contrasts with the UDAG pattern: there is statistically significant evidence that distressed cities (high poverty, low retail sales) were more likely to use EDA funds entrepreneurially than were cities using the UDAG program.[7]

CDBG Resources

The Community Development Block Grant program remains the single most important source of federal funds to cities today. City officials provided data on percentage allocations of CDBG funds for economic development in FY 1988. Again we find significant relationships between city economic and social characteristics and policy choices using CDBG funds.[8] But, again, these findings contrast markedly with the UDAG findings. Cities using CDBG funds for economic development activities tend to be distressed cities with lower and more slowly growing income levels, higher poverty rates, more female-headed households, and more renters than in other CDBG cities. In other words, the EDA and CDBG patterns indicate that stress encourages entrepreneurial choices, whereas the UDAG pattern indicates that slack resources make this more likely.

Overall Federal Resources

If we look at overall rates of local participation in these federal programs, rather than at the specific type of program funds, the contrast between cities is particularly evident.[9] On a per capita basis, federal economic development funds went to cities with low income, high poverty, declining population, a higher-than-average black population, higher-than-average teenage pregnancy, higher-than-average infant mortality, higher-than-average proportion of single-parent families, more crime, more elderly, decaying retail trade and employment, and problems in the housing sector. This is consistent with the poverty and economic distress criteria in many urban federal funding programs. These distressed cities got more national funds and were more likely to use EDA and CDBG funds in market-oriented ways. Of those cities eligible for national funds, the better-off cities were more likely to make entrepreneurial use of UDAG funds.

Characteristics of Cities Using Nonfederal Resources for Market-Based Strategies

Which kinds of cities chose market-based local economic development strategies after the federal funds and incentives to do so were largely removed? Two indices of nonfederal market-based strategies were created based on the following indicators: whether cities use revolving loan funds, venture capital, net cash-flow participation, interest subsidies, equity participation, equity pools established by public-private consortia, or program income to carry out economic development activities (see Table 3.2).[10] With the Combined Index, we can measure cities reporting any use of these market-based strategies at any time. In contrast, the New Index is more precise: it shows those reporting first use of these strategies since 1980. Independent variables similar to those employed to analyze federal fund use were also used to identify significant relationships between city characteristics and the choice of market-based strategies in the absence of federal resources. The findings displayed in Table 4.1 paint a picture of urban distress—relatively lower incomes, higher unemployment, higher infant mortality, lower sales, and so on, linked to city choices of market-based strategies. And contrasting Table 4.1 with the previous analysis of city characteristics and the use of federal funds yields interesting insights. Whereas better-off eligible cities tended to use UDAG federal funds for market-based strategies, distressed cities were more likely to use EDA, CDBG, and nonfederal resources for market-based strategies. Although it challenges conventional political economy arguments, this corresponds to Goetz's (1990, 1994) and Elkins's (1995) analyses of Type II policies.

Finally, cities that use entrepreneurial strategies also differ in the methods they use to assess economic conditions and evaluate the success of their economic development strategies.[11] The cities using more market-based policies focus strongly on the job market in assessing their economic conditions, but focus explicitly on program performance—securing good leverage, having strong loan repayments, and generating program income—in assessing their strategies.

Political Characteristics of Cities Using Federal Resources for Market-Based Strategies

Did cities making entrepreneurial use of federal funds have distinctive political characteristics? In the absence of systematic city-level data on political features, we turn to the Fiscal Austerity and Urban Innovation (FAUI) data set for measures of the local political setting.[12] More federal development funds per capita are more likely in cities with higher proportions of Democrats and nonwhites (particularly blacks) and partisan-affiliated representatives on the city council; these highly funded cities also score strongly on the Ethnic Political Culture Index, a measure of private-regarding or clientelistic political culture (Clark and Ferguson, 1983). These cities are more likely to have adopted (since 1978) fiscal strategies involving personnel reduction, export strategies, and (not surprisingly) seeking more intergovernmental funds.[13]

Table 4.1

Correlation analyses: Characteristics of cities using nonfederal resources for market-based strategies

r	Independent (characteristic) variable	Dependent variable
-.421	Per capita income change 1969–79	Combined Index
-.244	Per capita money income, 1979 (constant 1985 $)	Combined Index
.202	Total debt outstanding, 1985–86	Combined Index
.205	Infant deaths per 1,000 live births	Combined Index
.318	% of households with female head of household	Combined Index
.303	One-person households, % of all households	Combined Index
.257	% of births to mothers <20 years old	Combined Index
.230	Hospital beds per 100,000 population	Combined Index
-.193	% completing 12 years of school	Combined Index
-.214	% change, paid retail employees 1977–82	New Index
-.210	% change retail sales 1977–82	New Index
-.180	Housing permits issued per capita	New Index
-.199	New private housing authorized by permit 1980–86, % 1980 stock	New Index
.219	Civilian labor force—unemployment rate 1986	New Index
.207	% of manufacturing establishments with >19 employees	New Index
-.180	Per capita money income, 1979 (constant 1985 $)	New Index
-.173	Infant deaths per 1,000 live births	New Index

Note: All independent variables are standardized residuals from a trend surface analysis. Significance level <0.05.

These descriptive features of national largesse are intriguing but not surprising. Less obvious are the apparent links between these features and entrepreneurial use of federal funds. Cities attributing their financial problems specifically to the loss of federal revenues, for example, are likely to score highly on our policy measures as UDAG fiscal and social entrepreneurs. Cities with high UDAG social entrepreneur scores, however, are also cities scoring low on fiscal authority. It may be that these cities are constrained by state legislation from negotiating on fiscal matters but are free to negotiate on social conditions. Both policy indices are positively related with strong Ethnic Political Culture scores, suggesting that such cities are more amenable to group-based bargaining for discrete development benefits.

This politicized setting is amplified by analyses showing strong differences between cities in forms of government and entrepreneurial use of federal resources. Cities with mayor-council forms of government used federal resources with market-based strategies significantly more than did council-manager forms of government. Mayor-council forms of government were not only clearly more effective in receiving economic development funds from the federal government during the peak years of federal funding of cities, but they also distinguished themselves in using those funds more entrepreneurially.[14] These findings underscore the importance of political leadership in securing external funds and in undertaking potentially risky policy initiatives, including shifting federal funds to new uses.

Finally, there is a statistically significant difference between cities with relatively high per capita federal economic development funding and the presence of nonwhite mayors.[15] This means that nonwhite mayors are getting more federal economic development funds to work with; Elkins's analysis suggests that these mayors are more likely to pursue Type II strategies.

Political Characteristics of Cities Using Nonfederal Resources for Market-Based Strategies

These leadership measures also prove important in distinguishing cities' entrepreneurial policy choices in the absence of federal funds.[16] Once again, form of government is related to the use of these strategies, as it was in the federal period.[17] Again, mayor-council forms of government clearly favored entrepreneurial strategies relative to the choices of cities with council-manager forms of government. Similarly, the presence of nonwhite mayors distinguishes cities using market-based strategies, even when federal funds are less available.[18] Elkins (1995) has found comparable evidence of the importance of mayoral power and African American political representation.

Given that nonwhite mayors are relatively recent and rare features of American local politics, it may be that these newcomers are less obligated or at least less tied to entrenched economic interests of a white business elite. Although African American (Stone, 1989) and Latino (Judd and Ready,

1986; Saiz, 1991) mayors inevitably find they must align themselves with the business community in order to get things done, they also tend to have broader agendas. In many instances, these include greater economic integration of ethnic and racial minorities, the very types of policy objectives that would encourage market-shaping initiatives and discretionary benefits. This result is further supported by a statistical relationship between the active use of strategies and the proportion of the council that is black.[19]

Together, these statistical analyses provide evidence that there are significant relationships between city political features and city policy choices using nonfederal resources. An admittedly murky picture emerges: entrepreneurial strategies, particularly UDAG indices, being more likely in cities previously benefiting from federal largesse but now suffering from loss of federal funds, with strong minority representation on city council, strong mayoral leadership, political cultures valuing bargaining and negotiation of discrete benefits, and problem definitions centered on market performance rather than public sector allocations. The adoption of these entrepreneurial approaches occurs in a highly politicized atmosphere, one more charged than when adopting conventional locational subsidies (Elkins, 1995; Goetz, 1990).

Learning through Policy Networks

Our findings thus far indicate that these new policy strategies are not a function of policy history or policy competition. They do appear to be associated with more local contextual features, although these relationships beg the question: How *do* cities learn to use market-based policies? Because this is an exploratory mapping of city policy patterns, we are not able to address here a question about precise decisions in specific cities at this level of analysis. In chapters 5 and 6, our case studies allow us to examine individual cities more closely, but here we want to explore a city-level feature that came to light during our field interviews. Local officials emphasized the importance of participation in specialized policy networks as a source of new ideas and new skills. There are many such organizations, including the networking and training efforts of the National League of Cities, the International Council of City Managers, and the Council for Urban Economic Development.

The National Development Council Training Network

A major player in this skills network, one of the oldest, is the National Development Council, a national nonprofit organization specializing (since 1976) in providing training and technical assistance to cities. NDC began working with ten pilot cities, with federal support from HUD, EDA, and the Small Business Administration (SBA), to nurture development finance skills. By the time of our survey in 1989, fifty-eight cities were participating. NDC programs worked with the public, private, and nonprofit sectors to provide training and organizational strategies, such as bank loan participation programs, that encouraged cooperative ventures.

NDC, along with similar economic development networking organizations, had a formative impact on the capacity of American cities to participate in public-private partnerships. They created and disseminated the knowledge and skill base necessary for such new public sector roles. As change agents, they shaped the emergent local economic development "worldview" described here as a demand-side, market-shaping, entrepreneurial orientation. NDC's emphasis on deals rather than grants, its introduction of equity financing and credit analysis techniques, its techniques for devising long-term capital financing through packaging of discrete resource pools and leveraging both public and private funds, and its focus on performance goals and program management led local officials away from bureaucratic programs and toward more activist roles. Although these orientations and skills may have developed and disseminated in the absence of the policy networking role played by NDC and others, they accelerated these processes and provided more widespread, systematic coverage.

NDC's network was extensive: Cleveland, Tacoma, and Chicago participated in NDC training, but Berkeley (California), Kenosha (Wisconsin), and Mt. Vernon (New York) did as well. In our analyses, cities participating in NDC training and technical assistance programs were significantly more likely to have active economic development agendas and to have used market-based strategies at some point. They were also much more successful than other cities in garnering federal support for economic development.[20]

NDC's emphasis has been on finance tools rather than grant management; in a sense, NDC and other policy networks laid the groundwork for the diffusion of public-private partnership arrangements in American cities. It is important to recall that the public-private partnership rhetoric inserted in federal programs during the Carter administration was a novel concept for most local officials. Indeed, in most cities, a climate of mutual distrust and lack of knowledge about values and operations in each sector was pervasive. Carter's emphasis on the inability of the federal government to provide sufficient public resources for local development projects, and his subsequent cuts in federal funds to localities, was complemented by the argument that the private sector had the resources and know-how to make such projects work. Yet it was left to local officials to figure out how to make it profitable for private firms to meet local economic and social goals such as bringing jobs to ghetto communities or fostering the development of more housing for low-income people. With a few exceptions, such as Pittsburgh, Boston, and Chicago, most American cities lacked the development finance skills, experience, expertise, and institutional capacity necessary to find common ground with profit-seeking private sector firms.

NDC began to fill this void with a series of training sessions aimed at providing local officials with the tools to encourage private sector investment in small and medium-sized businesses, using both federal and local resources.[21] The four key courses were offered in weeklong sessions involving forty to sixty local officials; they were titled "Introductory Concepts in Economic Development," "Business Credit and Financial Analysis," "Real Estate Financing and Federal Loan Programs," and "Developer Deal Analysis and Equity Capital Financing." The introductory session, for example, went over development financing concepts; the roles of federal agencies (HUD, SBA, EDA), local economic development professionals, and local banks; the financing tools available for neighborhood commercial revitalization; the components of industrial job development; and the role of credit analysis in identifying viable deals.

In the process, NDC self-consciously set about creating and legitimating a new cadre of local economic development professionals (EDPs). In a local government world dominated by grantsmanship and bureaucratic management of federal programs, these newly trained local officials stood apart. Often this was literally the case: as we indicated in chapter 3, many cities moved toward establishing economic development divisions separate from grant-funded community development departments, or even moved these functions off-budget or into quasi-public organizations. Furthermore, NDC characterized these EDPs as working with an Economic Development Financing System, a set of tools capable of financing a range of types and sizes of borrowers. In contrast to local bureaucrats administering programs, EDPs wielded a portfolio of development finance tools in a new local government "delivery system." They influenced the composition of this emergent delivery system by their preference for working with umbrella groups bringing together neighborhood organizations, such as the Chicago Association of Neighborhood Development Organizations (CANDO) and lending consortia, as well as for utilizing 501c3 organizations. In working with Small Business Administration loan programs, NDC encouraged the use of local development corporations to coordinate loan packages submitted to participating financial institutions and to provide marketing and technical assistance to firms.

NDC acted as a change agent by articulating a coherent vision of a new local role, rationalizing the shift in terms of public goals such as job creation and slum revitalization, providing the necessary knowledge and skills, encouraging new institutional arrangements that facilitated public-private cooperation, and publicizing the successes of its participating cities.[22]

Not all these efforts were successes, of course. The new tools promoted by NDC and others contributed to overbuilding of downtown office space, oversupply of festival shopping malls, and the diversion of public funds from other local needs. NDC advocated more entrepreneurial, less risk-aversive strategies, although its programmatic orientation was toward small and medium-sized firms and neighborhood commercial and industrial development rather than the large speculative projects more likely to lead to such excesses. Our aim here is not to evaluate the effectiveness of NDC programs (see Goetz and Rich, 1983), but to underscore their importance in the emergence of local entrepreneurial orientations.[23]

Effectiveness of Groups of Strategies

Do entrepreneurial strategies make a difference? Policy effectiveness remains a thorny issue and complex goal. Although all local officials hope their policy choices lead to increased jobs and income levels in their communities, these are not necessarily their only concerns. They are well aware that global and national socioeconomic trends can overwhelm their efforts to make a difference in their cities' economic situations. Yet few cities choose to revert to the traditional role of service provision and infrastructure maintenance. City choices vary more than would be expected. This suggests differing beliefs about the effectiveness of various policy choices or, at a minimum, the images local officials hope to convey about their cities' position in a global economy (Pagano and Bowman, 1995).

Local officials are more likely to be realists, we suspect, than are the academics who bicker about dubious claims of policy effectiveness. Local development officials often implicitly adopt a "portfolio" approach to their strategy choices, well aware that some will fail for reasons beyond their control but hoping that enough will succeed to create an aura of success or at least momentum. As Pagano and Bowman (1995) demonstrate, changes in landscape or skyline are among the more important, but less tangible, measures of effectiveness used by local officials. These displays of local policy effort contribute to the differentiated image and niche a city hopes to create for itself in a changing economy. They also establish a climate conveying the values and priorities a city hopes to establish in the minds of investors and citizens. These symbolic politics are often as powerful as any cost-benefit analysis of individual strategies (e.g., Shlay and Giloth, 1987).

In the absence of empirical analyses of the effectiveness of local entrepreneurial approaches, great expectations prevail but little evidence exists (but see Bartik, 1991). Indeed, we must make a strong disclaimer, as is normal in statistical analyses, that it is impossible to infer causality and difficult to single out the effects of policy measures in such a complex situation. Yet simple analyses do provide some level of evidence for evaluating the impacts of policies. We address this void by exploring simple relationships between the level of entrepreneurial effort and changes in employment and income in the local community. Other secondary policy effects include the impacts on business starts and tax revenues. Our methodology promises more precise measures of effectiveness by measuring changes in outcomes while controlling spatially regular factors causing local economic change.[24]

Effectiveness of Market-Based Strategies Using Federal Resources

Did market-based strategies using federal resources pay off? This is admittedly a difficult question to answer without in-depth case studies. Yet aggregate analyses of variables that represent desired "effects" of these strategies can describe whether there is a statistically significant relationship between the market-based strategy used and the desired effect.[25] Again, in the complex socioeconomic milieu in which American cities find themselves, it would be inappropriate to argue that these identified relationships are causal.

Nonetheless, our analyses produce some intriguing findings. The statistical analyses indicate a positive relationship between cities ranking high on UDAG Social and Fiscal Entrepreneur Indices and healthy retail growth.[26] The negative relation with unemployment suggests that cities ranking high on the Social Entrepreneur Index are less likely to have unemployment problems. These findings allow us to reject the proposition that there are *no* significant relationships between use of market-based policies relying on federal resources and city fiscal and socioeconomic conditions. But we cannot determine the direction of this relationship. It is possible, for example, that these cities were able to be social and fiscal entrepreneurs with UDAG funds precisely because they had healthy commercial sectors and low unemployment.

Effectiveness of Market-Based Strategies Using Nonfederal Resources

Due to the newness of these strategies, it is too early to tell if they have been truly effective. It is premature both because of the time lag required for strategies to have effects and because of the limits of data availability. Despite these necessary statistical disclaimers, the analyses reveal evidence of positive relationships between policy choices and local effects. There are weak but statistically significant relationships between city use of market-based strategies using nonfederal resources and selected city fiscal and socioeconomic conditions.[27] These preliminary analyses suggest that cities introducing market-based strategies since 1980 also have significantly greater job growth and more fast-growing companies. The job growth is particularly heartening, given that these cities were characterized by high unemployment rates. Further, their fiscal situation is marked by lower taxes and expenditures. Again, although causality or even strong relationships cannot be claimed, the significant relationships make the case for further exploration of the effectiveness of market-based strategy use.[28]

Effectiveness of Individual Strategies

Some local development officials now have tool kits that include financial instruments, public-private partnerships, marketing strategies, institutional flexibility, and new types of public authority. Yet it is difficult to choose the appropriate tools from this array, given that many of the tools are relatively new and their general effectiveness remains uncertain. We analyzed the effectiveness of specific tools, in addition to our analysis of overall strategy use. The statistical tests compared mean economic conditions in groups of cities that ever used a particular tool with those in cities that never used that particular tool. Table 4.2 indicates that cities using these tools are more likely to enjoy specific growth features than are cities that never use these tools. This is especially interesting because our growth measures are not the aggregate income and jobs measures often used in scholarly analyses of policy effectiveness, but more relevant (to local officials) and more dynamic indicators of local job growth and business formation.

Perceived Effectiveness Measures

In addition to these "objective" effectiveness measures, we were interested in how local officials assessed these tools. Each respondent was asked to estimate the "overall effectiveness in promoting economic development" of

Table 4.2

Specific tools associated with effective economic development outcomes

Effective outcome / Specific policy tools	*t*-test significance
Increasing job growth rate	
Marketing and promotion	0.009
Cash-flow participation	0.014
Selling land	0.041
Fast-growing companies as high percentage of new firms	
Equity pools funded by public-private consortia	0.010
Cash-flow participation	0.017
Marketing and promotion	0.032
Community development corporations	0.044
Increasing relative business growth rate	
Enterprise zones	0.003
Interest subsidies	0.004
Land acquisition and demolition	0.006
Land leases	0.015
Loan guarantees	0.038
Increasing business birthrate	
Infrastructure as in-kind development contribution	0.043

Note: Significance level <0.05. The effective outcome variables are taken from *Inc.* magazine. For descriptions of the specific policy tools, see Appendix B.

each of forty-seven development tools (see Appendix B). As the following list suggests, the tools perceived as effective tend to either (1) involve capital financing programs aiding specific firms or areas or (2) establish self-financing development efforts. They also allow local control of benefits. From these responses, the rankings of a dozen economic development tools perceived as most effective by local development officials are as follows:

1. Revenue bonds
2. Tax increment financing
3. Earmarking tax revenues

    4. Enterprise funds for public services

    5. Revolving loan funds

    6. Infrastructure as in-kind development contribution

    7. Below-market-rate loans

    8. Industrial development authorities

    9. Capital improvement budgeting

    10. Industrial parks

    11. Local development corporations

    12. Using program income for economic development

In contrast, the dozen strategies perceived as least effective, listed below, are more likely to involve efforts to structure markets or expand the city's public investment role. Note that some of these fit our definition of entrepreneurial tools, and several are reported as "under study" in Table 3.5.

    1. Foreign trade zones

    2. Export production promotion

    3. Business incubators

    4. Cash-flow participation

    5. Trade missions abroad

    6. Procurement assistance

    7. Marketing and promotion

    8. Donating land

    9. Enterprise zones

    10. Tax abatements, general

    11. More metropolitan and regional cooperation

    12. Land banking

Some discrepancies between the statistical findings and perceptions of the local development specialists are provocative. In several instances, tools whose use appears to distinguish effectively between communities with fast economic growth and those with slow growth (Table 4.2) are among those rated least effective by the local specialists. The converse is also true: few of those tools perceived as most effective appear to be significant in the statistical analyses of policy choice and growth conditions.

This is an intriguing puzzle. Some possible explanations for these discrepancies come to mind, although this disjuncture merits more focused research. Because the data reported are from all responding cities, they include data from cities that are less inclined to use entrepreneurial strategies and may reflect skepticism or lack of knowledge about more entrepreneurial tools. Recall that these entrepreneurial strategies are relatively new and thus less familiar than older, more traditional strategies. With a few exceptions, the tools perceived as "most effective" have been available to cities for years. Also, the newer strategies tend to emphasize long-term growth and thus may be undervalued by local officials interested in immediate revenue streams and short-term improvements. The newer strategies targeting growth processes and markets also tend to feature less tangible results (therefore, less credit can be taken by decision makers); they are less likely, in themselves, to change the local skyline dramatically (Pagano and Bowman, 1995). Finally, these results reflect local perceptions in 1989; despite the wariness about globalization initiatives indicated here, our 1996 survey reveals much greater interest in the promotion of global-local links.

Conclusions

The framework developed here allows us to describe communities as more or less entrepreneurial in their approaches to economic development and to determine the conditions under which cities choose more entrepreneurial approaches. Local context matters, particularly the political dynamics pushing the search for new strategies. Our tentative efforts at assessing the effectiveness of these market-based orientations rely on sophisticated spatial analysis techniques to control for regional effects; the findings reveal links between strategies and impacts that may have been obscured by regional effects in other studies. Use of these market-based strategies appears to distinguish communities with (1) job growth, (2) new firm formation, and (3) fast-growing firms from less fortunate communities. This is not necessarily a causal relationship of policy choices and economic change, but it indicates a clear difference in the public investment climate in communities adopting market-oriented strategies and those with more conventional orientations. This climate depends on both business and government: few of the public entrepreneurial strategies are possible without business partners who are willing to share both risks and gains. The dissonance of these "objective" measures of policy effectiveness with local officials' perceptions of what works creates more questions than we have managed to answer here.

In the next two chapters, we consider a second aspect of the new work of cities: the search for institutional frameworks appropriate for mobilizing interests and making decisions about responses to this changing local setting. We do so through case studies of four cities—Cleveland, Jacksonville, Tacoma, and Syracuse—active in the federal era but now choosing different development paths.

5

Cities at Work

Cleveland and Jacksonville

Undertaking the transition to a global era involved more than changing local policy orientations. As cities struggled to adapt to the changing nature of competition in a global context, many began to rethink their arrangements for making and carrying out economic development decisions. The emergence of public-private partnerships is one of the more obvious organizational aspects of these new considerations (Harvey, 1989; Eisinger, 1988). This partnership focus does not, however, capture the significant transformations in the institutional organization of the local state in the last decade. These transformations go beyond partnership rhetoric to encompass governance strategies in the face of increasing complexity (Stone, 1989; Stoker, 1995; Lauria, 1997). The focus on governance acknowledges the collective action problem created by the growing complexity and interdependence of market and state interests: mechanisms and structures must be devised that encourage cooperation and coordination in areas of mutual concern, such as local economic development policy activities. Partnerships are one such mechanism, but only one element in a larger process of local institutional design.

From our perspective, these institutional design processes are *as important* as the new policy strategies described in previous chapters. They structure the power relations of both state and market interests, sketch out the possibilities for participation and representation in local economic development policy making, and shape the goals, preferences, and prospects of contending groups. As Horan puts it, institutions "define the context and substance of urban governance" (1997, 152). We believe that they significantly influence how effectively a city will anticipate and address its development needs *and* local citizenship issues. These institutional changes, therefore, are significant aspects of the new political arenas at the local level: they are context-specific changes with long-term consequences for local democratic practice.

Context-Structuring Processes

In this chapter and the next, we portray these searches for new institutional arrangements as *context-structuring processes*—they are reshaping the frameworks within which groups mobilize and negotiate economic development issues (Fuchs and Cox, 1991). This reminds us that cities pursue their economic goals not only through specific policy strategies but also by creating institutional frameworks and decision arenas where relatively stable bargaining and negotiation can take place. These institutional frameworks are more than sets of static, formal organizations; they structure relations of power among contending groups and shape the contingent goals, preferences, and strategies of political actors (Elkin, 1985; Horan, 1997; Stone, 1989; Thelen and Steinmo, 1992; Clarke, 1995).

This institutionalist standpoint counters tendencies to focus narrowly on the politics of coalition formation or the seductive appeal of "the deal." It reinstates the importance of the structures of market and state (Horan, 1997, 152), although the concern is not with particular organizations or institutional capacity per se. Rather, we ask how the institutional framework creates incentives for coherent and stable choices on policy issues and whether this creates bargaining advantages for certain interests (Kantor and Savitch, 1993). In short, how are diverse interests coordinated, and on what types of agendas, on what terms, and for whose benefit?

Searching for the Institutional Fix

These institutional searches—seeking the "institutional fix" appropriate for new conditions (Peck and Tickell, 1994)—are a critical element of the new localism. As Alan Scott (1992) describes it, local policies in economic development in the 1990s are not a matter of mimicking successful growth areas such as the Silicon Valley but of creating institutional infrastructures that deal effectively with the transaction costs associated with public-private development negotiations. These institutional arrangements "allow things to happen"; they are the "temporal steering mechanisms" that allow local governments some flexibility in avoiding intemperate choices and assuring the certainty necessary for long-range decisions. In Scott's view, they provide an infrastructure of collective order that establishes the cooperative base essential to healthy competition. Indeed, these are the contextual features driving the search for an institutional fix: the reduction of uncertainty, the minimization of transaction costs among discrete interests, and the anticipated mutual gain.

This argument goes some way toward explaining why cities are concerned with reconfiguring their institutional frameworks at this particular point in time. But it does not fully account for the trends in local institutional change, particularly the transition from more managerialist to more entrepreneurial strategies (Harvey, 1989; Leitner, 1990).[1] In lieu of reading these institutional changes straight off the economic landscape, we root them in the political history of American cities.

The Political Context

As American cities cope with the political and economic logic of global capitalism, new institutional arrangements are increasingly common. The increased fiscal dependency of American cities on private sector investment paradoxically compels them to seek new political frameworks for economic development decision making. Cities seek to overcome this dependency through structures that shape group bargaining and give public officials some control or influence. These coordination efforts become a means of maintaining some policy role, often through nonbureaucratic institutional arrangements that overlay existing arrangements.

This view emphasizes the intentionality of local development politics. It presumes that local officials are proactive and directive toward some vision (Pagano and Bowman, 1995) or notion of local economic well-being. It also assumes that they are able and willing to delegate political status and authority in order to accomplish economic policy goals. Local power resides in the authority to establish these frameworks and to structure the context within which groups negotiate. If we accept that globalization trends and regional trade arrangements smooth out the competitive advantages of nations and make local arenas more salient (Jessop, 1993, 1997; Parker, 1995), these frameworks become critical aspects of local economic development. In this sense, such institutional frameworks themselves serve as policy instruments, with significant variation in the extent to which the state—that is, local public officials—is willing neither to leave decisions to market forces nor to regulate interests directly through bureaucratic means (Crouch and Dore, 1990, 24).

The Federal Fix

When using federal resources, cities conducted most economic development activities through bureaucratic line agencies such as community development departments or economic development divisions. These agencies were well versed in channeling and monitoring federal funds; they could also be held accountable by both federal and local government. Project guidelines and eligible participants were determined in Washington, D.C. Although the actual procedures for making "deals" were often decided through interactions and negotiations between local and federal officials, these processes occurred within an arena structured by national officials. Essentially, the federal government decided the rules of the game and who could be "at the table."

As federal funds dwindled, however, continuing to lodge economic development functions in bureaucratic agencies became less necessary and—in many cities—less desirable. These agencies were staffed by civil service employees who often lacked the expertise and private sector experience that became increasingly salient in an era of public-private partnerships. They were also funded by city budget processes, which limited the scope of their activities as they competed with other city needs. These budget processes also hobbled the agencies' ability to pay top salaries in the competitive, mobile world of development specialists. In the absence of national guidelines, the players, the rules of the game, and the very frameworks for negotiation and bargaining between private interests and local state authority became salient, contested, local issues. As national influence declined, cities sought more flexible, more appropriate institutional arrangements.

The withdrawal of national funds and centralizing directives leaves questions of appropriate decision frameworks, objectives, and rules of the game to local discretion in American cities. Attendant fiscal pressures have meant that new relationships are being established between local governments and groups strong enough to cooperate in achieving mutual goals. Thus acquiring the new policy skills detailed in previous chapters was only one element of adapting to a new policy context. Each city needed to work out its own unique "institutional fix," or framework of market-state relations, for organizing and carrying out economic development activities.

These institutional frameworks are devised in the absence of federal program regulations and procedures and in the face of economic and political uncertainty. They are at least as significant as specific strategy choices; indeed, these frameworks shape the policy choices made and create the capacity to carry out some policies but not others. In the following case studies, our accounts of local development efforts put the analytic focus on these context-structuring processes: the crafting of institutional frameworks for mobilizing interests in local economic development policy making.[2]

Institutional Frameworks and Policy Orientations

This institutional perspective is a necessary complement to the previous focus on policy choices; it is especially useful in underscoring the power and conflict issues involved in making these choices. Relying on the rather awkward "context-structuring processes" label reminds us that these structuring processes (Stone, 1989) are momentous: they yield a framework in each city that spells out the players, decision rules, procedures, and values to be included in economic development decision processes.[3] Different frameworks present different incentives, bargaining advantages, and trade-off opportunities (Kantor and Savitch, 1993) that influence these goals and strategies, although, as Thelen and Steinmo put it, "institutions constrain and refract politics but they are never the sole 'cause' of outcomes" (1992, 3). These frameworks are open to challenge, of course, but they shape the development policy choices made by cities, the voices heard in the process, and who gains and loses from city efforts.

The Institutional Framework Typology

Although there are many salient dimensions to these institutional frameworks, we develop a framework typology based on two dimensions: (1) whether market or democratic institutional logics dominate decision arenas and (2) whether the elements of the framework are tightly or loosely coupled. These dimensions focus on the roles and values associated with decision making in the public and private sectors and the linkages within the framework itself.

Institutional Logics

The institutional framework typology we develop presumes conflict between what Friedland and Alford characterize as interdependent institutional orders with differing central logics and organizing principles (1991, 249). In their view, conflicts occur when there is disagreement over which institutional logic should guide particular activities and to which categories of people it should apply (256). Our fieldwork and interviews confirm this abstract point: given that local economic development is a relatively unsettled policy field, local conflicts center on whether the appropriate institutional logic is the accumulation and commodification practices of capitalism, the rationalization and routinization of state bureaucratic organizations, or the decision-making participation and popular control of democracy (see Friedland and Alford, 1991, 248).[4] Local economic development issues compel some type of institutional response: either the logic of the market is extended to the state and democracy or the logic of the state and democracy is extended to local markets. The former appears most likely, although, as we detail later, attempts to extend bureaucratic controls and popular participation to economic development activities are not as infrequent in American cities as one might think (see also Goetz, 1994; Kantor and Savitch, 1993).

But with the burgeoning of local economic development activities in the mid-1970s, market symbols and practices—the rhetoric of partnerships, leverage, entrepreneurs—are now rife. Institutional change trends appear to entail shifts in the institutional setting from one in which state bureaucracies manage development with the legitimation of democratic procedures to one in which market logic is pervasive. If market challenges to the institutional orders of the state and democracy prevail, either bureaucratic organizations adopt the practices and symbols of market logic or new quasi-public organizations better able to do so become dominant. If these challenges are rebuffed, economic development policies are more likely shaped by bureaucratic and democratic practices and symbols.

The typology begins to capture these struggles by characterizing city decision arenas as dominated by market or state/democratic institutional logic. Market logic, for example, prizes profitability, efficiency, and responsive command structures in decision making. Democratic logic in decision making, on the other hand, values accommodating different interests, participation and representation, and consensual decision processes. These are ideals, of course; private enterprises are not immune to inefficient decisions, and many public organizations fall far short of democratic practice. But the distinction allows us to characterize the institutional frameworks in different cities in terms of their values, symbols, and procedures.

Framework Links

The second dimension describes the links within the institutional framework. The aim is to characterize the local institutional fabric, particularly the "infrastructural power" or capacity (Horan, 1997) of public institutions to coordinate and carry out development decisions. We distinguish this infrastructural power in terms of tightly or loosely coupled local institutional links.[5] In more tightly coupled frameworks, for example, decision rules, procedures, and values will be more consistent and prevalent across organizations (DiMaggio and Powell, 1991, 29). Goals and strategies are relatively explicit and coordinated; this enhances the likelihood that plans will be carried out. Many acclaimed urban redevelopment "success" stories (see Wolman et al., 1992) feature relatively tightly coupled frameworks: Pittsburgh and the Allegheny Conference, the Baltimore Inner Harbor partnership, and, as we detail below, Cleveland and the Cleveland Tomorrow network. Tightly coupled frameworks can provide the leadership, focused attention, formal communication, coherent decision sequences, and organizational resources necessary to overcome the uncertainty and complexity of local decision making. Organizations are run by professionals, and interest designation is driven by organizational compatibility with dominant rules and procedures. Although the policy setting is more homogeneous and stable, more tightly coupled frameworks can lead to less variety and diversity in local economic development policy environments. Privileging some values and decision rules over others can limit the range and effectiveness of strategies available to other groups, such as minority and neighborhood interests. Thus tight coupling may make the local institutional structure more vulnerable to external shocks (DiMaggio and Powell, 1991) such as the loss of federal funds or credit crunches.

In contrast, more loosely coupled frameworks encompass varying organizational types with different values, decision rules, and procedures; multiple points of authority; formal and informal communication networks; and fragmented resources. Mustering coordination and cooperation under such conditions is notably difficult; "success" is more elusive, less coordinated, and probably slower in happening. There is more potential instability as organizations continually adapt to changing circumstances. Furthermore, there is more uncertainty, and possibly conflict, over turf issues and the appropriate rules and routines to use in different cases. Loosely coupled frameworks may be more flexible, however, in the types of projects and areas addressed, more able to adapt to changing conditions or new ideas, and more responsive to new opportunities. Finally, a looser framework may prove more accessible to groups seeking to challenge current priorities.

Variations in City Policy Orientations

These dimensions are interesting studies in themselves; we anticipate, however, that variations on these selected dimensions contribute to the different policy orientations cities develop. Here we are especially interested in how these framework dimensions shape a city's policy responses to restructuring trends, human capital needs, global-local links, and broader citizenship concerns.

The typology is used to explore differences in institutional frameworks and policy orientations across four cities—Cleveland, Tacoma, Jacksonville, Syracuse.[6] Several factors influenced their selection. They provide regional variation, similar degrees of social and ethnic diversity, and some similarities in political structure. Each is involved in making the transition from a more industrial economic base. With the exception of Cleveland (Swanstrom, 1985; Krumholz, 1982), they are not well-studied cities; each would be considered a second-tier city, although it is a relatively important regional economic center. All were active in federal development programs; they rank from very active to somewhat active in our indices of current policy strategies. To varying degrees, therefore, their institutional legacies are rooted in federal programs.

Most important for our purposes, their institutional settings vary on the two dimensions of interest here, with consequent differences in development policy orientations. In Cleveland and Jacksonville, market logic dominates the decision arenas and the public sector role resembles that of the opportunistic state. In Cleveland, the tightly coupled framework contributes to a sustaining, corporate-centered orientation, whereas the more loosely coupled network in Jacksonville provides a facilitative orientation. Democratic logics persist in the decision arenas in Tacoma and Syracuse, and the public role is attentive to value-added concerns. In Syracuse, the framework is tightly coupled around public sector agencies and quasi-public organizations and generates a bureaucratic/managerialist orientation, whereas in Tacoma a more loosely coupled framework allows an enabling orientation.

Table 5.1

A typology of policy orientations based on institutional linkages and decision logics

Linkages	Logic	
	Market	**Democratic**
Tightly coupled	Sustaining (Cleveland)	Managerialist (Syracuse)
Loosely coupled	Facilitating (Jacksonville)	Enabling (Tacoma)

By mapping these two dimensions of the institutional framework—whether the logic of the market or democracy prevails and how tightly coupled the framework is—we arrive at the characterizations of the policy orientations in each city noted in Table 5.1. The labels reflect how these two dimensions contribute to the overall tone of the policy approach.[7] The policy orientation in cities dominated by market logic arises from the *oppor-*

tunistic state roles of the public sector (Scott, 1992; Fuchs and Cox, 1991). These entrepreneurial orientations involve more activist public roles in structuring and positioning local economies but centered on creating the conditions for successful enterprise. The public agenda is subordinated to market opportunities, although the need for collaboration and cooperation presents conditions for accommodating public priorities as well.

Every American city must be sensitive to market logic, given the weak federal structure and privatistic culture. But some cities balance this market logic with democratic values more effectively through institutions and mechanisms for accommodating different interests, participation and representation, and consensual decision processes. In these cities, value-added orientations sensitive to local employment structures are more likely: the values and groups threatened by globalization can utilize different venues and procedures to push for policies that recognize different priorities.

In a sense, these institutional frameworks sort out differing definitions of local development problems; by privileging some definitions, or frames, and the attendant solutions, they increase access for some groups and limit it for others. They reflect some of the different paths possible and the importance of institutional frameworks for giving different groups a voice in economic transformation decisions.

A Caveat

These are not success stories. Even though the cities discussed here claim to be crafting entrepreneurial strategies or addressing human capital issues or bringing jobs to the community, it is rarely clear whether these policies really bring about the desired outcomes. Local officials, nevertheless, are political entrepreneurs (Schneider and Teske, 1992). Like other entrepreneurs, they are seeking returns on their investment of time and energy in terms of career enhancement; thus they naturally take credit for whatever "flies" (Rubin, 1988) and blame market forces for the rest. Even if they do not truly believe these local initiatives can counter forces beyond their control—and many of them are skeptical (Wolman, 1988)—they believe these efforts are necessary for symbolic and political reasons. As we demonstrated in chapter 4, and as other authors have shown, there is some evidence that some policies work in some situations (Bartik, 1994; Wolman, 1996). But, as noted previously, local officials are uncertain about which ones will work in their communities, and their perceptions of policy effectiveness may not jibe with empirical findings. In the midst of this uncertainty, they cope with the dual dilemma facing all local officials: catering to business needs and keeping voters satisfied (Friedland, Piven, and Alford, 1978).

It is not merely the uncertainty and weak effectiveness that make us hesitant to label these success stories. Although voters may be satisfied, or at least indifferent and not openly hostile, to local economic development efforts, there are few instances of local economic development efforts that mitigate the economic vulnerability of the four-fifths Reich (1991) sees as threatened by globalization. Maybe it is unrealistic to expect local officials to do so. Nevertheless, there are efforts at the local level to address the social costs of globalization; we note these here because they are counter-intuitive to the public choice logic that emphasizes the irrationality of local redistributional initiatives. While we remain reluctant to claim these as success stories in an absolute sense, they surely portray the inventiveness and tenacity of local officials coping with the uncertainty and polarization increasingly prevalent in their communities.

Cleveland: A Sustaining Orientation

The Cleveland story is almost an allegory: the events and dynamics occurring in Cleveland symbolize and illustrate many of the ideas and principles drawn on to describe the dilemmas facing American cities in the late 1990s. Cleveland underwent massive disinvestment, deindustrialization, and population loss in the 1970s; it suffers an extraordinarily high poverty rate and remains one of the most segregated cities in the United States. It lumbers under a highly politicized mayor-council system and operates under conservative state enabling legislation. Yet Cleveland is second only to Chicago as a regional financial center for the central Midwest, boasts of world-renowned cultural and medical care facilities, harbors symbolic analyst-related activities centered in universities and research institutes, relies on a continuing tradition of civic and corporate leadership, and is linked to the global web through international trade.[8]

Few other American cities find their disinvestment pains fodder for jokes, popular songs (The Pretenders' "My City Was Gone"), movies (*Major League* I and II), and TV shows (*The Drew Carey Show*). On the other hand, several fine analyses are available of Cleveland's tumultuous and painful shift from an industrial to a postindustrial economy and from a white ethnic to predominantly African American political base (Swanstrom, 1985; Keating, Krumholz, and Metzger, 1989; Krumholz, 1982; Schnorr, 1991). This account is different: we focus on Cleveland's efforts to fashion a response to the effects of globalization by restructuring the context in which economic development decisions are made.

Cleveland participated significantly in federal development programs and was an early innovator in public-private partnerships and entrepreneurial use of UDAG funds. The city's efforts to continue this entrepreneurial orientation are constrained by the conservative state enabling environment, which limits its choices, and the corporate framework in which local strategies are negotiated. Public-private partnerships and speculative ventures persist but are centered now on efforts to carve out a distinctive regional and national niche. Although neighborhoods play a prominent role in the development agenda, they operate in a tightly coupled institutional framework dominated by market logic and privileging certain organizational structures and thus particular voices.

The Local Context

In the past, Cleveland's fortunes rested on manufacturing, particularly steel and transportation equipment. The city reached its peak population of 914,808 in 1950; its physical borders were stopped at seventy-six square miles in the mid-1930s. The city suffered massive disinvestment in the 1970s, moving into a recession in 1979 more severe than any since the Great Depression. This resulted in substantial employment losses in the manufacturing, transportation, and utilities sectors. These severe economic dislocations continued through the 1980s; manufacturing employment fell by 18.3 percent from 1982 to 1987 and now constitutes only 23 percent of the labor force. With a population loss of 12.4 percent from 1980 to 1992, Cleveland's population in 1992 was 502,539—less than half its peak population of nearly a million (U.S. Department of Commerce, 1994b, 794). There has been significant suburbanization of both population and industry. The population loss was exacerbated by the availability of accessible, low-cost suburban housing.

Plagued by fixed city boundaries, severe riots in Hough in 1966, and accessible suburban land, Cleveland's downtown was hit hard by suburbanization. Middle-class families left in droves, leaving the poor and dependent behind. But the despair of the 1970s began to give way to a boom in downtown building in the 1980s. Public dollars, particularly UDAG dollars, were critical to this revitalization. The renovation of the Terminal Tower complex was a key trigger to new investment; it was followed by new office buildings for corporate headquarters for Standard Oil (Ohio), Eaton Corporation, and Ohio Bell Telephone (now Ameritech). Redevelopment of the waterfront as the North Coast harbor and the Galleria shopping mall as well as the transformation of the Flats industrial area into an entertainment area, and restoration of the Playhouse Square theater all served as attractions for middle-class suburbanites. This boom crested, eventually, with the construction of the Gateway sports facilities at Jacobs Field and Gund arena and the long-delayed opening of the Rock and Roll Hall of Fame (Benson, 1995). But as Mayor White said at the opening ceremony of the Rock and Roll Hall of Fame, "Baby, you ain't seen nothing yet" (quoted in Benson, 1995). By changing the image of the city from "the mistake on the lake" to a cultural, sports, and specialized retail center, the city hoped to bring back business and high-end residential investment.

Some claim that Cleveland succeeded in creating a dual city: a healthy, booming downtown and distressed neighborhoods saddled with declining schools and high unemployment.[9] Some of the inner suburban ring areas are now facing decline as well.[10]

After sliding below 1969 earnings levels in the early 1980s, the city began an uneven but steady recovery around 1983 (Conroy, 1992, 515). This recovery was fueled by growth in service sectors, particularly business and professional services, financial services, wholesale trade, and state and local government. By the 1990s, Cleveland was emerging as a regional finance, service, and health facilities center; hospitals and medical research centers are now the city's largest employers.

A strong core of cultural and educational facilities anchors revitalization efforts. The Cleveland metropolitan statistical area (MSA) enjoys a distinctive comparative advantage based on its publicly supported museums and botanical and zoological gardens, facilities with histories of high export potential in that they draw in tourists and dollars from outside the MSA (Mumphrey and Akundi, 1995, 20).[11] The downtown area flags in competition with the suburbs, however, especially as overbuilt suburban office space undercuts downtown rents.

While the economic base remains dominated by manufacturing, it is now more diverse; as Table 5.2 indicates, the transition to a service- and information-based metropolitan economy is well under way. As part of this process, 45 percent of the people in the area's workforce are employed by small businesses (Geahigan, 1994, 682).

But Cleveland's social needs are great: there is widespread poverty (28.7 percent below the 1989 poverty line in 1990), particularly among female-headed households (48.5 percent) and children (42.8 percent); a high infant mortality rate (seventeen per thousand live births); high dropout rates; very low proportions of high school (58.8 percent) and college graduates (8.1 percent—the second-lowest proportion among American cities); high economic dependency rates (30.8 percent on social security, 21.9 percent on public assistance); and an unemployment rate of 8.5 percent in 1991.

Cleveland has a mayor-council city government structure, with a city council elected by twenty-one wards. An electoral coalition including neighborhood groups put Mayor Michael White, an African American, and a reform-dominated city council in office in 1989 to carry out a neighborhood agenda. Indeed, White's election was the first time that neighborhood development groups were active in a mayoral campaign; they sat out Kucinich's campaign and recall election (Swanstrom, 1985). As of 1990, 46.8 percent of the city was African American and 4.6 percent was Hispanic. In 1966 and 1968 (but not in 1992), riots marked the city. Despite the prominence of several African American politicians, including the mayor and former city council president, Cleveland ranks as one of the most racially segregated cities in the United States (Massey and Denton, 1993).

Table 5.2

Cleveland metropolitan area earnings as measures of sectoral importance

	% local economy 1969	% local economy 1988	Index to national economy 1969[a]	Index to national economy 1988[a]
Construction	7.25	4.97	110.6	77.5
Manufacturing	42.86	32.39	152.8	159.6
Transportation /utilities	6.86	5.88	98.0	87.3
Wholesale trade	5.93	6.85	99.7	105.0
Retail trade	9.81	8.66	90.5	90.7
Financial services	4.20	5.04	76.3	69.3
Services	12.75	23.93	82.5	98.0
Business services	1.58	3.92	75.5	72.4
Government	9.13	11.18	56.2	71.5
State and local	6.91	9.04	71.0	82.8

[a]Index to national economy where 100 = same as importance in national economy.

Source: Conroy (1992, 521). Data from Bureau of Economic Analysis, U.S. Department of Commerce.

The Institutional Framework

Two venerable private institutions—the Cleveland Development Foundation (1954) and University Circle, Inc. (1960)—dominated development activities until federal economic development program funds in the late 1970s and 1980s enlarged the opportunities for city involvement. During the Kucinich administration in the 1970s, there was a short-lived attempt at "equity planning"; Mayor Dennis Kucinich appointed Norm Krumholz director of community development for a stormy year. Krumholz set out a social policy plan (Krumholz, 1982). Formation of neighborhood-based and housing-oriented local development corporations was encouraged as a means of planning from the bottom up. The city's Economic Development Department staff was cut back to two to three persons; as part of his antiabatement campaign platform, Kucinich ended tax abatements for development projects (see Swanstrom, 1985).

With Kucinich's defeat by a Republican candidate in 1979, however, these efforts to balance popular control and economic development came to a halt. Recruited by the business community to run against Kucinich, the new mayor (former lieutenant governor and now governor) George Voinovich embarked on an ambitious, downtown-oriented economic development program guided by a private consultant's recommendations (the "McKinsey Report") and inspired by James Rouse's call at a Cleveland conference in 1983 for a "civic vision." Voinovich signaled his intent by elevating economic development to a separate department; tax abatements were again available for downtown development (Swanstrom, 1985). Thus, after a twenty-year hiatus, a second wave of context-structuring activities moved over Cleveland in the 1980s, triggered by Voinovich's election and the availability of federal funds for local economic development.[12] As in the 1950s and 1960s, these efforts also led to establishment of development organizations outside the formal political structure. Although the public sector role became more prominent, thanks to federal funds, the emergence of a coherent corporate leadership organization and the diffusion of market rhetoric, symbols, and procedures through the federal UDAG programs contributed to the tightly coupled framework and corporate-centered sustaining orientations that persist in Cleveland.

The Federal Legacy

Overall, the local economic development context through the mid-1980s was structured by federal government program directives. Cleveland's economic development policy orientation was driven primarily by two sources of federal funds: (1) Urban Development Action Grants available for large-scale projects and allocated directly to public-private partnerships through city ordinances, and (2) Community Development Block Grants with more limited economic development uses and low-income beneficiary restrictions and allocated through city agencies and the city council. Because UDAG proposals and mini-UDAGs came before the city council as separate ordinances for specific projects needing approval, one city hall observer argues that they were perceived as individual deals rather than pools of capital. In contrast, CDBG funds came before the city council as a pool of projects, open to competition and negotiation. In contrast to local tax abatements and CDBG funds, therefore, UDAG funds provided leverage capital, contractual relations coordinating public-private actions, a set structure of development finance, and fewer political and administrative difficulties. In a number of important ways, the UDAGs lowered transaction costs for joint public-private development efforts. They also encouraged the diffusion of market logic and practices, in contrast to the more visible, political allocation dynamics of the CDBG program.

Cleveland's UDAG participation is notable for the entrepreneurial financing techniques that often put the city in the role of an equity investor. Other cities eventually began to adopt these techniques, but Cleveland was one of the first local public entrepreneurs; the support from the regional HUD office and a strong staff capacity allowed the city to push private developers for provisions in the UDAG grant agreements allowing the city to share in net cash-flow participation and to regain other forms of program income (Clarke and Rich, 1985; Rich, 1993b). Cleveland channeled most UDAG program income (or repayments) back into the city's Small Business Revolving Loan Fund, administered by the Cleveland Citywide Development Corporation (a 501c3 nonprofit staffed by the city). These funds are packaged with EDA Title IX and SBA funds to make small loans (less than $100,000) to firms in neighborhood and industrial areas outside the downtown area. Most of these were for small commercial and industrial projects, rather than the large-scale commercial projects favored by UDAG. To some extent, these priorities may reflect the National Development Council influence in Cleveland; Cleveland was an initial NDC pilot city in the late 1970s.

The Institutionalization of Market Logic

The McKinsey Report laid the foundation for formation of Cleveland's tightly coupled framework and corporate-centered economic development policy context. It recommended the formation of a citywide CEO-level committee (Cleveland Tomorrow) with the capacity to make the catalytic investments seen as necessary to continue the momentum stimulated by the UDAG program. There was a general perception that, in the absence of national funds, the city lacked the capacity to make such investments in the immediate future. Indeed, there was little sense that a city council-dominated policy process was capable of any coherent long-term development strategy, particularly one demanding joint public-private action in a depressed economy. Although a chamber of commerce-like group, the Cleveland Growth Association, was already in place, some argued that its mission was too broad to meet this need; a more specialized economic development focus and a CEO-level organization promised greater effectiveness.

Thus the impacts of a depressed regional economy and a sense of imminent political failure suffused the establishment of Cleveland Tomorrow in 1982. The institutional logic of corporate efficiency prevailed again in Cleveland: Cleveland Tomorrow formed in response to the perceived need for greater policy mobilization and coordination and the belief that the policy context structured by the traditional ward arrangements was inimical to such action. Corporate objectives, rules of the game, and areas of uncertainty became decisive in local economic development issues. A member of the McKinsey consultant team became executive director of a lean organization at Cleveland Tomorrow: a committee of more than forty CEOs, six permanent staff, and project liaison committees with eight CEOs assigned per project. Approximately thirteen CEOs of major corporations agreed to contribute $1 million each to an initial equity pool for Cleveland Tomorrow's public-private development projects.[13] They also set up a nonproject fund for catalytic investments. In both cases, transaction costs are lowered literally by the CEO-level operation and the limited partnership structure that allows corporations to make larger investments jointly than any one could afford individually.

A Tightly Coupled Framework

In Cleveland's tightly coupled framework, the concertation of business and government interests occurs informally, with the public sector in a sustaining but subordinate role to the corporate board. In terms of context-structuring processes, Cleveland Tomorrow structures participation in private policy making on limited, specific issues; allocates participation rights to corporate representatives; coordinates with public authority in these limited areas; offers mutual gain to participants; is oriented toward mobilization rather than self-regulation; and provides a stable forum for iterative bargaining, exchange, and deliberation among designated representatives.

Mutual development gains are possible only through this structure; although representation is limited to corporate representatives, a series of spin-off organizations, described below, bring in noncorporate voices.

Coordination of city and Cleveland Tomorrow activities occurs nominally with city planners and a steering committee supported by private investors; staff in the city Planning Office provide informal coordination. Cleveland Tomorrow coordinates its spatial targeting with areas identified in the Civic Vision 2000 strategic plan; although it makes investment decisions through its CEO board, officers claim it is unlikely it would adopt projects without city support—particularly tax abatements, capital improvement funds, and other financial support.

This tightly coupled framework expands the range and effectiveness of strategies available to business to the extent that they correspond to the interests articulated through Cleveland Tomorrow. Yet this is a narrowly based constituency, one dominated by large corporate and developer interests rather than small businesses. Furthermore, there has been a turnover in 65 percent of corporate leadership positions in Cleveland in the past eight years; this makes the corporate commitment to Cleveland Tomorrow more vulnerable than it might otherwise appear.

The city's strategies are increasingly constrained by limited funds and the competitive resources available through Cleveland Tomorrow and Neighborhood Progress Inc. Recent changes in state legislation may strengthen the city's hand. Until recently, Ohio cities were not allowed to own and disburse land; these constraints on their land development powers severely limited their economic development options. But in 1990, voters agreed to amend the state constitution to make housing a public purpose; this allows the city to lend funds to individuals and nonprofit organizations or builders who develop affordable housing. This new flexibility allowed Cleveland to create a Neighborhood Development Bond to support new housing construction with general obligation bond revenues and a series of revenue notes for construction financing on city-owned land. But the city cannot extend credit to private investors, so direct loans and loan guarantees using city funds are not possible.

Cleveland's city officials see the state industrial revenue bond program, eminent domain authority, linked deposits programs, tax increment financing authority, and earmarking of state liquor profits for small business development as particularly helpful state programs. Currently, more than three-fourths of the city is designated a state enterprise zone, with both new and existing industries eligible for generous tax abatements. In December 1994, Cleveland was designated a supplemental empowerment zone in the 1993 federal empowerment zone program. This promises HUD grants of $87 million, but not the tax incentives allowed in the six urban empowerment zones.

These gains in local flexibility occur under the most adverse circumstances: a recessionary economy, an overbuilt office market, and a shift toward regional rather than local policy arenas. The last of these is the most significant: economic development debates in Cleveland are framed increasingly in a regional context because of the political strength of suburban constituencies. As one observer has pointed out, just as the mayor and city council define their agenda in entrepreneurial terms, all the big city deals are done and the arena has shifted to higher levels. Even Cleveland's neighborhood housing orientation is driven by state legislation and federal Home Ownership Made Easy (HOME) funds for market-rate housing rather than the Cleveland Housing Network's original "Cleveland model" of low-cost lease-purchase rehab housing.

A Sustaining Policy Orientation: Neighborhood, City, and Business Development Links

This framework yields a policy orientation centered on sustaining corporate priorities and interests. It is not determinative of particular policy choices but affects the range and effectiveness of policy strategies available to different interests (Williamson, 1989, 169). The institutional framework in Cleveland is infused with the market logic of efficiency, as exemplified in biases toward performance criteria and "bricks and mortar" neighborhood organizations.

Cleveland stands out as a tightly coupled framework with a sustaining policy orientation, particularly because of the formal ties between Cleveland Tomorrow's spin-off, Neighborhood Progress Inc. (NPI), and neighborhood organizations. Such ties are sought after in other cities, for a variety of reasons, but Cleveland's historic neighborhood links are imbued now with market logic. As the UDAG program suffered cuts in the 1980s, large-scale downtown development projects became less viable in many American cities, and interest in neighborhood markets and projects increased. Also, the wave of bank mergers in the 1980s enabled community organizations to use the Community Reinvestment Act (CRA) to challenge lending patterns; as a consequence, many banks are setting up neighborhood development programs and seeking neighborhood-based groups to carry them out. Neighborhood development issues, therefore, became more salient across cities in the 1980s and 1990s; this led to conscious efforts to restructure participation and representation in neighborhood economic development policy-making processes.

Unlike the earlier generation of local development efforts in Cleveland, these new organizations included formal linkages with neighborhood development groups throughout the city. These organizational efforts included the entry into Cleveland of Local Initiative Support Corporation (LISC) (1988) and Enterprise Foundation (1984) staff; they also arose from new neighborhood initiatives resulting from bank mergers, such as the Ameritrust Development Bank funds. And some were public efforts: local development organizations blossomed during the Voinovich administration; now, a citywide umbrella group for the local development corporations, the Cleveland Neighborhood Development Corporation, provides technical assistance to the member organizations. In 1980, the city set up a neighborhood planning system that placed neighborhood planners in neighborhood development districts to act as liaisons with the city and, most important, to provide technical assistance and monitor the council CDBG allocations.

But, over time, these other efforts were dominated by Cleveland Tomorrow's launching of the Neighborhood Progress Inc. program in 1987, building on its earlier support of the Cleveland Housing Network (CHN) and the Cleveland Neighborhood Partnership Program. The CHN and the NPI reflect two different models of balancing democratic participation and corporate efficiency in decision frameworks. The CHN is a non-profit umbrella organization for neighborhood groups engaged in housing projects, both rehabilitation and new construction, in eleven neighborhoods. A core centralized staff provides technical assistance and capital support. Member organizations work extensively with the federal low-income housing tax credit provisions; this gives them financial acumen and a performance record unusual for neighborhood groups. Nevertheless, control over the CHN comes from the bottom up: the constituent organizations direct the group's agenda, and it retains a neighborhood focus. Over time, Cleveland Tomorrow aimed increasing amounts of support toward the CHN and collaborated with it on several projects. The director of the CHN, Chris Warren, was appointed head of the steering committee for the Civic Vision 2000 plan; when Michael White won an upset victory in the 1989 mayoral race, he persuaded Warren to join his administration as director of the Department of Community Development. Warren now heads the city's Economic Development Department and its enterprise zone project.

The NPI, in contrast, parallels Cleveland Tomorrow in structure, operations, and institutional logic. Cleveland Tomorrow set up NPI as a 501c3 organization to do neighborhood-based economic development in line with the model being used by the parent organization. The executive director was brought in from Pittsburgh; he works with a board that includes CEOs, foundation staff, city representatives, and elected neighborhood representatives. The presence of the neighborhood representatives is a result of pressure from neighborhood groups—they were not part of the original organizational design. Although six members of the fourteen-member NPI board are elected directly by neighborhood organizations, observers note that they are often "overwhelmed" by the expertise and resources controlled by their CEO colleagues. They do not vote as a bloc, although the continued presence of neighborhood representatives on the NPI board is periodically under attack by those who see them as a source of contention based in parochial interests.

Operating funds come from Cleveland Tomorrow ($3 million in 1991–93), other local foundations (such as the Gund Foundation), and the city. As one observer has pointed out, NPI lowers the transaction and information costs incurred by these groups in assessing risks of individual neighborhood projects. In return, NPI becomes the gatekeeper for access to the corporate and foundation communities.

Like Cleveland Tomorrow, NPI takes equity positions on projects and needs projects with rates of returns sufficient to generate the necessary revenue streams. These decision rules effectively constrain the groups NPI works with and limit the types of projects they can support. Project proposals are competitive, with about a 30 percent acceptance rate. Larger groups are more successful in gaining NPI funds; groups are encouraged to consolidate with neighboring associations to enlarge the scale of operations possible. And there is a growing resource availability gap between neighborhood groups engaged in "bricks and mortar" real estate development activities and those involved in more traditional community organizing and social service activities. Cuts in federal funds exacerbate this gap: as public resources dwindle, Cleveland Tomorrow and NPI loom as the access points to corporate and foundation assets for those neighborhood groups that fit their organizational criteria.

Given its resource base, NPI increasingly is capable of structuring the context for neighborhood economic development activities in Cleveland. It serves as an intermediary, buffer organization between some neighborhood organizations and the investment community; it limits participation to those groups carrying out housing and commercial development projects generating sufficient rates of return. Those groups able and willing to cooperate gain access to corporate and foundation funds and expertise; the city gains implementation of a neighborhood agenda it cannot afford to carry out itself. The neighborhood representation on the board thus far has offered some opportunity for exchange and deliberation among affected interests. Until recently, however, it could not be argued that public authority was delegated to NPI: resources primarily were corporate and foundation contributions, internal decisions were guided by market criteria, and there was only limited formal public representation in the organization. NPI has indicated an interest in becoming a quasi-public citywide development corporation, but that has yet to happen. So far, NPI operates alongside the city political and administrative structure; it relies on informal coordination with the city, using city Department of Community Development staff on its project selection committees but not directly influencing city relations with neighborhood groups. Those groups not successful in competing for NPI funds often turn to the city council for support.

But the White administration is attempting to reorient those relationships. Michael R. White campaigned on a promise to "rebuild city neighborhoods," emphasizing housing issues, but the meager resources available to do so were long captured by groups "locked into" ongoing council funding. City council control of the CDBG economic development funds meant that Chris Warren, the new director of the Department Community Development (and former head of the Cleveland Housing Network), had little flexibility for introducing new orientations or bringing new groups into the arena.

To counter this stalemate, White and Warren proposed creating a Housing Trust Fund of $1.5 million from the city's $25.1 million CDBG funds (1990). These monies would create a revolving loan fund for low-interest loans to developers willing and able to work with nonprofit organizations and to match city dollars three to one. This meant that groups could not count on city hall for 100 percent financing; they had to establish track records that would make them credible with private lenders. Warren persuaded the city council to cooperate by expanding the council's set-asides from $170,000 to $200,000 but requiring that some funds be available only for nonprofits; thus ward allocation totals were still nearly three times the amount approved for the new Housing Trust Fund, but there were more restrictions on the types of projects eligible and more emphasis on performance criteria. Warren also proposed devoting nearly 40 percent of the CDBG funds to neighborhood housing development. And in 1992, more than $2 million of the new federal HOME funds for rental rehabilitation became part of the Housing Trust Fund. Thus the city created a pool for support of capital projects independent of the traditional council CDBG allocation process.

Establishing a consolidated, competitive operations finance pool for general support of community staff and administration was a second innovation, and a Community Development Corporation Development Grant Program was a third. In the latter, the intent was to provide start-up funds for groups without sufficient track records to be competitive in NPI or Housing Trust Fund allocation processes; this would help groups develop capacity and programmatic ideas. As one city hall observer has pointed out, these nonincremental changes essentially introduced the logic of zero-based budgeting for neighborhood groups: performance criteria would supplement the entitlement criteria characteristic of most council members' CDBG allocations.[14] The changes also introduced a competitive development financing logic to council allocations and privileged nonprofit organizations in the allocation process. Rather than directly challenge the corporate-dominated orientation toward neighborhood economic development, White and Warren created a separate city mechanism to give access and channel resources to performance-oriented neighborhood groups.

By 1992, the NPI "model" began to penetrate city decision processes. Warren persuaded the city council to suspend the usual fund application process and to ask neighborhood groups to resubmit proposals according to new guidelines. Although the city vehemently denies these parallels to the NPI model, neighborhood groups point out that the new proposal forms and criteria are essentially identical to NPI's. As a result, there is increasing polarization between the performance-oriented "bricks and mortar" groups that now have privileged access to both NPI and city resource pools and all those smaller, non-development-oriented groups that compete in ward-based CDBG allocations.

Representation and Participation

As this market logic penetrates city allocation processes as well as those of Cleveland Tomorrow and NPI, there is little recourse available to groups involved in community organizing and social services. Groups are pushed to consolidate and merge, many enter entrepreneurial activities that do not necessarily correspond to constituency demands and needs, and overall there is a polarization of neighborhood groups that were able to act collectively in the past. Previously, groups such as the ad hoc Neighborhood Budget Coalition acted collectively on behalf of neighborhood interests in Community Development Block Grant budget hearings; they also, for example, tried to hold the city accountable for the use of UDAG program income and other discretionary revenue sources. Yet the new context structures representation and participation in ways that divide groups with access from those without it; as a consequence, less collective action for neighborhood interests is likely over the long run.

Despite these efforts to centralize and coordinate the decision context for local economic development, local political dynamics create challenges to these efforts from both within and without the decision frameworks. As city allocation processes more closely parallel those of the dominant for-profit and nonprofit organizations, there is increased polarization of neighborhood-based development groups. In Cleveland it tends also to split groups along ethnic and racial cleavages. Although NPI and the city argue for the need to allocate scarce resources according to performance criteria, many groups argue that political criteria continue to privilege certain groups. This is of particular concern to non-African American groups: with one exception, every Latino group suffered cuts in city funding in 1992. Because most Latino groups in Cleveland are involved in social agendas rather than development activities, they fear the future will only be worse. Such groups lack electoral clout, however, and there appear to be few grounds for countermobilization in the near future.

A more subtle concern is that the resources being pumped into selected neighborhood groups are a form of clientelism and patronage rather than empowerment. As one veteran observer has noted, capacity may be more important than resources: Cleveland groups have their roots in the conflict and advocacy organizations of the early 1970s, but they have gradually given up their political voice in favor of resources. Although the NPI framework has neighborhood representation, there is little capacity building involved: meetings are infrequent, neighborhood representatives are not cohesive, little neighborhood networking or information sharing occurs, and the focus is increasingly programmatic rather than group oriented. The current mergers and coalitions of neighborhood groups are seen as based on weakness and fear rather than success; thus the increased organizational scale is not likely to result in increased political voice, as it rarely reflects common ground or allows greater participation. Some groups fear that NPI is moving to supplant individual neighborhood groups by becoming a citywide development corporation for Cleveland rather than a voice for the neighborhoods. Advocates rationalize this strategy by arguing that neighborhood groups involved in carrying out development projects become enervated and lose important capacities in the process; they conclude that neighborhood groups should focus on making policy decisions and leave development to other intermediaries.

There is also concern that the corporate dominance of the decision context fails to affirm the perceived need for a viable manufacturing sector and overlooks the needs of small businesses. The Civic Vision 2000 effort, in particular, fails to address these concerns (Clay, 1988). This inattention is exacerbated by fragmentation in the city administrative structure; both manufacturing jobs and small businesses are concerns of many neighborhood groups, but they are in the Department of Economic Development's bailiwick, where neighborhood groups feel they have little access. Add to this the sense that corporate interests are beginning to define economic development issues in regional terms, and there is the potential for further volatility.

Although the city is commonly perceived as a junior partner in an economic development context structured by corporate interests, the city council's ongoing interest in neighborhoods and small business issues is another base for future challenges. According to one council member, "The focus on downtown has ended." There are growing demands that neighborhoods and small businesses get access to UDAG program income funds and CRA reinvestment funds. But the recent splits among neighborhood groups engendered by the new funding allocation procedures may reduce the clout of the neighborhood coalition. The main modification in the negotiating context, altering the NPI framework to allow for direct neighborhood representation, has proven to be primarily symbolic. The issue now is whether the mayor and council or NPI controls the framing of neighborhood development issues.

Positioning for the Fourth Wave

A sense of economic vulnerability and political failure prompted context-structuring efforts in Cleveland. It led to the formation of a nongovernmental economic development policy network that immediately overshadowed city hall in terms of resources and expertise. The public sector role was to sanction a framework for addressing economic development issues outside the city council; this framework legitimates the expertise and judgment of corporate personnel and the logic of efficiency for guiding development decisions. In order to achieve economic development success, the city has displaced policy responsibilities outside conventional political channels and has supported an institutional infrastructure that brings corporate criteria and operating procedures into democratic arenas. Given the vaunted achievements of this tightly coupled institutional framework (Kanter,

1995), how adaptive is it likely to be in responding to globalization demands and human capital needs?

Cleveland's civic leadership is positioning for the fourth wave through a development program aimed at consolidating the city's regional and global economic base. These projects anticipate a city economy with substantial growth in financial, health care, service, and tourism sectors; the old industrial core sectors are expected to ratchet down perhaps one more notch and then stabilize.[15] The environmental degradation and hazards associated with some of the old brownfield sites hamper redevelopment of these industrial acres for new economic uses. But these efforts are under way, as are many renovations of old warehouses and industrial buildings.

Some Cleveland Tomorrow members argue that city economic development is increasingly driven by county, special district, and state decisions, particularly the state's capital budgeting processes and development finance policies. They see Cleveland Tomorrow's focus shifting to government arenas beyond and beside the city. In May 1996 the city reached agreement with the town of Figgie and the Jacobs group for development of 630 acres of city-owned land in the eastern suburbs—the Chagrin Highlands. The long-standing dispute was resolved in favor of developing a research park patterned after the Research Triangle in North Carolina. This will be the largest economic development project in northeast Ohio; it resonates with a regional orientation for the city and an effort to capture service and knowledge-base jobs for the area.

These civic leaders also increasingly link the quality of local public schools and future labor force skills to their economic development agenda. Throughout the revitalization surge during Voinovich's ten-year tenure as mayor, the school district was ignored as attention went to redevelopment projects (Theiss, 1996). Neighborhood decline attendant to the city's disinvestment dilemmas undermined the traditionally strong public school system. By November 1995, many business leaders were arguing that reforming Cleveland's schools and attention to human needs should dominate the local civic agenda. The city's commitment to human capital received a severe test in March 1995, when U.S. Senior Circuit Judge Robert B. Krupansky put the school district under state control. The Republican judge criticized the school board for its lack of leadership and action, financial mismanagement, "politicized mismanagement," and Mayor White's efforts to back "reform" candidates in school board elections (Theiss, 1996).

Backed again by a report from the McKinsey & Co. group on reforming the district, Governor Voinovich advocated community, or charter, schools as the solution to the district's problems. The state is also funding an experimental $5.25 million voucher plan for Cleveland that will allow fifteen hundred children from kindergarten through third grade (chosen by lottery) to attend private and religious schools at state expense. By May 1996, Cleveland Tomorrow announced education reform was its top priority; it established an education support program to work with the Cleveland Summit on Education group, appointing a loaned executive from BP America to "manage the business sector's involvement" in education reform. The remarkable parallels in approach to economic development and human capital issues confirm the existence of a tightly coupled network, although it is not clear the values, procedures, and consensus that gave momentum to economic development projects will be as effective in this sphere.

Jacksonville: A Facilitative Orientation

Jacksonville ranks as an active user of economic development strategies in our national study (see Table 3.4). This characterization corresponds with other studies that depict the city as an aggressive user of subsidies and incentives to stimulate growth (Bowman, 1988; Turner, 1992; Swanson, 1996). Jacksonville was a late participant in federal development programs, in part because program criteria limited its eligibility. It relied primarily on CDBG to support economic development efforts, allocating relatively large shares of CDBG funds for newly eligible economic development activities. In our interviews, Jacksonville officials described themselves as continuing to use entrepreneurial development strategies actively; they also characterized their postfederal stance as one of being less risk averse because they have had a significant record of development successes. These successes build on a reputation for a low cost of living, a well-trained technical labor force, and a history of aggressive city support of corporate expansion and relocation. The city's continued entrepreneurial stance is grounded in active use of TIF mechanisms for downtown revitalization and the city's privatization of its economic development activities. This allows the city to continue to engage in speculative ventures, relying on private nonprofit associations and the chamber of commerce to form appropriate partnerships.

The institutional framework in Jacksonville is infused by market logic and is loosely coupled; that is, there are diverse organizational types with different values, decision rules, and procedures; multiple points of authority; formal and informal communication networks; and fragmented resources. Although market logic prevails, marshaling coordination and cooperation is not predictable. Neither public nor private organizations necessarily control sufficient resources to ensure that agreement can be reached and projects carried out. The facilitative policy orientation features a public sector role of vigorously aiding private investment initiatives (Turner, 1992), but with less capacity and coherence than in more tightly coupled arrangements. It is supported by an increasingly privatist state development finance infrastructure that provides substantial local financing authority.

Public-private partnerships in Jacksonville still center on land development as the city struggles to redefine its image. This has been enhanced by the city's ability to capture a National Football League (NFL) expansion team slot. These image shifts may be threatened, however, by local inequalities and racial tensions. Neighborhoods are not well defined, but there is persistent poverty in the historic "Northwest Quadrant," an African American community. Like other southern cities, Jacksonville features low-density sprawling settlement patterns with little public transportation to link areas or bring people to jobs.

Local Context

Jacksonville is a large (8,417 square miles), growing city of 673,000 (1990) on Florida's northeast Atlantic coast—"the First Coast"—with a distinctive consolidated city-county (Duval) governance structure. Jacksonville enjoys a certain amount of "place luck" (Logan and Molotch, 1987). The city is strategically located for access to major American producer and consumer markets in the Northeast, Midwest, and Southeast: a due-north line from Jacksonville points to Cleveland and the heart of the Midwest. The city is also at the westernmost point of the Atlantic coast, making it a natural transfer point for cargo. Rail and highway links to Los Angeles provide the shortest U.S. land distance between the Atlantic and Pacific Oceans (Jacksonville Community Council Inc. [JCCI], 1995b, 2). With its port facilities and air, rail, and highway links, Jacksonville is a key distribution point and the center of the First Coast region's manufacturing employment.

Jacksonville's image, nevertheless, has suffered from its northern Florida location and implicit assumptions of a blue-collar, "redneck" economy and culture more associated with rural southern Georgia than glitzy, affluent Florida (Valente, 1995). Indeed, in the past it was sometimes called "the Cleveland of Florida" because of its manufacturing base and heavy pollution from paper mills, chemical plants, and a regional sewage plant. These assumptions had some merit in the past as Jacksonville struggled with a port economy, the smell of paper manufacturing plants, and an unskilled labor force.

But Jacksonville is moving away from this northern Florida stereotype and indeed from the Florida image in general. Embedded in a state economy dominated by low-wage retail and service jobs connected to tourism and retirement sectors, Jacksonville's relatively diversified and stable economy is built on three naval facilities, JAXPORT maritime facilities, insurance firms, light manufacturing, transportation, banking, and medical care. Historically, small businesses have been a significant element of the local economic base: in the early 1990s, about 85 percent of all Jacksonville businesses had fifty or fewer employees; 41 percent of the private sector workforce was employed by small businesses (JCCI, 1993). Back-office services have been important since the 1950s, when Prudential Insurance Company opened a regional office that became the core of a cluster of major insurance firms and regional banks headquartered in Jacksonsville (Clary, 1991). The labor pool, historically including part-time, high school graduate, female workers at nearby military bases, attracted a new generation of financial services: AT&T's Universal Card Services, U.S. Sprint, and Merrill Lynch run clerical operations here, and America Online and SafeCard Services expanded into Jacksonville in the mid-1990s.

The seaport facilities along the St. Johns River—JAXPORT—handle more than five million tons of container, liquid, and bulk cargo annually. JAXPORT is the state's primary entry point for automobile imports. Steamship and ocean carrier service connects JAXPORT with South America, Europe, the Middle East, and the Caribbean; more than 67 percent of JAXPORT's tonnage is accounted for by trade with Puerto Rico and South America (Thuermer, 1991; JCCI, 1995b).

Jacksonville is benefiting from state growth patterns. As one local developer put it, Florida "is filling up like a big old sock," and both wealth and population are moving north up the coastline (Wilkie, 1994). From 1980 to 1988, its growth rate was 18.2 percent (Turner, 1992). As base closings begin to affect the local economy, and as the city's new (1993) National Football League franchise, the Jacksonville Jaguars, spurs construction and retail growth, job growth patterns are beginning to converge with the state profile. In 1995, the largest employment gains were in services, wholesale and retail trade, and government, with job losses in manufacturing. Construction job losses are momentarily stabilized with the NFL Jaguars boon. Both building permits issued and construction values jumped sharply in 1993 and remained at higher levels through 1995. The ten-year unemployment rate in 1995 averaged 5.6 percent; rates in recent years are below that average and below the state average of 7 percent.

The city's competitive advantage lies in its transportation and distribution networks, its medical base, and related industries such as transportation equipment, instruments and controls, information systems, and medical products (Crownover, 1991c). In the late 1980s the city decide to target biomedical, information transfer, and defense firms.[16] Downtown, the office vacancy rate in 1991 was 22 percent, thanks in part to two new office buildings (Jacksonville Center and Barnett Center) as well as mergers and downsizing among downtown employers (Longman, 1991). The city's industrial real estate market faces a jolt when Cecil Field Naval Air Station closes in 1998, leaving more than 10,000 acres open for redevelopment. More than 10,000 military-related jobs are also at stake, with 3,200 workers at the field averaging salaries of $40,000 (Johnson, 1995).

In 1990, *Fortune* magazine named Jacksonville the ninth-best city in the United States for business, noting its strong labor force. Although city officials proclaimed 1990 "the year of the deal," a local economist labeled the Jacksonville area as the "least promising" of Florida's metropolitan areas in 1991 because of trends indicating continued erosion of manufacturing jobs and growth in lower-wage service and back-office jobs, slowed employment growth, overbuilt retail and office space, declining sales tax revenues, and weak commercial construction (Longman, 1991). Although *Money* magazine named Jacksonville the "best mid-sized city" in the country in 1995, the development high of the 1980s began to sour. The policy issues now center on sustaining growth and pursuing more high-quality, high-wage (human capital) development (Longman, 1991).

The city of Jacksonville and Duval County merged in 1968; since 1968, Jacksonville has operated with a city-county consolidated structure. It is a council-manager city with a nineteen-member council, fourteen elected by ward and three at-large; mayors are limited to two terms. Throughout much of the period 1945–94 (with the exception of the Hazouri administration), Jacksonville was governed by "a consensual elite with a narrow distribution of power and a convergence of leadership ideologies" (Swanson, 1995, 13); through the mid-1970s the power structure was dominated by Ed Ball, a fiscally conservative politician with little interest in encouraging growth (Wilkie, 1994). Mayor Jake Godbold beat an old-line business candidate in 1979 on a populist platform. He came into office with a nonsuburban constituency of African Americans and blue-collar workers; he promised to increase African American representation and to circumvent the "good old boy" network by bringing in outside money through public-private partnerships. As soon as he took office, however, he established a working relationship with the chamber of commerce and set up a growth machine leadership in the 1980s that promoted substantial downtown revitalization. He literally threatened to disband the Downtown Development

Authority (DDA) and appoint new members if it failed to pursue his public-private partnership model for aggressive downtown revitalization strategies (Turner, 1992).

Subsequent mayors have continued this prodevelopment orientation and generally have been more proactive on development issues than the council. They lack Godbold's personalistic "machine," however. Jacksonville resembles many Sunbelt cities: the politicization of development issues found in other regions is less strident here, the economic cliques have given way to classic "growth machines" with little local resistance (Kerstein, 1995; Turner, 1992; Swanson, 1995). These growth machines constitute a consensual elite on many issues, but their efficacy tends to depend on individual personalities as much as organizational ties and coherent agendas.

But the traditional blue-collar electoral base and a growing minority voice prompt Jacksonville candidates to run on populist platforms (Turner, 1992). Once in office, mayors seek means to juggle private sector development needs through DDA and the social needs of their constituents through council channels. In 1991, Ed Austin was elected mayor after running against incumbent Tommy Hazouri; a majority of blacks voted for Hazouri. This appeared to disrupt the populist coalitions—and agendas—that supported Jacksonville mayors through the 1980s. Austin appointed Ronnie Ferguson, the Urban League president, as one of two deputy mayors. A Republican, John Delaney, followed Austin as mayor.

In 1995, the adoption of a unitary ballot that eliminated party primaries gave white suburban Republican voters an advantage in this once Democratic stronghold (Swanson, 1995).

Institutional Framework

Jacksonville was late in joining federal development programs due to state constraints and program ineligibility according to HUD's UDAG distress criteria and EDA's allocation formula (a familiar situation in many southern cities). Its institutional framework is loosely coupled, in part reflecting competing state legislative priorities on growth management and economic development. These state-level tensions produce local entities with competing agendas and often constrain local initiatives. Coordinating public economic development entities to "speak with one voice," as former deputy mayor and former Downtown Development Authority head Frank Nero puts it, has been a continuing priority. This fragmentation also stems from the often conflicting needs of the county and city areas encompassed in the consolidated jurisdiction. The state government itself does little to mitigate these fiscal and policy tensions: Florida has one of the very lowest rates of per capita taxation in the country and allocates funds to cities through a statewide distribution formula.

The Federal Legacy

As a result of its belated entry into the federal arena and its limited eligibility, the city primarily used CDBG funds for economic development. It became dexterous in using the CD "float," allowing it to stretch funds by drawing against future allocations and lending the money out for development projects. From 1985 to 1987, more than 50 percent of the city's $8.1 million in annual CDBG funds were used for economic development, primarily to cover financing costs for Jacksonville Landing. These allocations included provisions for minority vendors and construction firms as a condition of the allocation, but constitute a significant reallocation of CDBG resources.

The Institutionalization of Market Logic

Jacksonville's institutional framework, therefore, is not strongly rooted in federal development programs. It is built on state enabling legislation allowing active entrepreneurial local roles and a conviction that the resources and expertise needed to promote economic development lie outside government.[17] As a result, Jacksonville literally privatizes most of its economic development efforts by reimbursing the chamber of commerce for expenses involved in pursuit of economic development initiatives. The mayor has an aide for economic development who serves as liaison to the chamber and approves these expenses, about $250,000 in 1994. The council has no significant role in these miscellaneous appropriations other than through general budget processes. The council does, however, approve grants from a targeted Duval County economic development trust fund for infrastructure investment in the Northwest Quadrant; a similar citywide trust fund is administered by the Economic Development Division of the Planning and Development Department.[18] The city consolidated its economic development activities into the latter department in the early 1990s. The chamber's relations with this department, and other units, on economic development issues are informal and ad hoc (Turner, 1992).

Public sector roles are modeled after the corporate sector. The Jacksonville Area Economic Development Council, formed in 1990 with all private sector leaders appointed by the mayor, includes a 501c4 local development corporation capitalized by CDBG funds and UDAG program income: the Jacksonville Economic Development Corporation (JEDCO) is also supported by the mayor's office, staffed by the city, and targets existing corporations, predominantly minority-owned firms. JEDCO use CDBG funds and UDAG repayments to capitalize a revolving loan fund; it also uses SBA 504 loans to help small businesses buy or renovate property and equipment if it is tied to job creation. A revamped council with a fifteen-member board chaired by the mayor established advisory groups and took the lead in setting policy in the mid-1990s (JCCI, 1993).

Jacksonville's local incentives in the 1990s included the state enterprise zone program, in which businesses receive state tax credits and sales tax exemptions and a 50 percent city tax abatement on the municipal utilities tax, tax increment financing in downtown Jacksonville and at Jacksonville International Airport, and Duval County trust funds. The Economic Development Council claims that Jacksonville spends much less on recruitment—about $600,000—than other southeastern cities, such as Orlando, Tampa, and Atlanta (estimated at $2 million), and argues for more earmarked city funds for the chamber.

The major agency in downtown redevelopment efforts is the quasi-independent, state-chartered Downtown Development Authority. It is a separate and autonomous redevelopment agency, with a board of directors appointed by the mayor; the mayor and the DDA, therefore, are the locus of economic development negotiations (Turner, 1992). The city council is involved in designating the boundaries of blighted areas (in Jacksonville they include low-income residential areas), approving clearance and demolition plans, and issuing redevelopment bonds; nevertheless, the DDA is designed to be distanced from city council politics. The DDA is charged with designing projects within a special downtown district designated as blighted, bringing in businesses, and working to put together financial deals using public capital (Crownover, 1991b). Its revenue structure is based on three downtown increment taxing districts. Tax increment financing is available for use within the designated downtown area; it allows capture of incremental increases in ad valorem tax revenues—the gains beyond the predesignation revenues used as a baseline—to be used to pay debt service on redevelopment bonds issued by the city for development projects and to finance further projects within the district. The city council deliberately included some General Fund revenues in DDA's budget in order to maintain some fiscal control over TIF budgets and revenues. DDA is a powerful quasi-public organization; it has been instrumental in negotiating many of the deals transforming Jacksonville's skyline, using TIF and CDBG funds. Despite these successes, it has also been criticized for inefficiency and overemphasis on consultancies and studies (Crownover, 1991b).

The city's port facilities reflect a historic public-private partnership:

federal funding in 1912 for dredging of a deepwater ship channel in the St. Johns River was contingent on city construction and operation of publicly available port facilities (JCCI, 1995b). These docks were operated by a city port department until 1963, when the Jacksonville Port Authority (JPA) was created as an independent local public authority. Three of the seven board members are appointed by the Jacksonville mayor, the others by the governor. JPA owns and operates three airports, and two marine terminals (JAXPORT), and is planning a third terminal and additional port expansions. JPA operates primarily as a landlord for the marine facilities; private firms contract with the JPA for use of the port and storage facilities, and private dollars cover operating expenses. The port's initial construction (1913) and expansion (1966) were supported by general obligation bond financing from the city; since 1983, expansion and improvements have been financed by revenue bonds. JAXPORT, however, "lacks a dedicated source of revenue to finance large bond issues for capital improvements" (JCCI, 1995b, 11).

Although JAXPORT's economic impacts include nearly $50 million in local taxes and 18,000 jobs, JPA is not as prominent in local politics as Tacoma's Port.[19] Given its dependence on private revenues, JPA tends to focus its attention on its direct customers; until recently, JPA has not been an active partner in the city's or the chamber's economic development activities. Indeed, the acquisition of the NFL Jaguars appears to be at the expense of the port's expansion plans. As Gator Bowl renovation costs spiral, JPA will have to turn to the city council for other means of financing its expansion plans (Coletti, 1994). A half-cent sales tax increase earmarked for port expansion and improvements over a ten-year period is suggested by JPA; it would be subject to voter approval and the likely opposition of groups such as the Concerned Taxpayers of Duval County.[20]

In this privatized entrepreneurial order, the key player is the 110-year-old Jacksonville Chamber of Commerce, one of the largest chambers in the country, with more than 4,300 members. The chamber is charged by the mayor's office with responsibility for recruitment of new industry (JCCI, 1993). Its Economic Development Department has a staff of fifteen and a budget of $1 million (1991). From 1982 to 1990, it had its own political action committee (JAXPAC); it also features specialized units for small business and minority affairs and sponsors other promotional organizations, such as Up Downtowners. The chamber structures participation in economic development policy making and provides a decision arena outside public control where this occurs. The chamber's success in promoting downtown development in the 1980s brought gluts of retail and office space; it also raised the issue of the quality of the growth being achieved by the city (Longman, 1991).

Its internal governance structure, however, limits the chamber's ability to dominate economic development decisions. Annually elected chairs have little chance to develop agendas, much less carry out coherent strategies. In many instances, internal splits among members preclude the chamber's ability to take positions on issues. The chamber operates through more than fifty boards, committees, and task forces and eight Area Councils.

To some, the chamber is a weak link in any effort to run Jacksonville as a growth machine; the agenda is driven as much by the preferences of powerful individuals as by a corporate vision or set of coherent interests. Regional trade groups such as the First Coast Manufacturers Association, formed in 1990, are strong. There are tensions, however, between those involved in the emerging financial services back-office employment sector and those concerned with the loss of higher-wage manufacturing and port activities.

In 1990, the chamber abandoned the "committee of 100" structure common in Florida cities and created Cornerstone-Partners in Progress as the umbrella for its economic development programs. Cornerstone is a five-year strategic plan for business attraction. As the chamber's economic development arm, Cornerstone made a sharp break from the past by emphasizing targeted recruiting of business clusters rather than the wide-net approach used previously (Longman, 1991). Although the recruitment targets parallel the same types of firms that have moved to the area recently— manufacturing and distribution, medical products and services, financial and information services—Cornerstone plans to aim at smaller projects less likely to be incentive oriented. As of 1993 the goals included creation of fifty thousand new direct and indirect jobs, $3.2 billion in economic impact, and $1.5 billion in new capital investment by 1996 (JCCI, 1993).

A Loosely Coupled Framework

In Jacksonville's loosely coupled framework, economic development entities have overlapping goals and work together on a project-specific basis but "lack a commonly shared long-term vision, strategic coordination, and coordinated operational plans" (JCCI, 1993, 16). The coordination of business and public interests occurs through the chamber and the Downtown Development Authority. Local government has delegated public authority for economic development to these private (chamber) and quasi-public (DDA) organizations. The DDA's role blossomed with federal resources; its

TIF powers sustain the public authority role although debt service, and ongoing costs have weakened this position. As of early 1995, there were no regional economic development organizations for the four-county Jacksonville metropolitan area.

Given its modest involvement in federal programs, there is little experience with a directive public sector role in Jacksonville. Rather, that role traditionally has been a facilitative one in which public officials create the conditions for development, as those needs are defined by private sector interests. Participation in these decisions is structured through the chamber and the citywide development corporations on limited, specific issues identified by those groups. Substantial public authority for economic development is delegated to these intermediary organizations in the expectation that mutual gain will result. The decision arenas for iterative bargaining, exchange, and deliberation on economic development issues, therefore, exist outside formal political structures. Coordination and cooperation occur, however, primarily through negotiations among powerful business leaders and public officials controlling necessary resources; the loosely coupled framework inhibits more structured exchanges.

Alongside its pioneering growth management initiatives, Florida is increasingly characterized as making "an industry of industrial development" (Henderson, 1995). A privatist institutional framework at the state level sustains Jacksonville's orientation. Among the state programs important for local development is the public-private corporation Enterprise Florida, funded by private donations and the state legislature since 1992 to stimulate high-tech business growth and jobs creation. Enterprise Florida provides innovation grants to local groups, including Jacksonville's new Technology Center, which devises plans and matching funds in support of high-tech business development.[21]

Jacksonville's institutional infrastructure also responds to state enabling legislation originally aimed at managing growth but now focused on ensuring a high-tech economic base. The statewide growth management plan requires a city comprehensive plan with a mandatory master plan for downtown development. This includes Development of Regional Impact (DRI) Statements accounting for the land use impacts of large-scale projects. In Jacksonville the 1982 downtown DRI Statement of anticipated land use allowed the city essentially to create its own investment climate by establishing a DRI plan for all of downtown specifying what can be built and where; this makes DDA the "master developer" for downtown and creates a market in which DRI rights can be bought and sold. Also, all of Jacksonville's downtown and an area extending eight miles into the Northside, an African

American neighborhood, is in the state enterprise zone program, making firms eligible for state tax forgiveness. The state enterprise zone program is criticized as unwieldy, however, and many downtown firms do not take part in it; Jacksonville did not receive national zone designation. State bond programs are also used extensively in the city; previously the city was active in use of industrial revenue bonds, but now most bond issues are committed to housing. Finally, the state TIF provisions have been used extensively in the city since 1979 in lieu of federal program funds and tax abatements.

Representation and Participation

The city's extensive sprawling development patterns militate against the establishment of strong neighborhood identities. The city brought neighborhood organizations together in six Citizen Planning Advisory Councils in the city's planning districts. In recent years, residential neighborhoods throughout the city have been identified and mapped; the city provides one staff person to support neighborhood organizations (JCCI, 1996).

The city included six residential areas (two are low/moderate income) in its Downtown Action Plans setting out DDA's boundaries; these areas are eligible for TIF funds and other city funds, although priority is given to market-rate housing along the river (Turner, 1992). The poverty rate in these downtown neighborhoods was 45.6 percent in 1980 (Turner, 1992). The populist coalitions instrumental in mayoral campaigns in the 1980s encouraged the establishment of a citywide housing commission with a special committee on downtown housing (Turner, 1992). The CDBG funds providing loan guarantees for the Jacksonville Landing included social conditions attached to the loan guarantees providing for low-income housing (Turner, 1992). Yet most economic development decisions are made outside electoral channels. Although neighborhood activists and African Americans have gained electoral representation (several African Americans serve on the city council, and an African American served as city council chair in 1991), they remain outside the institutional framework for economic development. In the facilitative orientation governing those decision arenas, neighborhood and minority development concerns remain relatively underdeveloped. African Americans complain of a "closed-door climate" in Jacksonville, seeing themselves as lagging behind blacks in other southern cities such as Atlanta and Houston (Crownover, 1991a). There were race-related civil disturbances in Jacksonville in the late 1960s; a lawsuit on busing was in the courts through the 1980s. African Americans are relatively well organized and active, with a stable leadership cadre, in traditional organizations such as the NAACP and the Jacksonville Urban

League. There is a historic link between the African American community and the docks; African Americans have worked as longshoremen, and have had some voice through the International Longshoremen's Association.

The historic African American community—formerly known as the Northwest Quadrant—remains the most disadvantaged area in the city. Black neighborhoods nudge against the core of "old Jacksonville"; these areas suffer from high poverty and unemployment rates, prompting mobilization around jobs and infrastructure issues. Since 1986, the city has targeted infrastructure development to the northwest area that essentially also expands the old central business district into the quadrant. In the mid-1980s, the mayor created the Economic Development Trust Fund, targeting one-half the funds to provide infrastructure support to businesses generating more than five jobs in Northwest Quadrant neighborhoods. This trust fund is capitalized by bond issues; it provides grants to economic development projects screened by an appointed private sector advisory board and approved by the city council. In 1994 the city and the chamber sponsored establishment of the Northside Business Services Center to assist local businesses. An African American council member organized a community development corporation, but it has not been active; there are no neighborhood development corporations in Jacksonville.[22]

Most minority economic development support comes through state programs. In 1985 the state legislature established the Black Business Investment Corporation program, capitalized at $5 million, to provide matching funds to local corporations able to raise at least $500,000 in start-up capital. The Jacksonville citywide group the First Coast Black Business Investment Corporation started in 1987 and provides loans and technical assistance to new and existing local black-owned businesses. By 1992, it had made eighty-four loans, creating and maintaining more than 215 jobs.

Overall, the prevalence of market logic and values in decision arenas provides little nourishment for building social capital or tending to those marginalized by globalization and restructuring. But Jacksonville enjoys a significant organizational network concerned with exactly those needs and operating outside electoral structures. The Jacksonville Community Council Inc., a nonprofit civic organization, emerged from the 1974 Amelia Island Conference of one hundred community and business leaders concerned about the quality of life in Jacksonville. JCCI organizes citizen-based studies on community issues and follows up with volunteer advocacy to implement the recommendations. In the past few years, topics included community leadership, preparing for military downsizing, JAXPORT, and developing a regional economic development vision and structure. The

JCCI, along with the chamber, pioneered the city's Quality of Life effort; for more than a decade, it has tracked seventy-four indicators and benchmark measures to monitor sustainable development trends in the community. In the early 1980s, a JCCI study on the human services led to establishment of the Human Services Coalition (now the Human Services Council) to coordinate funding and delivery of human services. JCCI plans and coordinates human services for United Way of Northeast Florida and the Human Services Council. Current initiatives focus on the establishment of a regional economic development structure capable of developing and implementing a regional strategy sensitive to these quality-of-life concerns.

A Facilitative Policy Orientation

Jacksonville's institutional framework supports an active public sector role but remains privatistic, reinforced by a state institutional infrastructure that has shifted increasingly away from regulating growth to mobilizing for business development. The facilitative policy orientation emerging from this loosely coupled framework and decision arenas infused with market logic is nicely illustrated by the River City Renaissance plan for downtown.

The River City Renaissance Plan for Downtown

Prior to 1980, a "no growth" sentiment prevailed in Jacksonville. But the 26 percent growth rate in the four-county metropolitan area from 1980 to 1990, much of it at Jacksonville's expense, prompted rethinking of the city's future. Since the 1980s, there has been more support for development and a less adversarial political climate. Much of Jacksonville's development efforts continue to center on revitalizing the downtown area and countering its image as a cultural and economic backwater.

For years, Jacksonville lost companies to the surrounding suburbs. Interstate 95, with its tollbooths, cut through the downtown area, the St. Johns River was polluted, and the "smell of money" from paper processing and chemical plants hung heavy over the city. City officials invested heavily to curb this decline, drawing on a variety of state resources and investing in local projects to stimulate private investment. Jacksonville's growth previously had been on a north/south grid but had shifted to an east/west pattern on Morton Avenue, along the St. Johns River and away from the downtown area. The locus of their efforts, therefore, was an older downtown of low- and moderate-income housing and commercial buildings abutting the historic African American community in the northwest, a new downtown on the waterfront, and a mixed-use development south of the river.

The newly elected Mayor Jake Godblod in 1979 took the initiative in downtown revitalization and struck a number of public-private partnership deals. These speculative ventures included moving government buildings off the waterfront area, selling the city's largest public housing project, near the commercial district, and selling five city blocks on the waterfront for development. The city's River City Renaissance downtown revitalization program provided more than $230 million for more than thirty downtown redevelopment projects, ranging from street improvements to a new performing arts center and city hall to renovation of the Gator Bowl for the new NFL Jaguars franchise (Johnson, 1995).[23]

Jacksonville Landing illustrates some of the pitfalls of this entrepreneurial approach. After touring festival market and harbor redevelopment projects in other cities, Jacksonville officials launched JAX Landing in 1985 as a means of moving the city into the "big leagues." This is a Rouse multiple-use hotel and festival marketplace project, although local officials claim Rouse put in only a very modest share of the $43 million investment. The city owns the land and leases it to the developers; it also agreed to build a parking garage. Initial public financing also came from CDBG funds, using the float to provide no-interest loans to developers. CDBG funds proved critical in covering borrowing shortfalls and closing costs on the Landing prior to its opening in 1987. The city relies on such financing tools in lieu of tax abatements, which raise resistance on the city council. As an equity investor, the city participates in the net cash flow from the project as well as lease payments. Jacksonville Landing also is part of the Northbank West tax increment district (TID).

Although the center of downtown activity, the project contributed to the glut of office space downtown; individual projects remain troubled. Rouse's landmark building, the twenty-six-story Jacksonville Center across from JAX Landing, was 47 percent vacant and about to lose its major tenant in 1992, less than three years after opening (Horak, 1992b). Similarly, the Harbormaster's Restaurant on the south bank closed in 1992 after failing to make an interest payment on its $29 million city-backed loan. Downtown retail continues to be undermined by the opening of regional malls such as the Avenues; they bring new jobs to the area but have produced one of the most overbuilt retail markets in the country, with a retail vacancy rate in 1991 of 17 percent (Longman, 1991). Further downtown waterfront development is contingent on environmental cleanup.[24]

Many of these Renaissance projects were financed through tax increment districts. Since 1979, Jacksonville has relied heavily on tax increment financing. The city council created three downtown tax increment districts under state legislation allowing TIDs in blighted neighborhoods. Property taxes in each district were frozen at their existing levels; increased property taxes from new growth go into TID accounts for debt service and to support the Downtown Development Authority's district development efforts such as land acquisition. The goal is to have self-financing mechanisms available over the TIDs' thirty-year life span. The city encourages this growth through infrastructure, bonds, loans, and other inducements. Given the city's strong market and growth prospects, and coterminous taxing jurisdictions in the consolidated city-county government, TIF proved effective and uncomplicated in Jacksonville. Indeed, one local official claims TIF was used to revitalize the entire downtown area in the 1980s.

But little more than ten years after their creation, Jacksonville's downtown TIDs (Northbank West, Northbank East, Southbank) were strapped. No funds were available for new projects because each TID fund was tied up in debt service or DDA operations (Horak, 1992a). Faced with the need to continue the development pace in the TIDs, DDA was forced to turn to a reluctant city council to request General Fund allocations for specific projects (Horak, 1992a).

Nevertheless, the River City Renaissance plan is chalked up as a redevelopment success: it brought substantial capital improvements and new public facilities to the downtown. Even in the absence of substantial federal funds, the city continues to seek corporate relocations aggressively with a mix of locational, infrastructure, and entrepreneurial incentives. The state provisions for tax increment financing and state incentive programs prominent in the Renaissance program, and DRI rights, allow the city to take a stake in a project's success. When General Foods threatened to close the downtown Maxwell House roasting plant, for example, the state and city rallied with $1.3 million in state sales tax credits on personal property, equipment, and machinery; $550,000 for bridge construction; $500,000 in corporate income tax relief; a 50 percent public service tax exemption on electricity; and a 100 percent sales tax exemption on electricity. In response, the Maxwell House plant expanded, adding an estimated 50 new jobs to the original 380 (Barrett and Greene, 1991).[25]

Not all these speculative efforts pay off: after Jacksonville directed $2 million in state road funds, $1 million in county trust funds, and substantial job training support to American Express's card processing center at Deerwood Park in 1991, the company announced in 1994 that it was closing the facility in a consolidation move. As a consequence, the county now links its subsidies to development agreements specifying performance conditions for receiving funds (Barrett and Greene, 1991). Similarly, the city now structures its incentives to ensure the recipient repays if project performance is insufficient. Also, the chamber's Cornerstone initiative claims to be moving toward smaller projects (fifty to one hundred jobs) that are less demanding of expensive incentive packages (Thottam, 1994).

As the city moves into the late 1990s, its orientation is characterized by the chamber's targeting of business clusters and the city's use of DRI mechanisms for large projects, a reliance on TIF funding mechanisms, and use of the NFL Jaguars to reposition itself as a truly major-league city. The city's efforts to bring in an NFL franchise go back to the 1970s; its unexpected success in 1993 is equated with bringing American Express and the Mayo Clinic to the city (Thomas, 1991). Indeed, many now refer to the city as "Jagsonville." But more than $135 million in public funds went into upgrading the Gator Bowl for the Jaguars, although the city concedes that few jobs have been generated by the expansion team and the team receives all revenue from parking tickets and concessions (Navarro, 1995)

Positioning for the Fourth Wave

Although there are efforts to catch the fourth wave through human capital development, Jacksonville's primary emphasis appears to be on nurturing global-local links.[26] In the past, Jacksonville sought to attract new business through subsidies and incentives. With the leveling off of the high growth rates in the 1980s, the city became increasingly sensitive to the concerns of existing businesses, to the needs of its manufacturing sector, and to sustaining its ability to attract labor-intensive firms and its ability to compete for international maritime trade.

Jacksonville's globalization strategies hinge on enhancing the competitiveness of JAXPORT. To JPA planners, trends toward free trade within the NAFTA region, the potential opening of the Cuban market, the shift of East Asian import-trade activity toward Singapore and Manila, and even container ships for Far Eastern trade that must take western routes because they are too large for the Panama Canal are grounds for optimism about the port's future. JPA's master plan anticipates $934 million in capital improvements to meet these emerging opportunities. But the port is trapped by its dependence on revenue from user charges and leases for operating expenses and the absence of political will for public financing of expansion plans. It is hampered by the absence of both a major, dedicated revenue source for capital improvements and a revenue structure that can provide substantial net revenue. Raising additional private revenue from fees and leases is constrained by the highly competitive rate structures along the Atlantic coast. Along with the other thirteen deepwater Florida ports, and in contrast to competitor port authorities in Charleston and Savannah, the port receives minimal state funds;[27] Florida ports rely on net revenues and financial backing from local governments (JCCI, 1995b). And although port expansion is a familiar element in local economic development strategies, it often is supplanted by other projects.

The city's contribution to JAXPORT remains at the $800,000 amount set by the state legislature in 1966. Voters rejected a 1986 proposal to provide JPA with a dedicated funding source by allocating $1 million of ad valorem tax revenue to port improvements. In 1993 and 1995, the city supported two revenue bond issues for capital improvements (totaling $73.5 million); because the JPA's net revenues are leveraged almost to capacity for bonding purposes, these bond issues will also be paid off with revenue ($1.7 million) from the city's telecommunications tax (the "beeper" tax) and from a portion ($2.2 million) of the Jacksonville Electric Authority's annual contributions to the city (JCCI, 1995b, 12).

Market Logic and Institutional Frameworks

In Cleveland and Jacksonville, the institutional order and logic of the market dominates local economic development decision making. Market rhetoric, symbols, and practices are rife in both cities: public allocation processes are framed in terms of partnerships, leverage, and efficiency criteria. Business leadership collaborates in setting the goals and priorities for public policy making; in Cleveland, this influence is exercised through organizations with public-private representation, whereas Jacksonville privatizes its policy functions through contracts with the chamber.

Yet variations in the coherence of the institutional frameworks result in different policy orientations. The role of public sector officials is similar in Jacksonville and Cleveland in that it is subordinate to private interests—both cities hew to the "opportunistic state" model of sustaining corporate priorities and responding to market opportunities. These are activist public roles directed to structuring and positioning local economies, but they center on creating and sustaining climates amenable to corporate needs. But the capacity and coherence to carry out this sustaining role vary because of differences in how tightly or loosely coupled the institutions are.

In Cleveland, the tightly coupled framework provides the leadership, focused attention, formal communication, coherent decision sequences, and organizational resources that allowed the city to make its remarkable comeback. Organizations are run by professionals and interest designation is driven by organizational compatibility with dominant rules and procedures. As a result, the policy setting is relatively homogeneous and stable.

In Jacksonville, the greater diversity of organizations, the strong but factionalized state government role, and the difficulty in establishing coherent decision sequences hamper the city's ability to carry out development strategies. Even though it is a loosely coupled framework, participation rights are rather narrowly defined and designated representation is limited. The regional public sector infrastructure is underdeveloped. Elected officials coordinate public authority primarily through approval of land use agreements and budget expenditures for chamber activities. Iterative bargaining, exchange, and deliberation over development issues occur within the DDA and chamber arenas. Neither public nor private sector consistently dominates decisions, but neither is capable of mustering sufficient cooperation on a consistent basis.

This is not an argument for "best practices." Cleveland's acclaimed development success lacks a participatory and representative dimension, despite the city's phalanx of community organizations and groups. But Jacksonville's loose coupling does not promise more democratic voice; the groups and organizations concerned with community leadership and voice feel frustrated as much as thwarted. The diversity of organizational styles, decision rules, and procedures makes it difficult to hear any voice on a consistent basis.

6

Different Paths

Syracuse and Tacoma

Different frameworks and development paths are embraced by two cities where democratic logic persists: Syracuse and Tacoma. These cities were active in federal development programs; each has a history of past entrepreneurial strategy use, each has had to rethink its orientations and institutional frameworks as national funds have become scarce.

As the Cleveland case illustrates, the institutional frameworks devised for economic development decision making structure the choices likely to be made and the voices heard. They do so by setting out the rules of the game for negotiations and determining the arenas in which decisions on economic development policy are made. The Syracuse and Tacoma narratives sketch the contexts, institutional frameworks, and policy strategies in settings where democratic and bureaucratic values persist. In Syracuse this democratic logic is institutionalized in a tightly coupled bureaucratic framework, whereas Tacoma's more loosely coupled framework encompasses a diverse set of organizations and networks that span public, private, and nonprofit sectors. The activist public role in Syracuse is programmatic and bureaucratic; in Tacoma, it is an enabling role.

Syracuse: A Managerialist Orientation

Syracuse is active overall in economic development efforts, with long-standing use of entrepreneurial approaches (Table 3.4). Syracuse participated actively in federal development programs and engaged in the entrepreneurial use of these federal funds. In our interviews, city officials reported continuing use and adoption of new entrepreneurial strategies in the absence of federal resources. The dwindling of national program funds is significant, but Syracuse is bolstered by a state government institutional infrastructure oriented toward interventionist development finance programs. This state government programmatic structure stabilized the bureaucratic framework in Syracuse and minimized the disruption of declining federal funds. It is also redirecting local efforts to regional development and international trade priorities. The state role entails state funding and the development and transfer of knowledge and skills rather than efforts to structure local decision contexts. The Pataki administration's recent proposals to downsize this state institutional infrastructure may undermine the stability of the local bureaucratic framework and open it to new challenges.

Local Context

Known as the Salt City for its extensive salt fields, Syracuse's wealth came from manufacturing. Despite a brief postwar growth period, Syracuse has been facing manufacturing employment loss since the 1930s and steady population loss due to suburbanization since the 1950s.[1] As of early 1994, Syracuse's largest employers included the State University of New York Health Science Center at Syracuse (4,700), Carrier Corporation (4,294; air conditioning), Niagara Mohawk Power Corporation (NiMo) (3,400), Martin Marietta (2,900; sonar and radar systems), St. Joseph Hospital Health Center (2,860), and New Process Gear (2,700; auto transmissions), all with roots in the area going back at least sixty years.

Nevertheless, the local economy is more diversified and stable than those of other central New York cities such as Rochester and Buffalo; recessions tend to hit later and recoveries lag behind the national economy. Even though commercial manufacturing continues to exit the area, many of the same firms retain their research and development and product development units in or near Syracuse (Bender, 1992). Recently, clusters, or "hot pockets," of information-technology companies have been emerging around the Rome Laboratory and its links with research universities in central New York, including Syracuse University. The local skilled labor force, with its strong productivity rate, is seen as one of the city's strengths.

Between 1985 and 1989, the number of business establishments in the Syracuse area grew by 10.7 percent, compared with a state increase of 6.2 percent; private sector employment growth during this period was 8.4 percent, nearly double the state figure (Ballman, 1991). The number of manufacturing firms and payroll is relatively stable, but manufacturing employment is in decline. However, the city has yet to make the transition to a service-based economy; indeed, local business leaders argue that "manufacturing matters." As one put it, "We're not going to make it pressing each other's pants." Many local firms have been dependent on defense spending; defense spending in the area is the key national policy issue, rather than particular programmatic priorities. Repeated revenue shortfalls have driven the city to cut services and to consider privatization strategies for many public facilities, including the Syracuse Hancock International Airport.

Although there were signs of decline in the central business district by the mid-1970s, the area remained reasonably healthy through the mid-1980s. As the move of businesses to the suburbs accelerated in the late 1980s, both residential and commercial property downtown lost value.[2] Looking back, local officials calculate that this decline began to turn around in 1991. The last department store left downtown that year, signaling "the end of an era" and the beginning of the downtown's transition to new uses. Syracuse's struggles to transform its local economy entailed ominous economic and environmental problems. Beginning with the 1992 renovation of the Hotel Syracuse, much of this transformation involved rehabilitation and renovation of historic properties. It also involved construction of a new convention center (1992) and a Museum of Science and Technology (1997) in the historic Armory Square section. Tensions continue between downtown redevelopment and city investments in the northeast, including the Inner Harbor, or "Oil City," project: development of the Oil City project on the lakefront will yield total retail space dwarfing that available in the entire downtown (Roberts and Schein, 1993, 29).

City officials estimate that nearly half the property in the city is tax exempt, limiting their ability to stimulate revitalization. They see much of their growth as "internal" and small business oriented, as there is little land available for development; recently, greater attention has been paid to retaining existing manufacturing firms. Although there is not much foreign investment to date, this is likely to change in the near future. Syracuse is two and a half hours from the Canadian border as well as centrally located to major markets in Boston and New York City, standing at the juncture of highways I-81 and I-90. Between 25 and 40 percent of goods produced in the central New York region are exported; the GATT agreement is seen as a boon to international firms in Syracuse, such as Carrier, Ambassador Group International, and Lamson, although local blue-collar jobs may be at risk (Grossman, 1994).

Syracuse is a mayor council city, with the Common Council including at-large and district members. The city was governed by a county-based Republican party organization through the 1940s, leading to its portrayal as having a loose pyramidal power structure with a businessman-attorney—

Stewart Hancock, "Mr. Syracuse"—at its head (Martin, Munger, et al., 1961). By the postwar years, however, this power structure began to fragment and the Republican Party lost central control. The Democratic Party gained control of local government in the 1960s; in January 1994, Roy Bernardi, a Republican, was elected mayor after more than twenty years of Democratic control. In their classic study, Roscoe Martin and Frank Munger found a series of decision areas rather than a monolithic structure; they acknowledged that economic interests had the most influence but saw these groups acting through community representatives, particularly lawyers and party officials (1961, 316). Even though describing Syracuse politics in the early postwar years, Martin, Munger et al. note that decision making on real estate development is "not private in any restrictive sense, but rather private-public, or perhaps in the end public-private" (1961, 259). This sense of a partnership relation between a strong private sector and a capable public partner persists in our analyses.

Institutional Frameworks

The Federal Legacy

Syracuse was an early and consistent participant in most federal development programs, including urban renewal, model cities, SBA 7a, 502, and 503 loans and loan guarantees, CDBG, HUD Section 108 loans (8), and UDAGs. Syracuse was in the initial round of Neighborhood Development Corporation cities: NDC provided technical assistance from the late 1970s to the present, emphasizing job creation and development financing skills. As in Cleveland, almost all of Syracuse's UDAGs involved equity partnerships and payback provisions; the resulting program income is used to support general community development projects.

Institutionalization of Democratic Logic

By the 1980s the city began to rethink how it used its money, according to one official; it reorganized its economic development functions and began to support these with CDBG funds once that became an eligible activity. In 1994, the city was granted $129,000 in HUD's Economic Development Initiative (EDI) program to subsidize HUD Section 8 loans in distressed neighborhoods.

In the absence of significant national development funding, Syracuse officials see themselves as somewhat active in using entrepreneurial strategies. Indeed, one official claims there is "very little they don't do." Although the state of New York is typically seen as a "hard sell" because of taxes, labor costs, and utility costs, there is growing emphasis in local economic development strategies on the quality of the labor force, the established infrastructure, the sophisticated community of economic development professionals, and access to one of the world's biggest markets (Hardley, 1995).

A Tightly Coupled Framework

Business and public interests come together in organizations with more than thirty years of development experience in Syracuse. Line agencies and major organizations in the public sector (the Department of Economic Development, the Syracuse Industrial Development Authority [SIDA], the Downtown Committee) and the private sector (the Metropolitan Development Association, the chamber of commerce) coordinate sectoral interests. Some public authority for economic development has been delegated to these private organizations, although not as substantially as in Cleveland or Jacksonville. Together, these public, private, and quasi-public organizations structure participation in economic development policy making and provide decision arenas outside of, but accountable to, elected officials (see Ferman, 1996). Participation rights are broadly defined; the continued bureaucratic role permits indirect public accountability. Together, these public and private organizations structure a stable, recognized forum for iterative bargaining, exchange, and deliberation on development issues. Until recently, top leadership positions in both public and private organizations were often held for years by the same individuals. Key managers move between positions in public and private sector economic development organizations. Elected officials coordinate public authority and negotiate with participants in a number of different arenas. The public sector role includes developing a framework for addressing economic development issues in coordination with state and county initiatives. Increasingly these organizations, and New York state agencies, frame growth issues in regional terms.

Syracuse's institutional framework is relatively stable; there have been few changes in the organization of public sector agencies since the federal era. The city's economic development policy-making responsibilities are centered in the Department of Economic Development; there is also a Community Development Department, with both supported by general fund revenues. The quasi-public, fifteen-member, mayorally appointed Downtown Committee of Syracuse receives special assessment funds from downtown property owners, state grants, and revenues from a downtown parking lot operation; it operates through a private nonprofit corporation of the same name. Initially, its focus centered on streetscape improvements and marketing; it is now seen as a major vehicle for downtown revitalization master planning and projects. In addition, Rebuild Syracuse, Inc., administers the city's state economic development zone and distributes state funds to minority businesses.[3]

Additional public actors are the Syracuse Industrial Development Agency, with tax-exempt bonding authority and the ability to grant state and local tax breaks, and the Syracuse Economic Development Corporation (SEDCO), the city's certified development corporation for assisting businesses, including equity investment ventures, marketing and administering SBA 503 loans for small businesses.

This extensive public sector infrastructure is paralleled by private development groups. In 1959 the private Metropolitan Development Association (MDA) was established to broker arrangements among developers, tenants, and financial institutions; its corporate members provide funding for a professional staff of three. The MDA conducts strategic planning for its members and acts as a developer of last resort. It has taken a lead role in direct foreign investment efforts, including the recruitment of expanding Canadian firms to the area.[4] It is also a key player in lakefront development and industrial park development, now through participation in the Lakefront Development Corporation.

The Greater Syracuse Chamber of Commerce represents three thousand members in and around Syracuse, covering about 60 percent of the employed workers in the area. Recent priorities include retention of existing firms and promotion of international trade. The chamber is also a major force in the newly formed Economic Growth Agenda organization.

In some ways this stable, tightly coupled organizational framework has exacerbated turf problems over the years. In an effort to overcome such tensions and provide a more coherent voice on economic development issues, public and private leaders formed the Central New York Economic Growth Agenda in the mid-1990s. It is a regional public-private organization encompassing area stakeholders in economic development, including businesses; universities; city agencies; elected state, county, and local officials; MDA; the chamber; and private associations. A council of twenty-seven representatives and an executive Policy Committee supports the practitioner group; representatives from public and private organizations meet twice a month to address local development issues and jointly approach development prospects.

In contrast to the regulatory state government stance in Washington and the enabling but privatist state government approach in Florida, New York State provides a panoply of programs and organizations to support local economic development. These state agencies and programs are an important aspect of Syracuse's institutional terrain; in particular, these state units have been important sources of development financing and staff resources.[5] At both the state and county levels, public organizations often become limited partners in local firms and projects through equity investments and subordinated loans. The Pataki administration is signaling a shift to using trade associations as the contact point, however; it also promises to strengthen regional state Department of Economic Development offices dealing with start-up and small firms ("New DED Commish," 1995).

State enabling legislation provides for Payment in Lieu of Taxes (PILOT), a tax increment financing-like program, a state enterprise zone on the near west side, urban development corporations, job development authorities, and industrial revenue bonds. PILOT schemes are significant elements in attracting firms to the area; they defer placement on tax rolls through formulas calculating payments on reduced assessment rates. The chamber of commerce used the state urban development corporation and job development authority programs in developing business incubator projects in two business parks in the late 1980s. In 1988, the state established a state enterprise zone program granting tax breaks for job creation in areas with high unemployment and poverty and available vacant land.[6] Designated as an area hit hard by the recession, Syracuse was one of the first 19 state zones created (34 zones as of 1993) and one of the early leaders in firms participating (62) and jobs created (339 as of January 1991). The city expanded zone boundaries in 1994 to encompass two square miles of downtown and adjacent neighborhoods.

But the transition from the Cuomo administration to the Pataki administration in 1994 (supported heavily by Syracuse voters) signaled a retrenchment in state economic development staff and resources, a withdrawal from large projects dependent on public financing, and plans for decentralization of staff and decision autonomy to regional offices, including Syracuse and Albany. Charging waste and spending splurges during the last year of the Cuomo administration, Pataki cut the state economic development staff by 25 percent once in office. Nevertheless, in Syracuse the institutional ties with state and regional agencies appear to have withstood these disruptions.

Beginning with joint meetings of county legislatures and economic development officials in 1991, Onondaga and Syracuse officials began working toward a regional economic development approach. This includes a nonprofit regional development corporation (COMCO) representing five central New York counties. In 1992, Niagara Mohawk Power and the state Department of Economic Development created a regional public-private partnership (based on NiMo's service area)—the Upstate New York Economic Development Partnership—to encourage expansion of Canadian businesses into upstate New York and to promote exports to Canada ("Local Economic Developers," 1992). NiMo created its own economic development department in 1994; the efforts to recruit companies for its service areas and aid the retention and expansion of existing firms now includes helping firms gain access to global markets (Fitting, 1996).

Representation and Participation

The bureaucratic presence links neighborhoods and the city. Although there are strong electoral links through the Common Council's district structure, the city economic development efforts center on upgrading commercial neighborhoods through the Neighborhood Business Area Improvement program.

Housing rehabilitation has been a CDBG priority since the 1980s, generally garnering nearly half the CDBG allocation. The city leverages private funds for housing by making deposits of CDBG funds in local institutions willing to make low-interest and deferred-payment loans within its targeted neighborhoods. The Neighborhood Housing Services, working initially in the Brighton neighborhood, also work through a relationship with the city, neighborhood residents, and local financial institutions. The Syracuse Model Neighborhood Corporation, a nonprofit housing corporation created under the Model Cities program, continues to acquire and rehabilitate units for low-income housing. In 1993, Syracuse became a demonstration city in the affordable housing initiative sponsored by the National Association of Realtors and the U.S. Conference of Mayors. The project requires local boards of realtors and mayor's offices to work on public-private sponsorship of affordable housing. The city is also rehabilitating low-income housing through NDC's Corporate Equity Fund investment program. Other support for neighborhood projects comes from UDAG program income and tax amnesty funds. A city Neighborhood Advisory Council participates in allocations of a UDAG program income pool. The city's tax amnesty program allows it to collect delinquent taxes and deposit them in the Syracuse Development Fund, to be used for housing and development projects. The funds are volatile, however, and insufficient to support long-term projects.

A Managerialist Policy Orientation

The stability of Syracuse's framework and policy orientation stems from a strong state institutional infrastructure supporting public sector activism and entrepreneurial interventions. Federal resources were instrumental in developing Syracuse's economic development capacity, but not determinative. Nor have they been necessary for Syracuse's continued entrepreneurial orientation. State programs and resources sustain these efforts and allow Syracuse to continue to use public capital to leverage private development funds.

This institutional infrastructure balances an orientation toward mobilizing economic development interests with continued public controls over development. This managerialist orientation is exemplified in Syracuse's downtown and lakefront revitalization efforts.

Linking Revitalization and Brownfield Recovery

In 1992, Syracuse's efforts at downtown revitalization won an award from the International Downtown Association. For Syracuse, the arduous path to this recognition was shored up with substantial state and county support. In the mid-1970s, a special assessment district for the downtown was created (1975) and administered by the quasi-public Downtown Committee of Syracuse; the special assessment tax levies are determined and allocated annually to the Downtown Committee with the approval of the Common Council—the city council—and the mayor. Along with CDBG funds, these levies fund the Downtown Loan Fund, a revolving loan fund for rehabilitation of downtown commercial businesses in the district; SIDA makes the loans after rating by the city Department of Community Development.

First steps to turn around the downtown area centered on abortive efforts in 1979 to rehabilitate a downtown landmark, the Hotel Syracuse, renovation of the War Memorial, and more successful revitalization of Armory Square.[7] The Armory Square revitalization was pivotal to downtown recovery, spurred by historic renovation projects and a vision of making the area into Syracuse's "Soho." These include new residential units in older historic buildings such as the Dome Hotel and new commercial/residential ventures such as the Center Armory building. Although the Downtown Committee's initial efforts centered on streetscapes and improvements, the committee and the city increasingly became involved in brokering new construction and rehabilitation projects. By 1996, the Downtown Committee claimed that $425 million had been invested in the downtown in the past ten years (MDA, 1996). Much of the difficulty in moving downtown office space is attributed to the slack market outside of Syracuse; boosting the regional economy would help the downtown market recover. More explicit criticism is targeted, however, at the city's attention to the lakefront area at the northern edge of town. This public investment dwarfs the efforts at downtown revitalization. There is substantial public construction in the downtown area, but highly visible state and national funds continue to come to the city for infrastructure development and environmental cleanup necessary at the lakefront site.

Brownfield recovery is an important aspect of Syracuse's revitalization plans. The city characterizes its Industrial Commercial Development Strategy (1982) as preserving the city's industrial base by promoting the expansion and retention of existing local firms. Oil City is a 180-year-old industrial district between the downtown and Onondaga Lake featuring numerous oil storage tanks that dominated the cityscape. Thanks to unfortunate highway developments in the 1960s, the city was effectively cut off from its lakefront; as the manufacturing plants closed down in the 1970s and 1980s, the area became derelict and marred by toxic waste deposits. In the mid-1980s, the city joined with the Pyramid Companies (the largest shopping center development company in the Northeast and based in Syracuse) to redevelop the site and recover its lakefront access. This tract is seen as the key to development of Syracuse's north side. The seven hundred-acre area is being transformed into Syracuse's "Inner Harbor," replete with renovated historic office buildings, a hotel and marina, residential communities, a rehabilitated regional market, a two million-square-foot shopping mall (Carousel Center), the ubiquitous aquarium, and a new rail station and regional transportation center (the Intermodal Transportation Center, benefiting from federal ISTEA funding and state Thruway Authority funds). In April 1997, the city's new Triple A baseball stadium opened in the Inner Harbor area, despite Governor Pataki's earlier threat to cut off such projects.[8]

The city granted $75 million in tax concessions as its contribution to the public-private partnership charged with the Inner Harbor redevelopment of Oil City (Roberts and Schein, 1993). In the absence of the federal funds that supported Syracuse's earlier redevelopment efforts, these concessions were critical to the implementation of Pyramid's plans. The "Oil City Deal," struck in 1988, relied on SIDA to broker the negotiations. As an off-budget agency with tax-exempt status, SIDA issued bonds to finance Pyramid's construction, including a $55 million loan to help build Carousel Center (Gallagher, 1991). It also became an equity partner in the Oil City project on the city's behalf and to the benefit of the private developer. SIDA is able to take advantage of the state's PILOT program to channel funds to the city to support infrastructure development around the lakefront project. In 1996, $15 million in state Thruway Authority funding played a critical role in pushing the project forward. Approximately $30–50 million in public improvements is invested in the lakefront development.

City support of lakefront development is criticized by some as contributing to a decline in central business district property values. The impact of Carousel Center on downtown retail sales since its opening in 1990 is unclear. One view is that most downtown retail depends on downtown workers and tourists, so that Carousel's biggest impact has been on other suburban shopping malls, where vacancy rates are increasing (Gallagher, 1991). The use of SIDA for retail rather than industrial development is credited with the "over-malling" of the Syracuse area (Gallagher, 1991).

By 1996, momentum for Syracuse's Inner Harbor lakefront development was picking up steam. Syracuse will be the hub of the state's revitalized canal system; the goal is to convert the canals from shipping to primary use as a recreational facility. With $15 million in funding from the State Thruway Authority, and another $4 million from the city and the federal government, the city director of development reported a target ratio of three private dollars for every public dollar for harbor reconstruction. The city and the Metropolitan Development Association set up the Lakefront Development Corporation as a nonprofit entity to direct and oversee development of the entire lakefront area; it is the preferred developer for coordinating the work handled by the private sector (Levin, 1996).

Positioning for the Fourth Wave

Syracuse is positioning for the fourth wave by creating public initiatives for linking telecommunications and economic development initiatives and by nurturing its international trade role. The national 1996 Telecommunications Act restructured the telecommunications marketplace; cities are now trying to figure out what their appropriate roles are and how to maximize their market positions. Among the telecommunication initiatives under consideration is one for Syracuse to become a demonstration "Smart City" in the telecommunication spine being laid out from Buffalo to New York City by a private firm. As a loop in this spine, Syracuse could tie in all city offices and some private firms in the downtown area to this fiber-optic network. This is a low-risk option for the city; it would provide permits and approvals, but the major financing would come from the public utility, Niagara Mohawk, and the private carrier.

Another window of opportunity opened through a rate settlement with NYNEX in the mid-1990s. As part of the settlement, NYNEX created the Diffusion Fund to provide telecommunications access to distressed communities in the central New York region. Capitalized with $50 million over five years, the Diffusion Fund covers construction and capital costs of putting telecommunication infrastructure into disadvantaged neighborhoods. Seeking "community-driven planning," NYNEX establishes a community consortium in each city to determine where the infrastructure will go and what type of access will be provided. Together in this Syracuse consortium, the city of Syracuse's Economic Development Office, MDA, and NYNEX held public forums before selecting inner-city projects in summer of 1997. Although the neighborhood selection process is driven by distress criteria, the neighborhood links will include churches, social organizations, and other informal organizations. Although the Diffusion Fund pays for the infrastructure, the sustainability of these telecommunications links depends on who pays for the operating costs. This issue has threatened the viability of Diffusion Fund projects in other cities, such as Buffalo; it is a stumbling block as Syracuse strives to catch the fourth wave.

These public initiatives are strengthened by the growth of information technology clusters in the Syracuse area, supported by educational institutions and technical infrastructure as well as the skilled labor force. But local economic development officials have not yet constructed a coherent strategy for promoting the area's human capital assets (Hadley, 1996). In a sense, many of these human capital policy responsibilities are borne by state agencies rather than left to the city.

In 1986, member firms of the Greater Syracuse Chamber of Commerce formed the Greater Syracuse International Trade Council (ITC) to foster the growth of exports for small and medium-sized manufacturing and service firms interested in access to a global market. Funds come from chamber members and from the state Economic Development Commission. In recent years the ITC has shifted its emphasis from global "awareness" programs to focus on working more directly with companies with high growth potential in international markets (Cordeau, 1996). Participation in trade missions is increasing, with recent trips focusing on China, Taiwan, and Asia. With a state grant in 1991, the chamber also established an Office of International Trade within the Department of Economic Development to focus on trade prospects of small and medium-sized companies (Van Fleet, 1992).

Syracuse is part of the Buffalo customs district, one of the nation's busiest ports in 1995, with a strategic location on the Canadian border. Much of the $59.7 billion import-export traffic involved Canadian trade; automotive industries and office machinery account for much of the trade. However, there is a sense that trade goes through the area but is not necessarily captured there (Debo, 1996); an economic development plan that builds on the region's clusters in education and medical manufacturing to create value-added production processes is being advocated.

Tacoma: An Enabling Orientation

Tacoma ranks among the most active entrepreneurial cities in our national study (see Table 3.4). Tacoma participated significantly in federal development programs, including numerous public-private partnerships, and engaged in the entrepreneurial use of these federal funds. In our interviews, city officials reported continuing use and adoption of new entrepreneurial strategies with nonfederal resources. Nevertheless, there has been a lag in establishing direction for the postfederal period. The decline of Tacoma's national champions and fragmentation in the business community left a vacuum in which local public officials searched for an appropriate development path. The context increasingly is shaped by state policies requiring regional cooperation on comprehensive land use planning and greater coordination among service providers. Tacoma is compelled to take on an enabling role in managing growth impacts within state guidelines and distributing the costs and benefits among neighborhoods within the city. Along with these direct context-structuring processes on the part of the state government, Tacoma's state representatives and local leadership pulled substantial state government resources into the city in the 1990s.

Although the scale and scope of the institutional setting may be state driven, the players, decision rules, and values are informed by Tacoma's political history. In the past, Tacoma's politics were dominated by locally owned national champions, such as Weyerhaeuser, and strong labor unions; although this contributed to an adversarial political climate, it also delineated a tradition of democratic control and broad representation in public decisions. This has kept neighborhood and social issues on the local agenda, although their prominence depends on shifting council coalitions. Neighborhoods in Tacoma are less well-defined than in Cleveland, but the persistent poverty in the African American community, despite years of targeted federal funds, keeps minority economic development concerns on the city's agenda.

Local Context

Although exploration and European settlement of the Puget Sound area date to 1792, Tacoma's official birth date is 1873. That was when the Northern Pacific Railroad chose an area at the head of Commencement Bay as the western terminus of its Transcontinental line. Until recently, Tacoma coped with a job-poor economic base dependent on outside forces; key features include the Port of Tacoma (the sixth-largest port in North America), extensive landholdings in military installations at Fort Lewis, and national shipbuilding and lumber corporations. Until the late 1970s, Tacoma could still be described as a "labor town," with more than half the workforce unionized; the political tradition is blue-collar and Democratic. Labor lost its edge as locally owned businesses merged with national corporations, the local smelter finally closed down, and the Port Authority operations became subject to greater scrutiny. Police and fire-fighting forces remain unionized, however, and labor support is still critical in local elections. Manufacturing losses have also had impacts on local tax revenues: the Business and Occupation Tax is the largest single revenue source for the city's general fund. In the 1990s, Tacoma and Pierce County's economic base has become less dependent on manufacturing; service industries and, increasingly, high-tech industries are locating in the area. Even as the unemployment rate gets closer to the national average, however, the working poor remain a persistent problem.

Weyerhaeuser, producer of timber products and responsible for much of the "Tacoma aroma"—the noxious smell traditionally associated with Tacoma—ranked twenty-fourth among American industrial exporters in 1993. As in New York, cities in the state of Washington are increasingly trade oriented. In addition to Boeing's strong international trade position, the ports of Seattle and Tacoma together are the second-largest container ports in the country.

Tacoma runs on the nonpartisan mayor-city manager model. Since 1993, elections of five city council members are by district; three other council seats are nominated and elected at-large. Both women and African Americans have held council seats and served as mayor, although it is a weak mayor office. A separate school district is governed by a board elected at-large. With a population of 176,664, Tacoma is 11 percent African American, 6.9 percent Asian, and 3.8 percent Hispanic. The city spreads on steep hills above the bay, similar to San Francisco (even equipped with cable cars in the past), and features magnificent Mount Rainier looming above the city.

Institutional Frameworks

Tacoma is marked by the sights and smells of a railway terminus and working port—a waterfront dominated by wharves, sawmills, and industrial fittings, including numerous large, smelly, polluting smokestacks. In 1873, city officials rejected Frederick L. Olmstead's plans for parks and boulevards as too impractical (Reese, 1973). Local officials have been more receptive to redevelopment plans since then, but with only mixed results. Tacoma's downtown suffered from the opening of the Tacoma Mall, a few miles south on the newly extended Interstate 5, in the 1960s. Although the mall is within city limits and thus contributes to the tax base, the exit of major retail stores devastated the downtown. Nearly half of Pierce County's population now lives within a five-mile radius of the I-5 corridor site. In the early 1990s, the addition of 1.5 million square feet of new retail space, mostly warehouse retailers and roughly equivalent in size to the original mall site, dashed any lingering hopes of a downtown retail revival (Szymanski, 1994). Empty storefronts remain downtown a quarter century later, despite numerous city initiatives.

A series of efforts to revitalize downtown followed but were stymied by the burgeoning residential and retail growth in the suburbs. A staggering increase in crime rates downtown through most of the 1980s scared off both investors and customers. Furthermore, Tacoma's downtown is distinguished by a surfeit of property owners; the largest concentrations of downtown property are owned by public agencies—the University of Washington and the city itself (Cafazzo and Szymanski, 1995b). As local historian Murray Morgan recalls, the defeatist attitude was summed up by the saying "You could get arrested for optimism in Tacoma" (quoted in Popham, 1995).

The Federal Legacy

Despite these trends, Tacoma's many downtown revitalization strategies have tended to focus on commercial and retail initiatives, particularly during the federal period when UDAG funds were available. Tacoma was more active in federal development programs than Seattle, although its efforts to secure urban renewal and Model City funds stirred up local right-wing groups, including the John Birch Society, in the 1960s (Baarsma, 1973). Tacoma's institutional structure is a series of overlays from past federal initiatives, including Urban Renewal, Model Cities, CDBG, UDAG, and substantial EDA Title I investment in the port of Tacoma. It ran these federal programs through city hall, drawing on a cadre of long-serving civil servants with extensive program experience. Many of them participated in National Development Council training programs; Tacoma was in the initial round of NDC pilot cities in the late 1970s. Tacoma also was one of the first cities to use federal programs for business assistance and is consistently recognized as having one of the most comprehensive sets of financial assistance tools in the state.

Institutionalization of Democratic Logic

Although federal programs gave public officials a prominent role in struggling to recapture the city's commercial base, the absence of these funds and the irrefutable trends toward suburban retail development left public officials without a clear sense of direction. As federal largesse and influence dwindled, a progressive coalition gained control of the city council. A neighborhood activist was elected mayor in 1990 and a new city manager appointed; this prompted a reorganization of city policy priorities in the early 1990s. In 1990, economic development was downsized from a separate agency (created in 1986) to a unit in the new Planning and Development Services Department. Housing issues came to the fore. The 1990 council committed 65 percent of CDBG funds to housing. The council wanted to earmark UDAG repayments for affordable housing rather than channel them to the development agencies as in the past; they also wanted to enact a new excise tax for the same purposes.

Although this appeared to signal a new institutional order, no new decision arenas were created to sustain these priorities, nor were there initiatives from the business community to push development issues outside governmental channels. Rather than an institutional strategy, in the early 1990s the city replaced the Planning and Development Services Department director and staff who had steered the city through years of federal programs with administrators with more private sector experience. Although housing priorities remain high on the city's agenda, by 1994 the council agreed to restore economic development programs to permanent status in the city budget.

A Loosely Coupled Framework

Overall, the local decision arena for economic development in Tacoma is relatively fragmented and diffuse. But the contours of a new framework are emerging as state legislation for comprehensive land use planning structures new decision arenas. To date, the concertation of business and public interests occurs informally, increasingly framing growth issues in regional and neighborhood terms. There is no one organization in Tacoma comparable with Cleveland Tomorrow, structuring participation in economic development policy making or providing a decision arena outside government where that might occur. Indeed, that is the tenor of recent critiques of Tacoma's approach, and initiatives to consider such a structure are now under way. Although public sector officials are not dominant, neither are they subordinate to corporate interests as in Cleveland. In terms of context-structuring processes, the city and county increasingly channel participation in policy making on issues framed by the state. Participation rights are broadly defined, and every development organization includes public and private representation. Elected officials continue to coordinate public authority and offer mutual gain to participants in a number of different arenas. The city and county councils remain the forums for iterative bargaining, exchange, and deliberation. The public sector role remains one of developing a framework for addressing economic development issues within the county and city councils, in line with state regulations. In balancing the costs and benefits of growth, city decisions are guided by state growth management legislation requiring that broader community and environmental needs be taken into account. Even its supporters do not claim that this institutional infrastructure is particularly effective in mobilizing economic development interests, but it permits a measure of democratic control over development.

As of 1995, the key organizations active in economic development included the Local Development Council (LDC), a nonprofit corporation funded by the downtown Business Improvement Area, a special taxing district (since 1988) of 350 property owners in an eighty-block area of the central business district; the City Center Council, a Tacoma-Pierce County Chamber of Commerce unit formed to encourage investment in downtown neighborhoods as well as the central business district; the Executive Council for a Greater Tacoma, a leadership group of fourteen public officials and private sector executives that was instrumental in creating the downtown theater district and encouraging development along the Thea Foss Waterway; the Economic Development Board (EDB), focused on job creation and retention in Pierce County; the University of Washington; and city agencies, primarily the Economic Development Division in the Planning and Development Services Department and the Department of Community Development (Cafazzo and Szymanski, 1995b).[9]

In 1993, the city drafted (updated again in 1994) its Economic Development Plan, an optional element in the required Land Use Management Plan. It considers the development options appropriate for a "built" city and sets a "high-skills/high-wage" (human capital) focus. The plan advocates targeting recruitment and retention efforts in international trade, health services, retirement industries, environmental management, new materials, and robots plus machine tools (City of Tacoma, 1993).

Although local efforts remain open to criticism, it is worth noting that there were no moves from the public or private sector in Tacoma toward establishing new institutional frameworks for economic development until 1995. A 1995 report diagnosed downtown revitalization efforts as suffering from the absence of a single organizational locus to coordinate public and private efforts (Fysh, 1995). Until then, there had been no calls for the formation of a nongovernmental economic development policy network that would mobilize resources and expertise. Key decisions remain within the public arena; a Public Development Authority (PDA) was rejected for Union Station on precisely these accountability grounds. This in part reflects what one observer has referred to as the "populism and parochialism" characteristic of Washington politics: there is a healthy belief in popular involvement, an aversion to top-heavy government institutions, and a disinterest in concerns beyond the city limits. State legislation is imposing a regional perspective to correct this parochial view.

In this diffuse setting, two context-structuring processes are currently in play: state pressures for comprehensive regional land use planning and the continued efforts of historic preservation and neighborhood activists to reorient development priorities. Through the 1980s, Pierce County gained notoriety for explosive sprawl development. The policy framework in Tacoma is increasingly set out by state legislation and programs aimed at these regional problems. The 1990 state Growth Management Act legislated clustered development patterns, with the goal of steering development toward urbanized areas to preserve remaining open space. To support job creation and discourage sprawl development and commuting, industrial zoning is encouraged to preserve large parcels of land for future development (Rushton, 1994). Each county was mandated to devise land use plans designating rural and urban growth areas, housing densities, and areas for commercial and industrial development; this heightened the role of the elected county councils, which have major land use and transportation responsibilities. Pierce County's new plans went into effect in January 1995, the first change in countywide land use planning since 1962. Because of restrictions limiting large-scale residential development to urban growth areas, the long-term impacts on Tacoma neighborhoods are likely to include increased pressures for affordable housing and neighborhood conflicts over growth impacts, but also increased property values. Fourteen mixed-use centers now are identified as urban growth areas within Tacoma.

In this new landscape, the Tacoma-Pierce County Economic Development Board is a key player, funded by both private and public sources. Founded in the late 1970s, its efforts include recruitment and retention, although it sees growth coming primarily from retention of existing firms in the county. The EDB relies on a thirty-member board of public and private leaders to maintain contacts with the business community and coordinate efforts. In 1995, it scored a major coup by persuading Intel to locate in the Tacoma suburb of Dupont.

Within the business community, the Tacoma-Pierce County Chamber of Commerce is another significant actor seeking to structure the context for local development decisions. In 1992, the chamber organized a communitywide "vision" group to bring different community sectors to the table to discuss ideas and lay the foundation for a future working group on specific issues (Fysh, 1994). The intent was to bring the stakeholders together and develop their capacity to reach consensus on issues. Many chamber leaders are also members of the Executive Council for a Greater Tacoma, an organization of local CEOs and public officials focused on improving the local economy.

A new decision arena for neighborhood representation is emerging. Karen Vialle, Tacoma's first female mayor, comes from an old Tacoma family and a strong history of neighborhood activism. When she took office in 1990, she brought this orientation to a city with a tradition of citizen activism. In the 1990s, there were more than fifty-five active neighborhood organizations; United Neighborhoods of Tacoma (UNOT), a federation of these groups, had been active since 1979. Vialle organized Tacoma's first Community Summit in 1990, preceded by a community survey identifying top issues for the city. Top issues included crime (1), educational quality (2), drug and alcohol abuse (3), and children, youth, and family (4). Downtown revitalization ranked a distant thirteenth, below neighborhood preservation (11). At the Community Summit, neighborhood enhancement was identified as a key issue; four strategies were identified to enhance neighborhoods, including a proposal to establish neighborhood-based "community councils."

Neighborhood enhancement ultimately became part of the city's strategic plan. As a result, an ordinance was adopted in 1992 creating a neighborhood council program and defining residential neighborhood council areas.[10] As of 1995, eight nonprofit councils existed citywide and advised the city council on matters relevant to their areas. The city set aside 5 percent of CDBG funds (about $160,000 in 1995) to provide funds allowing the councils to make decisions about neighborhood improvements and projects; each council must provide a 10 percent in-kind match in services or resources. The original umbrella coordinating group folded into the United Neighborhoods of Tacoma, which transformed into the new Community Council; each neighborhood council sends three representatives to the Community Council, a citywide coalition of the neighborhood councils in which the city manager also serves.[11]

A parallel structure exists to represent neighborhood business interests—the Cross-District Association of Neighborhood Business Districts. Many neighborhood businesses lost their customer bases when their anchors moved out to newer shopping centers. In 1991, the Neighborhood

Business District Revitalization Program, part of Tacoma's Planning and Development Services Department, started up with general fund and CDBG support. It tailored the Main Street USA model to neighborhood business districts rather than downtown main streets. The aim is to work with neighborhood business associations to create markets that reach beyond the neighborhood's residents. There are now six neighborhood business districts (only three existed prior to 1991); these are designated by the city as mixed-use centers in the state-mandated growth management plans. Depending on the financial strength of local businesses, some of these districts (e.g., South Tacoma) have formed local improvement districts; the central business district is a special assessment district with designated subarea uses of business and occupational taxes paid to the city. But the organizational capacity varies, especially in areas such as the Hilltop, where business survival is paramount. To avoid competition among these districts with uneven capacities, the Cross-District Association also formed in 1991 to act collectively in dealings with the city council. On issues such as parking and higher neighborhood zoning densities stemming from the state growth management directives, the neighborhood councils and business districts often have conflicting agendas.

With the initiative coming from within city government, supported by neighborhood groups, a new institutional link of neighborhoods and city decision structures is emerging. Tacoma is not a city of neighborhoods, but the construction of neighborhood identities is prompted—even promoted—by these institutional changes. They correspond to the city's identification of mixed-use growth centers under the new growth management initiatives; they also reflect the small-scale development orientation in the city.

Representation and Participation

Historically, the local public role remained one of satisfying the demands of business and the priorities articulated through the city council and the Urban Policy Committee. Tacoma's Model Cities participation institutionalized citizen participation through the UPC, although the role of citizen participation, as well as in CDBG activities, waned as deregulation set in. Federal funds were project oriented; they did not require a more strategic local role in distributing the costs and benefits of development, nor did they necessarily require a broad range of participants. The emergent state-based framework may finally sustain the new voices and visions for the city's future that surfaced with the waning of the federal period.

The weakening of national influence and the impetus of state legislation has allowed other voices to be heard, particularly those of the historic preservationist and arts community and human services coalitions organized around children's interests and housing needs. The necessary updating of the city development plan in line with the state Growth Management Act is increasing the access of new groups, such as the efforts of the Tacoma 2010 task force, established by arts groups in the Cultural Coalition, to integrate cultural projects into the city's overall economic development plan.

An Enabling Policy Orientation

Tacoma has moved ahead by redefining success (Cafazzo and Szymanski, 1995a). It shifted to an arts renaissance strategy in the face of suburban retail competition. In contrast to the large, federally subsidized efforts of the 1980s, it now targets the smaller-scale enterprises and specialized services generated by its new public facilities and cultural amenities. Tacoma's move corresponds to the policy shifts noted by many of our survey respondents: in the absence of federal funds, many reported turning to smaller, more diverse projects with smaller public shares of development costs.

An Arts Strategy for Downtown Revitalization

The decline of federal funds coincided with the emergence of electoral coalitions concerned about housing, safety, historic preservation, environmental quality, and neighborhood well-being. With some electoral clout, these groups sought to reorient development priorities and the distribution of development benefits. Their efforts were bolstered by an American Cities study commissioned by the city in the late 1980s that pointed out the futility of competing for retail and urged a strategy of urban renewal through the arts. Although other cities have adopted this revitalization strategy, Tacoma seemed an unlikely prospect. The timing, however, corresponded to a new advocacy in the arts community of economic returns to investment in the arts (McLennan, 1993) and its ability to bring people back downtown, if only for the evening. It also dovetailed with the availability of historic rehabilitation investment tax credits enhanced by the 1981 Economic Recovery Tax Act (ERTA). These tax credits stimulated investment in thirty-three surveyed buildings in Tacoma's central business district between 1982 and 1984 (Kipp Associates, 1985). For city officials, they allowed renovation of landmark buildings and opened the door to increased property and construction sales tax revenues at the federal government's expense in forgone tax revenues.

Like other cities, Tacoma was searching for nonpolluting, nonretail, high-multiplier enterprises with high export potential to support a new downtown economy. It also hoped for a new image, for the arts to "help us understand who we are as a community," as the city's Cultural Resources Division manager put it (quoted in McLennan, 1993; see also Pagano and Bowman, 1995). Unlike many cities, its downtown was graced by two historic jewels—the Pantages Theater and, a block away, the Rialto Theater—and the city itself was home to more than fifty-three arts organizations and twelve major arts institutions. ERTA tax credits allowed restoration of the Pantages in 1983, followed by renovation of the Rialto in 1991. The Rialto renovation benefited from the involvement of a private donor who bought the theater and contributed $1.3 million to its renovation; the city and state contributed about $535,000, and private donations paid the remaining costs (Ortega, 1991). The opening of the new 302-seat Theater on the Square in 1993 brought life back to the city's Broadway Center Theater District. With the help of private security patrols financed by downtown businesses, the numbers of serious crimes reported downtown fell by half between 1988 and 1993.

By the mid-1990s, retail and entertainment activities in the Broadway Plaza area and the "art renaissance" initiatives were beginning to take off. In 1991, the arts employed 277 workers in Tacoma, constituting a $12 million industry, not including money generated by new shops and restaurants (McLennan, 1993). By 1993, the new theaters, galleries, and branch campus workers totaled 525 (Cafazzo and Szymanski, 1995a). Although corporate support has been significant, particularly through the regional Corporate Council for the Arts and the Executive Council for a Greater Tacoma, the partnerships among the arts community, historic preservationists, and the public sector have been the key to this new direction.

This development path and image of the city as a cultural and educational hub gained further ground with the state government's agreement to locate two major facilities in Tacoma: the state Historical Museum and an expansion of the University of Washington campus. Both facilities capitalize on local restoration of another historic landmark, the Union Station rail terminal (built in 1911), as the site of a new federal courthouse, offices, and a waterside restaurant. The initiative for the Union Station renovation came from within the community, with significant leadership and backing from the corporate community and historic preservationists. Many of those involved in efforts to save the Pantages Theater in the late 1970s turned their attention to rescuing Union Station (Kipp Associates, 1985). In its rehabilitation of the Union Station rail terminal area, the city rejected the idea of setting up a Public Development Authority because of local concerns with the city's ability to control PDA finances. The trade-off of governance capacity for financial flexibility led to the establishment of the Union Station

District Development Association, a CDC-like private nonprofit organization with no specific financing authority.

By the late 1980s and early 1990s, the face of Tacoma began to change
with renovation of Union Station, the $100 million expansion of the Univer-
sity of Washington–Tacoma campus on an adjacent downtown site, and
settlement of the Puyallup Indian land claims, which stabilized ownership
in the Tidelands industrial area and allowed new port development.[12] From
the perspective of those working in shelters, this revitalization destroyed
many low-income housing areas, pushing the homeless out of the developed area. This revitalization is public sector driven, with joint efforts by
state and local government. The public resources, infrastructure development, and initiative garnered some private investment, particularly through
the historic ties of Weyerhaeuser and the inducements of the ERTA credits,
but the business community remained relatively passive. Individual business leaders, such as Fred Haley, were instrumental in gaining state support
for the branch campus and other facilities, and the Executive Council for a
Greater Tacoma was important in the theater district revitalization, but the
local business community did not take the strong, visible leadership role
evident in Cleveland. Indeed, it may remain captive to vestigial thoughts: a
chamber study group in 1995 attributed the city's downtown difficulties to
the tax and regulatory environment; the lack of housing downtown; the
lack of retail, restaurants, and entertainment downtown; the lack of manufacturing jobs; and a negative image (Fysh, 1995).

The Hilltop

Historically, the city's political geography encompassed a more affluent,
more Republican and "good government"-oriented north end and a more
working-class, more Democratic and labor-oriented south and east side
(Crockett, 1974). Many feel these voting patterns and representation biases
persist today. At least six distinct city districts exist: Proctor, Stadium, Sixth
Avenue, Upper Tacoma/Hilltop, Tacoma Dome, and Lincoln. The first three
are relatively prosperous; Lincoln is a multicultural district and, historically, many African Americans have lived in the Hilltop area north of downtown. Hilltop is now home to a growing population of Asian immigrants
and refugees as well. In 1990, the Hilltop area had approximately 13,000
jobs, although many were in hospitals in the area and required skills beyond the levels of most Hilltop residents. Unemployment in the neighborhood ranges from 14 percent to 27 percent, double to quadruple Tacoma's
average rate of 7.4 percent (Clements, 1995a).

Until the 1993 changes in voting procedures, candidates ran in district races for the primary, but in at-large races for the general election. This resulted in few people of color winning citywide office. So, effectively, Tacoma's neighborhood links were structured by the political geography noted above, with little actual neighborhood representation other than persistent concerns about the Hilltop. As a result, Tacoma's revitalization efforts have been bifurcated by an emphasis on the traditional downtown core and a concern for the primarily African American Hilltop area. Due to high poverty, unemployment, and substandard housing rates, the Hilltop has been the focus of many city-run federal programs. As these federal funds diminished, economic development activities were carried on by the Upper Tacoma Renaissance Association (UTRA), a nonprofit organization founded by the Urban League in 1985 and subsisting on city grants and contracts, League sponsorship, and LISC support. In late 1994, UTRA closed down for lack of funds. The historical lack of strong economic development organizations in the Hilltop is seen as one of the barriers to community-based economic development.

Federal funds promise to return with the designation of the Hilltop area as part of Tacoma's enterprise community (EC) in 1994. Tacoma was named an enterprise community with $3 million in resources targeted to an EC area including the Hilltop, portions of the eastside, downtown, and the Tidelands port/industrial area. In this ten-square-mile area of 20,494 residents, the poverty rate is 46 percent, unemployment tops 18 percent, and the crime rate is among the city's highest. The city is committing 60 percent of its CDBG funds to housing projects in the EC area; this includes support for training in home ownership, help in qualifying for home purchase, and working with private lenders on 204(k) rehabilitation loans (White House, 1994).

Positioning for the Fourth Wave

Tacoma now enjoys a certain "place luck" (Logan and Molotch, 1987) in its positioning for the fourth wave. The city's global-local links are secured by its strategic position relative to Pacific Rim trade as well as by the emerging binational Cascadia region's response to NAFTA incentives. These natural advantages are fortuitous: the city has little direct role in the Port Authority and is subordinate to state policy on the environmental issues dominating Cascadia debates. With the revitalization of the port and Thea Foss Waterway, the city continues to strengthen its international trade position. Its major policy initiatives, however, are directed at human capital concerns.

State legislation mandating greater coordination of human services prompted formation of Tacoma's Human Services Coalition and the development of the Strategic Plan for Human Services, resulting in significant increases in general fund allocations. In 1990, the City-County Commission on Children, Youth, and Their Families was established as a citizen advisory board to the city and county. These issues rose to second place in a 1991 community survey of important issues. The commission is preparing a countywide strategic plan to address issues that affect children—particularly dropout rates, child abuse and neglect, and poor birth outcomes—but it also claims an advocacy role in making children and families a political priority. The aim is to focus on local government's leadership role in coordinating these efforts. The needs and resources are seen as localized: possible funding strategies under consideration include establishing a special district along the lines of a public development authority dedicated to children's issues, earmarking taxes for children and family services, and periodic levies, in addition to more familiar fund-raising and Children's Trust Fund arrangements (Tacoma-Pierce County Commission on Children, Youth, and Their Families, 1992).

The city of Tacoma historically has been more attentive to job training and employment issues than has Pierce County. Both city and county are required to come up with a strategic plan for human services, and that state requirement has prompted some coordination. In 1995, Tacoma's citizen advisory group, the Urban Policy Committee, developed a human services strategic plan and took it to the city council for approval. As a result of this plan, the city shifted allocation priorities and funded several new areas. The city funds a number of human capital initiatives, including the work of the Washington Women's Employment and Education Organization.

Housing remains a priority issue. Nonprofit organizations are central to housing initiatives, as they are for Tacoma's larger social service agenda. This is especially so with the FHA 203(k) Mortgage and Improvement Loan program, which offers nonprofit organizations roles in housing development, rehabilitation, technical assistance, and marketing. With an ambitious goal of 60 percent home-owner occupancy in the Hilltop, the city committed $136,000 in CBDG funds for down-payment assistance to borrowers earning 80 percent or less of the area median income. Tacoma is relying on Habitat for Humanity, the Martin Luther King Housing Development Association, and the Hilltop Homeownership Development Center, among others, to carry out these rehabilitation and ownership programs. LISC is also active in the Hilltop area, working with CDCs, Washington Mutual Savings Bank, and Seafirst to provide permanent financing for affordable multifamily rental housing projects. These efforts were boosted with the Enterprise Community plans in 1994 for affordable housing rehabilitation and construction with national funds.

In addition, the Pierce County Coalition for the Homeless is developing a "continuum of care" model to compensate for declining national funds. The institutional goal is to get "all the people at the same table" to target funding sources and programs. The Greater Tacoma Community Foundation and United Way are important sources of support for these groups.

State government is a critical element in the development of Tacoma's new institutional framework. This occurred not through elaborate development finance programs, but through traditional infrastructure and amenities initiatives and a regulatory environment requiring regional cooperation. These state directives are recasting local decision arenas at a different scale and with a broader scope of actors. The need to coordinate city and county initiatives brings together elected officials with different constituencies and diverse private interests. Similarly, by focusing on the performance of service providers, they extend the scope of their decisions to include nonprofit organizations as well as city and county agencies. Although nonprofit organizations are recognized as intermediaries in these processes, public officials maintain control of allocation. Public-private partnerships in Tacoma now are often intergovernmental and extragovernmental. The regional decision arena has dampened the need to commodify place (Harvey, 1989): future growth will be channeled into urbanized areas by state land use plans.

Democratic Logic and Institutional Frameworks

In Syracuse and Tacoma, the institutional order and logic of the bureaucracy and the state are incorporated into local economic development decision making. Business leadership is important, as in any American city, but public sector leaders are often involved in setting economic development goals and priorities. Historically, this public leadership was situated in bureaucratic agencies; in both cities, there is a slow movement toward reliance on organizations with public-private representation, with Syracuse having more experience with this quasi-public organizational form.

Here again, variations in the coherence of the institutional frameworks result in different policy orientations. The role of public sector officials is similar in Syracuse and Tacoma in that it is directive and accountable through democratic channels for decisions on development. To some extent, both cities reflect a concern with value-added processes, in terms of both building on existing economic clusters and higher-wage jobs. This is similar to the opportunistic state model of efforts at structuring and positioning local economies, but in Syracuse and Tacoma there are relatively coherent public agendas guiding this process. Admittedly, elements of these value-added agendas were imposed by the respective state governments, but they also reflect concerns with retaining the knowledge and skill base from manufacturing activities and a traditional blue-collar workforce. Syracuse's tightly coupled framework is experienced in carrying out this value-added role, but it also appears locked into a particular set of solutions. Syracuse leaders themselves sought to increase the coherence of their regional voice with the formation of the Economic Growth Agenda. This tight coupling may make the local institutional structure more vulnerable to external shocks (DiMaggio and Powell, 1991), such as the loss of federal funds or the election of state officials with less expansive development agendas.

In Tacoma, there are overlays of citizen groups from the federal period, new neighborhood councils, coordinated neighborhood business associations—in short, a great diversity and range of organizations with different values and procedures; a strong and coherent state role; and a mobilized, consensual younger generation of community leaders in the human services. In the economic development arena, this loosely coupled framework produced the slower, less coordinated "success" expected in such settings. But this framework appears more suited to human capital and social service issues; it appears more flexible in the types of projects addressed, more able to adapt to changing conditions or new ideas, and more responsive to new opportunities. The city and county's experience with both the arts and the human services communities suggests that a looser framework may also prove more accessible to groups seeking to challenge current priorities.

Institutional Logics and Frameworks

In this chapter and in chapter 5, we have compared local institutional frameworks for local economic development policy making in the absence of the national regulations and procedures that have shaped decision arenas in the past. These local institutional designs are as significant for the work of cities as the policy choices detailed previously. They provide the arenas and structures through which leaders and citizens work out how to adapt to their new global context. Indeed, these institutional arrangements influence policy choices and outcomes by regulating formal and informal access to decision processes and by shaping the formation and expression of views toward local development issues. They provide different incentives and opportunities for mobilization and, in the process, take cities down particular development paths.

These institutional frameworks limit decision access to designated representatives (Syracuse, Jacksonville, Cleveland) or provide broader access in both formal and informal channels (Tacoma). They influence whether and how neighborhood and minority community concerns figure in city economic development deliberations. As the Cleveland case demonstrates, hinted at as well in Tacoma, they also shape those views or make some voices more audible and relevant than others. By privileging some definitions, or frames, and the attendant solutions, the frameworks increase access for some groups and limit it for others.

Actual institutional change was less evident than we anticipated. We anticipated that some cities would continue to choose entrepreneurial paths because they now had the capacity and expertise to do so. Our statistical analyses suggest that there may also be a *need* to do so—less well-off cities appear more likely to use nonfederal resources in entrepreneurial ways. Yet it is also reasonable to expect cities to be more risk aversive when their own resources are at stake; thus we anticipated that some cities would retreat to more traditional strategies and abandon the more speculative ventures possible with federal resources. Although logical arguments can be made for anticipating either outcome, we can understand the paths taken only by examining the local political, economic, social, and regional contexts. Federal policy history does not appear to determine recent adoption of entrepreneurial strategies, but it did provide the skills and institutional base for activist, market-oriented approaches. These sunk investments increased the costs of reverting to more conventional orientations as well as the costs of choosing a radically different policy path.

Institutional change is most dramatic in Cleveland and Tacoma, where the corporate community and state government, respectively, restructured the decision arenas. The resilience of institutional arrangements is not to be underestimated; with overlays of institutions crowding the landscape, ascendance of new organizations is more likely than outright displacement and substitution. This underscores the importance of state enabling legislation and state programmatic infrastructure in stabilizing local institutional arrangements. It also casts a perverse light on the importance of business organizations: without coherent business organizations, a directive public voice is less likely to be effective.

In chapter 7, we consider the policy options and institutional designs demarcating the fourth wave of innovation and adaptation hinted at in our studies. This overview is tentative and exploratory, but it foreshadows the continuing search for new ways to adapt to changing local contexts. Here the challenges stem from the globalization of economic processes and technological developments that appear to subvert our very understanding of the meanings of distance and locality.

7

The Fourth Wave

Global-Local Links and Human Capital

A fourth wave of local policy initiatives will center on linking localities to global webs and investing in human capital.

Up to this point, our empirical data and case studies show that cities are more active and salient as economic development actors than the initial globalization models anticipated. They also choose more entrepreneurial and divergent paths than conventional political economy models would suggest. To some extent, American cities appear to be complementing their historic land-site development policy orientation with a business- and enterprise-led development strategy more familiar in European cities (Begg and Whyatt, 1994). Given the territorial biases of American local politics, this is of some interest. Other studies confirm this diversity and complexity in local economic development choices (Elkins, 1995; Goetz, 1994; Miranda and Rosdil, 1995). Whether these policy approaches constitute a paradigm shift (Osborne, 1988) or merely a maturation in policy orientation, as Hanson (1993) puts it, there is growing consensus that localities are shifting toward more interventionist and more differentiated approaches to development (Eisinger, 1988).

A fourth wave of local policy initiatives aimed at integrating local economies into global markets, developing local human capital resources, and increasing use of telecommunications as a development tool is anticipated by our theoretical framework. In this chapter we report on recent empirical work that supports these expectations. This emerging evidence of fourth-wave approaches suggests that local officials are beginning to move beyond vestigial thoughts that put sole priority on the importance of physical capital and the local industrial base in wealth creation processes. We do not claim that this has occurred in all American cities, but we find intriguing evidence that local officials are moving toward an orientation that recognizes global-local links and human capital concerns.

Rethinking City Limits

As outlined in chapter 2, most models of urban politics emphasize the limits and constraints imposed on city choices by the twin logics of federalism and capitalism. These models of city limits may be less appropriate in a global era because several economic assumptions no longer hold: that growth occurs within politically bounded and relatively closed economies; that investment circuits are national; that productivity comes from factor-driven competitiveness, that is, a dependence on economies of scale and full utilization of relatively inflexible means of production; that high-volume production is the basis of economic growth; and Peterson's (1981) controversial argument that there is a unitary local interest in economic development. Globalization processes certainly undermine the first two assumptions: the decision context for local officials is now broader than local or national boundaries, and finance capital is not necessarily or solely domestic. Two aspects of changing production structures further challenge assumptions about economic growth processes: Scott's (1992) argument that productivity increasingly stems from minimizing the costs of transactions and innovations and Reich's (1991) contention that wealth is created increasingly through high value-added production processes rather than high-volume production.

These more economistic models of city limits slight local political factors and thereby misspecify the impacts of a changing economy on local policy. The reorganization of markets on a global scale entails the renegotiation of public/private roles at every scale. For example, as Goetz (1994, 88) and others note, these larger economic changes and globalization trends are likely to undermine the political hegemony of the local growth machine. More particularly, these trends contribute to the erosion of local citizenship through polarization and increasing inequalities in communities. These equity and polarization issues may drive policy change when citizens link spatial and social concerns with, for example, housing (Goetz, 1993) or job issues. Uneven development within cities, in particular, appears to create a charged political context in which alternate policy options may be pursued if viable demand mechanisms are in place (Elkins, 1995; Goetz, 1994). Thus there is an emergent political dimension of globalization as groups and politicians struggle to form coalitions around strategies that might manage and minimize the harmful domestic repercussions of globalization trends.

This dimension directs attention to the political rationale for attending to social needs and human capital concerns, complementing the economic rationale for human capital investment provided by Reich and others. This logic could include, for example, a focus on distributive policies and their effects on local reelection chances, the logic of dispersion or spreading benefits around to construct local coalitions, and politicians' need to recognize and respect past obligations as well as future needs (Goetz, 1993; DeLeon, 1992). This political logic could support a broader range of policy options than anticipated by the simple globalization models, including more "progressive" policies than expected from local political dynamics (DeLeon, 1992; Goetz, 1994; Elkins, 1995; Miranda and Rosdil, 1995). There may be more latitude for social and human capital policies than the city limits model suggests, and this may be more widespread than anticipated by world city models (Knox and Taylor, 1995).

We suspect that academic research now falls behind local practices in this shifting policy arena. The city limits model does not anticipate local concerns with human capital, nor does it accommodate economic growth processes based on human capital and information. To date, the evidence generated by scholarly research indicates that the current wave of local entrepreneurial strategies is responsive to the changing nature of economic competition and increased capital mobility but slights two increasingly important aspects of wealth creation—human capital and information (Castells, 1989; Parker, 1995). In the next wave of local economic development policy change—the fourth wave, by our count—we anticipate greater attention to the integration of human capital and economic development concerns and to the trade links and information infrastructure necessary to link local economies with the global web.

The Fourth Wave of Policy Innovation

The Transitional Ethos for the Fourth Wave

Despite our expectations for a new fourth wave of policy innovation, third-wave strategies remain important features of local agendas, as shown in chapter 3 (Table 3.6). Third-wave entrepreneurial policies reflect significant changes in the worldview of local officials and their assessment of appropriate public roles in local economic development strategies.

The local policy context is transforming in ways that echo some of the scholarly speculation described previously. Substantiating our 1989 survey, 88 percent of the cities responding in 1996 claim they are more active in economic development in the postfederal period than they were in the federal period, and 71 percent of these cities profess having stronger local economic development capacities now. These findings also support the "hollowing out of the state" prediction: 59 percent of our cities say economic development decisions have shifted down to the local level in the 1990s, with 26 percent reporting policy decisions mostly moving up to regional and state government levels. In particular, the majority of cities (57 percent) claim that their state governments are now paying more attention to urban areas.

More broadly, 70 percent of cities confirm that their local development orientations are changing in the 1990s, with 62 percent claiming they are becoming more aggressive in pursuit of economic development. Although the traditional development goals of business attraction (47 percent) and retention (53 percent) continue to dominate economic development orientations, these goals increasingly are pursued in a global context.

The Arrival of the Fourth Wave

Our 1996 survey of cities clearly points to a fourth wave of policies that targets two dimensions: (1) globalization links through trade and telecommunications initiatives and (2) human capital development.[1] Although some cities are located more advantageously than others for global trade, telecommunications technology celebrates "the death of distance" (1995): cities can forge telecommunications links with global marketplaces in lieu of direct trade links. Indeed, once the legalities and technical considerations are settled, strategies for information infrastructure may prove easier for localities to work out than the human capital initiatives.[2] In the following sections we briefly describe responses we received from city officials when we asked how they address these aspects of wealth creation—human capital and global-local links—in a globalizing economy.

The fourth-wave strategies we encountered include the following (strategies marked with asterisks are those also identified in previous waves):

Human capital

job training

job training targeting specific economic sectors

city/college collaboration

business incubators*

youth internships

school-to-work programs

Globalization

foreign trade zones*

export promotion*

trade missions abroad*

sister cities

international development planning

international tourism initiatives

links with universities/colleges on improving global
   competitiveness

attracting international direct investment

world trade centers

Telecommunications

fiber-optic networks

using Internet resources

home pages on the Internet

linking government offices via e-mail

public access to job and education information

public access to the Internet

telecommunications access to low-income residents

Human Capital Investment

Although the federal Private Industry Council (PIC) job training model remains important, many communities in our 1996 survey report local policy designs to target specific concerns. Minneapolis, for example, set up a task force to work on linking human capital and economic development; pushed by state legislation requiring reports on jobs created with public funds, the city passed a resolution establishing a wage guarantee (a minimum of $8.25 an hour) for city-aided job-creation projects.[3] Other cities also report making development assistance contingent on specific job creation and training efforts. Portland, Oregon's efforts to link new and expanding businesses with local labor pools in the late 1980s evolved into a separate Workforce Development Department by the mid-1990s. With the incentive of state funding support, Oregon counties can form alliances to support workforce development and training programs.

The majority of cities we surveyed in 1996 are involved in some form of job training. Interestingly, several cities target specific economic sectors in their human capital initiatives. Ann Arbor's and Stamford's training programs are targeted at software; Mesa's and Portland, Oregon's strategies are aimed at semiconductors; and Greensboro has a program focusing on metalworking. Many of these cities mention difficulties of matching skills and jobs and coordinating training efforts with business. Collaboration for city training efforts is often found with local community colleges. The sheer cost of human capital efforts limits what cities can do; cities are drawing on general funds, Community Development Block Grants, debt financing, state support, payroll taxes, and even lottery funds to support these programs.

Global-Local Links

Somewhat to our surprise, globalization is generally perceived as a positive trend by cities. Only 16 percent of the cities in the current survey mentioned local costs (predominantly loss of jobs) due to globalization. Meanwhile, 64 percent saw benefits (primarily increases in exports). About half of the cities surveyed had export promotion strategies (55 percent) and foreign trade zones (51 percent), strategies often mentioned in the third wave (see Table 3.6). Many cities remain at the awareness stage—pursuing activities to increase the local understanding of these new trends and to assess the local potential for benefiting from them. These awareness strategies include attending seminars, joining regional and international trade associations, participating in sister city programs (92 percent),[4] linking with universities and colleges to improve global competitiveness (57 percent), and conducting trade missions abroad (50 percent). Other frequently noted efforts include policies to attract international direct investment and international tourism initiatives. Cities as different as Durham, San Diego, Lexington, and Lubbock now have world trade centers. Dallas, Tampa, Oklahoma City, and Portland, Oregon (among others), have engaged in international development planning.

Portland is a good example of a city with development policies explicitly focused on global-local links. It is a leading port on the West Coast, and after a long history of trade with Asia, the city has expanded its working relationships with Europe. Its international programs include thirty sister cities, multilingual signage in the city, and the recent creation of an international development plan. This plan includes trade relations, education, technical assistance to business, and even a policy to make infrastructure internationally "friendly."

Telecommunications

Although our survey found a surprisingly diverse range of cities pursuing economic global-local linkages, not every city enjoys competitive advantages in the global marketplace. For many cities, telecommunication strategies provide a means of linking with the global web independent of trade relations. As Graham and Marvin (1996, 125) put it, cities are the "informa-tion switching centres" of the global economy or, in Scott's (1992) terms, the transactional nodes. "Quality of telecommunications" was ranked as the second most important location factor (behind easy access to markets, customers, and clients) in a recent survey of five hundred European com-panies (Graham and Marvin, 1996, 340). From a locational perspective, telecommunications is where the "sizzle" is for new businesses; an innova-tive and useful telecommunications policy may supplant cities' current "edifice complex." Image building of future cityscapes (Pagano and Bow-man, 1995) may take place in cyberspace rather than through construction of high-rise office towers, sports stadiums, and convention centers. Fur-thermore, some cities also see telecommunications as a means of building social capital and meeting the needs of different communities.[5] Non-governmental groups and "freenets" are becoming involved in these initia-tives (Schuler, 1996). The Milwaukee Associates in Urban Development (an association of 240 nonprofit organizations), for example, offers training and technical support to nonprofits on telecommunications possibilities.[6]

We found that cities recognize the need to integrate telecommunica-tions policies with local economic development strategies (76 percent), but less than half responding have actually adopted explicit telecommunica-tions policies. This is likely due to the continuing uncertainty in the federal and state telecommunication policy environment. For many cities, possi-ble telecommunications roles await state legislative decisions (Clarke and Saiz, 1995). Short of a full-blown local telecommunications policy, cities actively embrace new information technologies: fully 84 percent of cities responding use Internet resources, 78 percent have home pages on the Internet, and 78 percent use e-mail in city hall. Other telecommunication policies reported include providing electronic access to job and education-al information (54 percent) and providing public access to the Internet (46 percent). Some cities, such as Oklahoma City and Tacoma, are considering initiatives to provide telecommunications access for low-income citizens as part of their enterprise community plans.

In the following sections we consider the larger context of political, economic, and technological conditions shaping these local issues. It is not immediately obvious why these aspects of wealth creation—human capital and information—would be on local agendas. As we hope to make clear, they emerge at the local level at least in part as a consequence of institu-tional frameworks and political dynamics that make it difficult to formulate coherent national policies on these issues.

Redefining the Human Capital Issue

As both Karl Marx and Adam Smith would agree, the wealth of nations resides in their human capital. With globalization, international competition,
and economic restructuring altering value-added processes, this reality
ironically is truer now than it has ever been historically. Yet our ideas about
human capital and the political arrangements through which we respond
to human capital needs lag behind these new realities.

Attributes of Human Capital

Reframing local development policy orientations must begin with a recognition of the ways in which human capital is significantly different from
physical capital. Although analogies exist between traditional concepts of
physical capital and human capital, human capital is sufficiently different
from physical capital that neoclassical economic growth models dealing
with "capital" may not be applicable (see Table 7.1). Investing in a continuously learning, mobile, freedom-loving, nonownable human is only re-
motely similar to buying fixed plants and machinery. Yet our social and economic policies have been slow to adjust to this new reality. Policies that
target this productive sector of the economy will be different from policies
that previously targeted the physical capital-dominated manufacturing
sector.

Table 7.1

Comparing human and physical capital

Trait	Human capital	Physical capital
Mobility	Relatively high	Relatively low
Returns over time	Increase	Diminish
Premium pricing	Increases	Decreases
Assets	Non-ownable	Ownable
Flexibility	High	Low
Measurability	Difficult	Easy
Main constraint	Limited education	Limited resources
Federal policy	Minimal	Capital gains exemptions, investment tax credits
Postinvestment lag	Long	Short
Global economic importance	Increasing	Decreasing

In contrast to the "catch-up syndrome," in which initial advantages in returns on physical capital investment and premium pricing are eroded as competition encourages substitutions and additional entries into the market, individuals have incentives to invest in their own human capital development. For individuals with sufficient information, certainty, and resources to take advantage of opportunities to invest in themselves (Reich, 1983), their returns over time increase and premium pricing also increases. In the human capital world, those with an initial advantage are able to combine their initial education with increasing experience such that their returns do not diminish, but increase. Their premium pricing will usually increase as their specialty skills and reputation for problem solving and innovation become more widely known, versus the decline in the value of the best manufactures as their secrets become learned and imitable. By investing in their children's human capital through premium education, they may pass this advantage on generationally (Reich, 1991, 109).

Underinvestment in Human Capital as a Policy Problem

Transferring this individual rationality into public policy choices, however, is more problematic. Both market failures and the difficulties in measuring opportunity costs contribute to underinvestment in human capital.

Recognizing Market Failures

A diverse set of scholars concur on the importance of recognizing underinvestment in human capital as a pattern of market failures.[7] Robert Reich (1991), in *The Work of Nations*, clearly targets human capital resources as the key to generating wealth and maintaining American competitiveness. Eugene McGregor Jr. (1994) and Hornbeck and Salamon (1991) also recognize that relying on market forces alone will tend to encourage underinvestment in this strategic resource. Recent work on conditional convergence theories of economic growth emphasize the critical role of government policies and institutions in determining how well resources are used and put special emphasis on human capital investment. As economists bring institutions, intentionality, and policy choices to the fore in accounting for growth differentials, the public role in human capital investment becomes increasingly salient.

The underinvestment issue is especially striking when we compare the United States with Europe. Table 7.2 compares the United States and the European Community in terms of their educational achievement and skills base in human capital stock. The United States ranks first in the world in terms of the mean years of schooling of its populace over the age of twenty-five and first in total public funding per college student. It ranks second only to Canada in the percentage of college graduates (of graduation age). Yet Europe is increasing its public education expenditures at a rate almost double that of the United States, thereby narrowing the funding gap. Further, Europe is far ahead in the percentage of students taking scientific and technical education; this will result in a concomitantly greater scientific and technical sector in their future labor force.

Table 7.2

Comparison of human capital in the United States and Europe

Human capital variable	United States	European Community
Mean years of schooling of those age 25 and over 1992	12.4	10.1
College graduates (as % of population of normal graduation age 1990–1991)	29.6	12.6
Public expenditure per tertiary student 1991	$13,640	$6,310
Change in total education expenditure (as % of GDP) 1960–91	+32	+61
College natural and applied science enrollment (as % of total college 1990–91)	14	34
Scientists and technicians per 1,000 people 1986–90	55	81
% of 19-year-olds still in full-time education 1990–91	38	50
Earnings disparity: ratio of earnings of upper half to lower half of labor force 1991	5.6	2.9

Note: European Community here includes Belgium, Denmark, France, Germany, Greece, Ireland, Italy, Luxembourg, the Netherlands, Portugal, Spain, and the United Kingdom.

Source: United Nations Development Programme (1994).

Americans assume that they are members of a highly educated populace, yet only 38 percent of our nineteen-year-olds are still in full-time education, compared with 65 percent for Germany, 61 percent for France, and an average of 50 percent in the European Community (United Nations Development Programme, 1994, 192). Although educational structures differ internationally (among advanced industrial countries, the United States is distinctive for decentralized responsibility for education policy), in most cases nineteen-year-olds are at the stage where they should be developing complex human capital. In both Germany and Japan, continued vocational training is strongly supported after the period of formal education ends. In Germany this is done through a government-supported apprenticeship program, and in Japan it is accomplished largely through training programs in business and industry (Glazer, 1993, 35–37). The earnings disparities resulting from lack of education in the United States are almost double those of Europe. America's relative underinvestment in human capital undermines the continued competitive advantage of the U.S. economy.

Although human capital investment strategies are often criticized for increasing public spending, we have presented the counterargument: failing to invest in human capital development is an inefficient use of an important source of potential future wealth and international competitiveness. We now consider the opportunity costs problems associated with failure to develop unmet human capital potential.

Measuring Opportunity Costs

In addition to familiar calculations of the direct costs of human capital investment, it is also useful to estimate the opportunity costs of *not* investing in human capital. What are the social and economic costs of allowing our potential human capital stocks to remain untapped?

By couching the policy issues in terms of the opportunity costs of underinvesting in human capital, we clarify the problem but face complex measurement issues. To begin with, we must identify the current supply of human capital and its contribution to economic well-being, then assess the increased well-being possible with various levels of investment in human capital. The gap between the current level of productivity and that possible with increased human capital investment indicates the unmet human capital *potential* available in different communities.[8] Addressing this gap by calculating "where marginal resource outlays would yield maximum welfare gains" (Lehnen and McGregor, 1994, 20) should be the focal point of public policy initiatives.

Unmet Human Capital Potential

Unmet human capital potential is the difference between the net value added to society after optimal investment in human capital and the current value added attributable to human capital. The value added of both the optimal and current *stock* of human capital needs to be evaluated over time.[9] Optimal human capital investment would be determined, in pure economic terms, when all investments are made where marginal benefits (evaluated over time) are equal to or greater than marginal costs (evaluated over time).

The task of measuring unmet human capital potential is fraught with difficulty, given the dynamic nature of demand in a changing global economy and the uneven quality of the supply of human capital resources. This is especially true if concerns for the quality of human capital are incorporated. As the economy adjusts to globalization, it becomes increasingly difficult to discuss an optimal supply of knowledge, skills, and training relative to demand. There will undoubtedly remain a demand for a mix of services and talents. Not everyone will—or should—become symbolic analysts: some lack the needed talent to achieve that end, the market would likely not bear the influx of the increased supply of talent in that sector, and the prices of needed ancillary services would increase as the labor supply diminishes in other areas. Further, human capital keeps redefining itself in terms of it qualitative attributes.

Admittedly, the unmet human capital metric is primarily a supply-side measure. Yet it is reasonable to argue that the national economy, operating within the global market, could profitably absorb better-trained human capital—that we could gainfully employ a better-trained labor force without suffering significant losses in returns to labor based on increased supply factors. To make one rough estimate of the potential economic changes possible, let us make an initial assumption: that a better-trained labor force would retain its "educational advantage" in income; that is, a dynamic and growing global economy would be able to absorb the additional talent without discounting its income. Studies consistently point to the high correlation between income and education (although this becomes much more complicated when disaggregated by race and gender).

Using a recent U.S. Census report (1996) of 1993 data, we know that, on average, a person who is a high school graduate and did not continue his or her education makes average annual earnings of $12,960, compared with $6,096 for a person who did not graduate from high school. For further comparison, a person who holds at least a bachelor's degree has mean earnings of $28,068. The unemployment rate for those not graduating from high school compared with that of those successfully graduating from college is *five times* as high (United Nations Development Programme, 1994, 195).

Now if, for heuristic purposes, we assume that we are able to enact national human capital investment policies such that we increase the proportion of our population graduating from high school by age 25 to 90 percent (from the current 81 percent) and increase the population graduating from college by age 25 to 35 percent (it was 20.3 percent in 1991), what would be the expected annual increase in national income based on such a change in education if we make the heroic assumption that the increased capacity can be absorbed into the labor market without a decline in relative wages? A rough calculation yields an *annual* increase of approximately $200 billion for the increase in high school graduates and $250 billion for the increase in college graduates. Of course this is a simple analysis, and we have not introduced the temporal factors of lags and discounted income streams, or relaxed the assumption of the impact on incomes of increased labor supply. Nonetheless, even the introduction of these complexities, using reasonable estimates, including reduced labor absorption rates, would still yield annual benefits that measure in the hundreds of billions of dollars.[10]

Constraints on Addressing Human Capital Concerns

At first glance, the policy solutions to underinvestment seem simple (Fosler, 1991): invest in people directly or encourage the rationality of individuals investing in themselves to improve their productivity and their capacity to add value to the economy. Yet several constraints hamper the translation of this underinvestment concern into effective investment in human capital and encourage avoidance and suboptimal choices.

The Leaky Bucket Dilemma

As Reich (1983) puts it, the costs, processes, and returns from investments in human capital are "inescapably social." The logistical difficulty of capturing returns complicates investment in developing human capital. The mobility of human capital, its flexibility, its "non-ownability" and the long time lags involved before returns are realized serve to discourage local public and private investors. This is especially so in the American federal system, and dramatically so for cities. Americans are among the most mobile people in the world, with the average American moving sixteen times over a life span, including five major (intercity) moves. This mobility increases with education; the most skilled human capital is seldom wedded to a particular location. Given this mobility, local interests may have less economic incentive to invest in human capital at the local scale. Both public and private interests may see it as much more in their interest to lure already educated people to their cities and businesses, thus profiting from investment elsewhere. This "leaky bucket" dilemma—the risk that those who invest in human capital may not necessarily capture all the benefits of their investment—underscores the social dimension of human capital policy. As a public good, human capital investment is something from which we all would benefit, but it appears "irrational" for any one firm or city to support it. To local officials, policies designed to attract the best and the brightest—through cultural amenities, leisure activities, festival shopping areas—may appear to promise greater payoffs than policies designed to produce them.

The Joint Decision Trap

The appropriate geographic scale for human capital investment is a compelling issue: our decentralized responsibilities for human capital development guarantee frustration for those seeking more coherent approaches. The need for joint decisions between different levels of government on investment in human capital creates a joint decision trap (Scharpf, 1988) in which suboptimal policy decisions result from these institutional conditions.[11]

As the indicators in Table 7.2 reveal, the consequences of the joint decision trap are especially troublesome in the education arena. Institutionally, primary responsibility for education remains at state and local levels. Yet there is a strong national interest in improving education so that children will be competitive in a global economy and, incidentally, in providing their parents with some relief from the costs of doing so. At best, the national government can provide a bully pulpit for advocating school reforms and supporting state and local innovations. Increasingly, Congress and the White House have agreed on increasing student aid and loans for higher education (Katz, 1996), but more direct steering of education policy has been hampered by political constraints (King, 1995) and institutional fragmentation (Weir, 1992).

The Political Context

The political dynamics of our federal system not only hinder joint decisions, they encourage discrete and localist strategies. Many of the most basic social provisions have originated at the state level, as legislative responses to organized pressure groups, such as mothers and soldiers

(Skocpol, 1992), and through ballot initiatives (Tolbert, 1995). By the beginning of the 1930s, the planning and implementation capacities for social policies were "relatively well-developed at the sub-national level"; they remained restricted at the national level until the late 1930s (Amenta, 1991, 183). Ironically, the combination of subnational capacities, weak national capacities, and a national "left-center coalition" in power led to legislation providing national financial support for subnational programs. As these programs became established and entrenched, they became obstacles for later national reform initiatives (Amenta, 1991, 185).

The dynamics of national electoral coalitions during the 1930s also favored decentralized national-state programs; discretionary local administration provided latitude to those seeking to ensure that the distribution of benefits reflected local values. This was especially important in southern states; the combination of federalism and race relations provided powerful incentives undermining any efforts to strengthen or standardize job training and social services provisions (King, 1995).

Piven and Cloward (1993) point out that the limited national welfare state development in the United States gave primacy to employment-based social benefits and created resentment among organized workers over contributions for tax-financed public welfare benefits. From one perspective, the political coalitions formulating past urban poverty initiatives sought to avoid conflict with white working-class constituents by supporting what Piven and Cloward describe as "localizing and particularizing" concessions to African American groups rather than universalistic human capital programs. Weir (1992, 98) sees this as less a matter of intentional outcomes and more a consequence of the "collision" of the War on Poverty with the movement for black political empowerment. Nevertheless, particularistic, race-sensitive programs such as those opposing housing discrimination and those supporting school integration and affirmative action antagonized many whites and created resentment among other racial and ethnic minorities concerning perceived special privileges accorded to African Americans. The historical impacts and continued presence of these class and race dimensions to human capital policy cannot be underestimated (see King, 1995). As employment shifts to suburban locations and restructuring and flexible production strategies squeeze employer-based benefits packages, these workers are even less likely to support further benefits to enhance the unmet human capital potential of the urban poor. Increasingly, the fate of the urban poor and our future human capital stock is in the hands of a suburban, primarily white, electorate.

A History of Bounded Innovations

Long noted for the absence of universal, comprehensive social programs, U.S. policy history on welfare and employment issues contributes to the current dilemma (King, 1995; Weir, 1992). The difficulties of linking labor market policies to economic policy are not peculiar to the United States (King, 1995), but Weir (1992, 167) portrays American employment policies as an arena of bounded innovations: sequences of policy decisions and institutional designs that bound the range of alternatives considered in later policy making.

With the establishment of the Council of Economic Advisors following the 1946 Employment Act, the federal government set in play a focus on the macroeconomic factors influencing unemployment and the inadequate job skills of the poor that persisted through the 1970s. Recurring questions of low wages, underemployment, the eroding power of organized labor, shifts to flexible employment, dual labor markets, and the emerging international division of labor were subordinated to addressing unemployment. During this same period, the institutionalized state-level system of vocational education rebuffed national initiatives to link vocational education more directly to the labor market and integrate it more clearly with a national employment policy (Weir, 1992).

During the 1970s, the consensus behind the macroeconomic problem definition began to deteriorate in the face of globalization, economic restructuring, and income polarization. Struggles between Congress and the White House over more decentralized human resources training programs resulted in the 1973 compromise over the Comprehensive Employment and Training Act: it gave the Republican president a decentralized program in which operating responsibilities were delegated to local governments as "prime sponsors" while Democrats gained the public service provisions they sought for areas of high unemployment (Weir, 1992, 118). Although support for CETA collapsed in the face of corruption and mismanagement charges and a shift in program constituency toward the structurally unemployed, CETA left behind a legacy of an underdeveloped national labor policy infrastructure and the rhetoric of local control.

This institutional legacy and political rhetoric continue to mark national policies. To a significant extent, government intervention in employment issues was defined as part of "the problem" in the 1980s; indeed, unemployment lost its salience as a political issue as it became redefined as a matter of individual adjustments to a changing economy (Weir, 1992). The historical reluctance to create national initiatives permitted passage of the modest Job Training Partnership Act in 1982 and its successor, the Private Industry Councils (PICs). PICs symbolize the dominance of business definitions of employment and labor problems: they are public-private partnerships for local (often county) employment and training programs.

The National Stalemate

Although the scale issue argues for increased federal involvement, the 1980s brought a retreat from this responsibility. In the first year of the Reagan administration, federal investment in human capital declined by 21 percent (Juffras and Sawhill, 1991, 332). As the Clinton administration moved into its second term, this trend began to reverse. Clinton's FY 1996 budget proposed $47.3 billion for education and training, an increase of 13 percent over 1993 levels (U.S. Office of Management and Budget, 1995). Yet these modest national human capital initiatives may be eclipsed by recent workfare initiatives. Clinton signed so-called welfare reform legislation in 1996 that effectively ended sixty-one years of federal entitlement to public assistance. By converting Aid to Families with Dependent Children into a state-managed block grant program (Temporary Assistance to Needy Families, or TANF), tying future benefits to job-seeking efforts, and putting lifetime caps on benefits, Clinton moved the United States closer to the "Schumpeterian Workfare State" predicted by Jessop (1993).[12]

In the past, the political fragmentation and electoral calculations inhibiting national policy action have been overcome, Cloward and Piven (1998) would argue, only through "dissensus politics" in which disruptive protest won concessions (see also Brintnall, 1989). It is generally recognized that the urban riots of the 1960s spurred action on numerous urban programs, resulting in an increase in federal aid to cities from $10 billion in 1960 to $26 billion in 1970 to $47.2 billion by 1980 (Rich, 1993a). The limp national response to the Los Angeles riots in the early 1990s indicates that even such extraordinary crisis conditions may be insufficient now to prompt national action (Johnson, Farrell, and Jackson, 1994; Rich, 1993a).

The Governance Problem

To Weir (1992) and others (e.g., Heclo, 1994), the limited scope of and continued policy stalemate on employment policy derive from the interplay of ideas, politics, and administrative capacity in American politics. Although the fragmented political structure permits new ideas to surface, existing institutions encourage the bounded innovation and privileged problem definitions Weir describes. The historic difficulties in reformulating links between schools and the labor market exemplify the joint decision trap dilemmas haunting human capital agendas. Add to this the prevalence of vestigial thinking on economic growth and economic well-being, the political appeal of deficit reduction, an apparent lack of political will, the absence of constituency mobilization, and the pervasive race and class divisions in American society, and the prospects for a national policy breakthrough seem even more daunting. In the absence of well-organized parties, bureaucratic capacity, and incentives for political leadership on issues of work and skills, little national movement seems possible.

Weir, nevertheless, concludes with an argument similar to ours: that new policy orientations may emerge if human capital issues are linked to growing concerns about American competitiveness, the quality of public education, and the social costs of growing inequalities. Similarly, she also portrays the stalemate as a collective action or governance problem rather than a peculiarity of American exceptionalism: new approaches must build cooperation between private and public interests, broadly redefine employment problems, and reconfigure institutional links across policy arenas (1992, 178). In light of the national context sketched here, such policy orientations and governance issues will be recurrent elements of the local setting.

Rethinking Human Capital and Cities

American cities appear ill equipped to respond, however. For the first two-thirds of the twentieth century, cities had their fates tied to their traditional assets of *physical* capital. In the knowledge-based economy of the twenty-first century, cities will have their fates inextricably tied to their *human* capital assets. This sets a daunting task. To date, the dominant trend at the local level is also underinvestment in complex human capital. The average child in the United States is poorly equipped to compete in the global economy. Reich (1991) argues that less than 20 percent of our youth receive strong educational preparation. Those who do are children receiving primary and secondary education in elite private schools or high-quality suburban public schools and proceeding to a university system emphasizing the four basic symbolic analytic skills of abstraction, systems thinking, experimentation, and collaboration. This small group will be the highly privileged symbolic analysts of the future, while the majority of urban schoolchildren receive, at best, educations dooming them to the sinking boats of production workers and the barely afloat boats of service employees (Kozol, 1991; Kotlowvitz, 1991).

Complex Human Capital in American Cities: A Report Card

We illustrate the scope of the local underinvestment issue by taking a few first steps toward constructing a complex human capital report card for American cities. As Lehnen and McGregor (1994) argue, report cards allow us to benchmark in terms of the production and retention of the basic and complex dimensions of human capital. Basic learning includes acquisition of a general knowledge base at preworkforce stages. Given the mobility and leakage issues noted above, it is more likely that cities would focus their efforts on improving complex learning—the reasoning, problem-solving, synthesis, and other skills Reich identifies with symbolic analysts. And as Lehnen and McGregor report, high complex learning ratings appear to be the best predictors of state economic development.[13] The percentage of the population with college educations is the dominant measure of complex human capital used by Lehnen and McGregor.

Table 7.3 shows the current urban distribution of complex human capital based on the percentage of population that are college graduates. Figure 7.1 reveals that many of the cities with the lowest stock of complex human capital are precisely those cities that thrived during the heyday of manufacturing dominance of the economy. Other than the university cities, most of the cities with high stocks of human capital are outside the traditional manufacturing belt, many of them in the Sunbelt. Lehnen and McGregor (1994) find similar spatial patterns in their analysis of complex learning in state human capital stocks. Five states—Colorado, New Hampshire, Oregon, Utah, and Vermont—score high on both basic and complex learning indicators; a cluster of East Coast states and California score high on complex learning.

As Lehnen and McGregor point out, the mixed picture of pockets of citizens with complex learning skills and a general population with basic learning deficiencies argues for context-specific, targeted measures rather than universal policy strategies. Complex human capital is positively correlated with low unemployment, positive income change, increasing populations, employment increases, and the percentage of the labor force working at home.[14] Again, one cannot imply causality from such analyses. This is, of course, further complicated by urban definition problems and a variety of other control factors. But the correlations are not exceptional and parallel other findings. In the massive restructuring of the global economy, a new urban hierarchy may be evolving based on the geography of human capital.[15] This is one more reason to reconsider human capital strategies at the local level.

Table 7.3

Complex human capital in American cities

Percentage of people 25 years or older with a bachelor's degree or higher

>40%	30–40%	25–29%	20–24%	15–19%	10–14%	<10%
Ann Arbor	Seattle	Fremont	Springfield, Illinois	Phoenix	Akron	New Bedford
Berkeley	Sunnyvale	Greensboro	Montgomery	Beaumont	Milwaukee	Canton
Cambridge	Tempe	Fullerton	Columbus, Ohio	Bakersfield	Evansville	Detroit
Alexandria	Pasadena	San Diego	Garland	Shreveport	Hartford	Hammond
Madison	Durham	Lakewood	Richmond	Chicago	Waterbury	Gary
Tallahassee	Stamford	Albany	Livonia	Riverside	Toledo	Paterson
Raleigh	San Francisco	Denver	Peoria	Fresno	Erie	Newark
	Eugene	Glendale	Nashville	Hampton	Pueblo	Fall River
	Austin	Lincoln	Sacramento	Rochester	Independence	Youngstown
	Huntsville	Albuquerque	Cedar Rapids	Des Moines	Las Vegas	Cleveland
	Washington	Charlotte	Long Beach	Anaheim	Oxnard	Hialeah
	Huntington	Baton Rouge	Omaha	Tampa	Miami	
	Columbia	Boise City	Los Angeles	Rockford	San Bernardino	
	Torrance	Honolulu	New York	St. Petersburg	Bridgeport	
	Lexington	Colorado Springs	Wichita	South Bend	Dayton	
	Salt Lake City	Oakland	Orlando	Sterling	Portsmouth	
	Little Rock	Winston-Salem	New Orleans	Newport News	Elizabeth	
	Minneapolis	Dallas	Reno	Lansing	Santa Ana	
	Boston	Jackson	Cincinnati	Chattanooga	Trenton	
	Arlington	New Haven	Topeka	Jacksonville	Flint	
		Atlanta	Kansas City, Missouri	Amarillo	Warren	
		St. Paul	Syracuse	Corpus Christi	Kansas City, Kansas	
		Aurora	Abilene	San Antonio		
		Irving	Fort Lauderdale	Chula Vista		
		Concord	Yonkers	Memphis		
		Lubbock	Indianapolis	Louisville		
		Portland	Knoxville	Waco		
		Tulsa	Oklahoma City	Chesapeake		
		Virginia Beach	Providence	Norfolk		
		San Jose	Fort Worth	Columbus, Georgia		
		Houston	Mobile	Savannah		
			Jersey City	Birmingham		
			Worcester	El Paso		
			Mesa	Garden Grove		
			Spokane	Buffalo		
			Grand Rapids	Modesto		
			Tucson	Tacoma		
			Springfield, Missouri			

Table 7.3 *(continued)*

>40%	30–40%	25–29%	20–24%	15–19%	10–14%	<10%
			Davenport	Hollywood,		
			Pittsburgh	Florida		
				Fort Wayne		
				Roanoke		
				Baltimore		
				Macon		
				St. Louis		
				Allentown		
				Philadelphia		
				Stockton		
				Springfield,		
				Massachusetts		

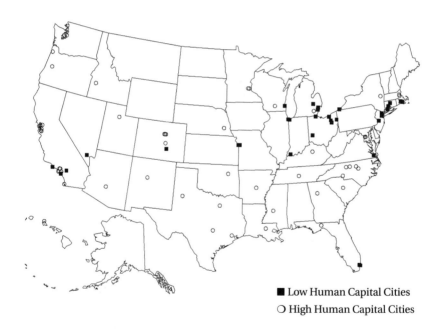

■ Low Human Capital Cities
○ High Human Capital Cities

Figure 7.1. High and low human capital cities (more than 25 percent and less than 15 percent, respectively, of people twenty-five years old with a bachelor's degree)

Local Human Capital Policy Agendas

What human capital initiatives are possible at the local level? The national stalemate leaves cities with little policy guidance, and the local context is complex and uncertain. New interests and ideas complicate local choices.[16] Demographic trends indicate that the new workforce in urban areas will be dominated by minority groups and immigrants, the very groups excluded by past practices (Glazer, 1993). To be competitive economically, communities must address human capital needs, particularly improvement of the skills and work experiences of these groups previously excluded from productive employment. To shore up local citizenship, cities must protect the economic well-being of local citizens in order to ensure their opportunities to participate in the social and political life of the community.

Counter to the predictions of the city limits story, there has been a resurgence of human capital initiatives and poverty reduction efforts at the local level. They reflect an approach that Wolman et al. (1992) characterize as supply-side, productivity-enhancing policies: strategies to increase a city's competitiveness by strengthening its human capital. These policies seek to improve the productivity of the factors an area supplies to the production process; in a global era, the strategic local factors increasingly center on the labor force and the infrastructural capacities in an area (Wolman et al., 1992; Clarke and Gaile, 1992).

It appears there is growing recognition that community development policies centering on programs for education and training of the smaller, more ethnically diverse future labor force in cities will be preconditions for effective local economic development (Bendick and Egan, 1993). Even though the dilemmas of scale and "leakage" make this problematic, some cities, such as Baltimore (Orr, 1992), Pittsburgh (Jones, 1994), and Boston (Glazer, 1993), are committed to developing strong educational systems and environments as amenities in their development strategies. Where school districts are independent entities, the institutional links capable of generating cooperation across sectors become critical (Stone et al., 1994). In every city, the intergovernmental links with state and county governments are increasingly determinative of successful education strategies. This resonates with the institutional design issues and context-structuring processes detailed in the preceding chapters.

School-to-work models are especially apt examples of the importance of this local infrastructural power. The Boston Compact, for example, forged a partnership between the city and its businesses linking attendance, school performance, and job access. The Compact showed students there was connection between school and work; it resulted in increased school attendance but was eventually weakened by bureaucratic conflicts (Drier and Keating, 1990; Glazer, 1993). Boston's City Year is a model for the national service program, and its Project ProTech emulates the German apprenticeship program (Drier and Keating, 1990). Baltimore modeled its Baltimore Commonwealth plan after the Boston Compact, seeking business collaboration in providing guaranteed job interviews, remedial post-high school training, and mentors for students.

Directly relevant to Reich's arguments and the human capital concern, there is a clear record of local programs and institutions to promote employment and income generation among the unemployed and the poor.[17] Although this is not a new concern for local governments, O'Regan and Conway (1993, vi) distinguish recent local initiatives from past efforts by their emphasis on empowerment, on linking poverty alleviation directly to broader economic development goals, on pursuing market-based strategies that are often sector specific, and on seeking to become sustainable elements of the local economy rather than third-party assistance entities. In fact, they characterize these efforts as new paradigms that constitute new, local development systems for the unemployed and the poor rather than merely different programs.[18]

Rethinking Local Links with the Global Web

Localities, to date, frequently slight an increasingly important aspect of wealth creation—information (Parker, 1995). Yet some have shown remarkable initiative in attempting to benefit from rapidly evolving telecommunications technology. Information technologies and the infrastructures to sustain them are distinctive features of a postindustrial economy and intrinsic to globalization processes.

An indication of the newness, the promise, and the uncertainty about the interaction between telecommunications technology and the city can be gleaned from new taxonomies in the research literature. Books and journals are full of anticipatory argot, from the early "global village" (McLuhan and Powers, 1989) and the "informational city" (Castells, 1989) to more recent technopoles, telecities, intelligent cities, wired cities, virtual cities, telecommunities, teleports, telecolonies, science cities, Cybervilles, electronic neighborhoods, electronic public places, and even postmodern hyperspace.

Scale again becomes an issue in public telecommunications policy. Provision of information highways remains a contested issue in American politics, and there are clearly major roles to be played on both national and state scales.[19] A few countries have embarked on ambitious telecommunications strategies, notably Japan, France, and Singapore, with mixed success (Castells and Hall, 1994). At the U.S. national scale, Henry Cisneros, then secretary of the Department of Housing and Urban Development, announced HUD's intention to restructure housing subsidies to incorporate learning centers and on-line access in government-supported housing to create "learning communities" (1995). Some states, such as Iowa and North Carolina, are moving ahead to develop statewide fiber-optic networks as a state economic development strategy (Clarke and Saiz, 1995). Many cities have major initiatives under way to make public investments in information infrastructure strategies that would improve their competitive advantage. Often these local initiatives are prompted by the seemingly mundane issue of the renewal of existing cable and telecommunication contracts. Faced with signing off on long-term contracts for service in a volatile industry marked by rapid technological innovation, many cities are considering establishing their own telecommunication utilities in order to ensure access, control costs, and provide adequate services.

This new path to global competitiveness is prompting the reconfiguration of local growth coalitions around "electronic public spaces" rather than traditional land use issues.[20] Partnerships such as the Greater Austin Area Telecommunications Network often include city, county, and state officials as well as public school districts, higher-education institutions, and local utilities. City partnerships or contracts with private corporations such as Time Warner Cable and SpectraNet raise issues of universal access, which must be provided by public utilities. Yet local initiatives to build and operate municipal fiber-optic systems often are challenged by private firms on the grounds of unfair competition. Furthermore, many cities are limited in planning for the "virtual city" by state laws and prohibitive costs. To avoid these political and fiscal hazards, cities are adopting new organizational structures: Milpitas, California, set up the country's first municipal telecommunications commission in 1995; San Diego is seeking private sector proposals for a public-private partnership to build a regional telecommunications network called San Net; and twenty-one northeastern Ohio communities are considering formation of a nonprofit corporation to operate a telecommunications network.[21]

Yet there are barriers on this path to stronger global-local linkages. Gearing up to meet these new infrastructure needs is beyond the fiscal capacity of most localities, but it is increasingly unlikely that corporate investors will take the initiative in the absence of partnerships with municipalities, states, and private investors.[22] Further, parallels may be made between the anticipatory promise of cable television and the current hopes pegged on advanced telecommunications technology. Newton notes that urban telecommunication policies are often ill informed and overambitious because "urban policy makers and technologists both tend to share the common trait of believing that they have more control . . . than they actually do" (1991, 57). Blind optimism often leads to a "technology push" atmosphere, wherein policies are unsustainable because they fail to meet the needs of the users and rely too much on subsidy (Graham and Marvin, 1996, 343). A further complication for urban telecommunications policy involves dealing with the free-rider problem, as neighboring communities can often access this expensive infrastructure over local phone lines.

Nevertheless, numerous cities have embarked on this development path—engaging in initiatives to "wire the city" for the telecommunications future. The following list hints at several different pathways to linking with the global web through telecommunications policies (Neumann, n.d.):

Anaheim, California, has completed an $8 million fiber-optic network to monitor electricity and negotiated with SpectraNet to provide fully interactive fiber-optic link to all citizens of the city. The city is laying fifty miles of fiber-optic lines to communicate with twelve power substations. Sixty companies are bidding on the extra capacity. The city may reap up to $10 million per year in revenue by leasing space on the network.

Bellevue, Washington, is constructing twenty miles of fiber-optic cable in a cooperative project that involves city, school district, and seven companies. The network will serve Boeing and Microsoft.

Denton, Texas, is installing a fiber-optic control ring, and plans are in place to extend the ring to schools. Real-time electric load monitoring has savings potential.

Madison, Wisconsin, is linking its city computers with the Internet. A fiber-optic network has been installed in municipal buildings.

Milpitas, California, has created the country's first permanent municipal telecommunications commission, which has recommended putting sixty-six cellular transmitters on phone poles, at no cost to the city.

New York City is developing its own fiber-optic system.

Palo Alto, California, is building its own communications utility with fiber-optic links to every home and business.

Philadelphia, Pennsylvania, has installed a fiber-optic network (City Net) that links seventy agencies and departments.

San Antonio, Texas, is experiencing a dispute over a twenty-five-year contract given to a Denver company that allows use of part of a fiber-optic network being built by a city-owned utility.

Seattle, Washington, offers fiber-optic companies use of city-owned rights-of-way on telephone poles and conduits. In exchange, the city wants low-cost access to the World Wide Web for all residents.

Other cities actively considering "getting wired" include Austin, Texas; Glasgow, Kentucky; Hampton, Virginia; Memphis, Tennessee; Murray, Utah; New Orleans, Louisiana; Northeast Ohio communities; Pinellas Park, Florida; St. Louis, Missouri; San Diego, California; and St. Petersburg, Florida (Neumann, n.d.).

Bolder steps in this direction have been taken with the building of "telecommunities"—residential subdivisions with the latest in telecommunications infrastructure designed to enable the human capitalist telecommuter to function efficiently and with ease (Warson, 1995). Montgomery Village, Ontario, Canada, is one of the first such communities in North America. These environments also provide the face-to-face externalities that Reich deems still important in the new human capital economy. Other urban futurists anticipate "network cities"—small groups of cities as far away as Japan and the Netherlands are now linked by the latest in communications technology—that could transform the entire urban system (Batten, 1995). These networks would allow a policy reorientation toward a mixture of competition and collaboration (Graham and Marvin, 1996, 355).

The broader impacts of telecommunication strategies are unclear. More telecommuting may have beneficial impacts on traffic congestion and air pollution. Similarly, the services that cities provide may increasingly be information based and more accessible. But it is also possible that telecommunications may finally bring about the "death of distance"; more telecommuting could change the need for centralized places of business, contributing to further central-city decay. It is also possible that telecommuting would free people to seek amenity locations, many of which may be small urban or rural areas. Recruitment of "lone eagle" telecommuters (also known as "modem cowboys") is an active strategy in many western communities. Short of these spatial changes, telemarketing may erode the retail sectors of some cities. Most seriously, there could be greater urban socioeconomic inequalities if the poor have minimal access to telecommunication services. The rich can more effectively secede from cities and enjoy stronger links to a global web. At this point, however, there seems to be no correlation between complex human capital status and cities' telecommunications initiatives, although this may well be due to the newness of these policies.[23]

The scale transcendency aspects of telecommunication technology argue strongly for policy cooperation at all spatial levels—local, regional, national, and international. Infrastructure provision is a historical function of American communities, albeit one with significant federal and state financing. It is valued highly by business, creates tangible, fixed assets for the community, and brings short-term and long-run employment gains to the community. To many, community networks—or freenets—offer new opportunities for a form of electronic democracy; the costs of grassroots mobilization may be reduced and the access to public officials increased through such networks (Schuler, 1996). Santa Monica, California, established the first modem system linking citizens, the city council, and city hall in the late 1980s; it is now estimated there are more than three-hundred community networks providing local information. Charlotte's Web, in Charlotte, North Carolina, successfully provides on-line service, including job information, through terminals at libraries, Boys' and Girls' Clubs, and other sites throughout the city ("Charlotte's Virtual Community," 1996). The community and noneconomic benefits stemming from a more active local government role in information infrastructure investment appear promising if these networks are inclusive and accessible.

Yet this potential boon is not without its dark side: the prospects for creating cleavages between technological "haves" and "have-nots," the impacts on governance of reduced information and access costs, the social and cultural reverberations of participation in virtual communities in virtual space at the possible expense of local participation, and the spatial consequences of the death of distance will loom large on future local agendas.

Conclusions

Our fieldwork, surveys, and other analyses persuade us that a growing number of local officials are seeking ways to devise orientations that integrate globalization, information, human capital, and economic development concerns. This fourth wave of policy innovation is grounded in an economic sensitivity to new growth processes and a political awareness that increases the costs of continuing to ignore unmet human capital potential in the community.

It is also prompted by a realization that "reinventing government" is an insufficient solution to urban problems. Our work underscores the need to push the political debate beyond "reinventing government" to reconstructing citizenship (Staeheli, 1994; Staeheli and Clarke, 1995). Rather than seeing the poor and unskilled as a cost, we argue that those fully understanding the economic and geographic changes of the twenty-first century will recognize these urban groups as presenting opportunities of unmet human capital potential. Local citizenship in a global era presumes citizens with the social and economic means to participate in a viable, responsive local government. In the absence of a fuller understanding of the new work of cities in the twenty-first century, local citizenship will continue to erode.

8

Reinventing Citizenship

*Inattention to the erosion of citizenship and decline in
social capital will undermine local development efforts.*

Reich's (1991) *The Work of Nations* provides a compelling starting point for
thinking about the consequences of economic and social changes in American society for cities and citizenship. In Reich's account, several trends
stand out:

The U.S. economy is being reshaped by trends toward globalization and new production systems featuring flexible
organization and high value-added processes.

These new forms of economic organization underscore the
importance of human capital resources but also create stark
differences among workers and citizens and increased social
segregation.

These new economic and social conditions reduce Americans'
sense of a shared future and transform the meaning of local
citizenship through social polarization and segregation.

Relying on market forces to respond to these problems leads to
underinvestment in human capital and insufficient technological, social, and institutional innovation.

To this we add:

Local officials engage in the transformation of their local
economies through strategic policy choices responding to
these economic and social trends.

Local officials have to adapt to these changing contexts with little
guidance on the likely consequences of new policy directions. The goal-

posts are continually shifting, and the choices are marked by complexity and uncertainty. Using data from federal programs and our national surveys of recent policy choices, we have traced the evolution of waves of local economic development policy strategies through the 1970s and 1980s, and into the 1990s.

Locational incentives historically dominated city agendas as cities used their land development and taxing tools to attract or retain the national champion corporations that were the backbone of the economy. During the federal partnership era, some local governments began to experiment with strategies involving capital as well as locational incentives. Cities were encouraged by several federal programs to act entrepreneurially with public capital—to share both risk and profit alike with private enterprises in local economic development ventures. City participation in federally supported economic development activities often yielded future income streams that were then used to capitalize revolving loan funds or venture capital funds for other local projects.

In the midst of this shift in local roles, the Reagan and Bush administrations in the 1980s orchestrated what amounted to the federal abandonment of cities (Rich, 1993a). This period was also marked by a growing interdependence between city well-being and the global economy. These national budget cuts and increasing vulnerability to global economic trends gave rise to growing local uncertainty. Cities needed to increase their fiscal stability and reduce the vulnerability of their local tax bases. They were also operating in an increasingly politicized local setting, one beset by the polarizing impacts of these global economic changes. Rather than crafting a deductive argument about the effects on cities of these changes, our empirical work asked what local officials chose to do in the face of these trying circumstances.

Cities' diverse and often entrepreneurial responses to these conditions chart new policy ground in ways unanticipated by urban theorists or national policy makers. In chapters 3 and 4 we have chronicled these strategies and the conditions under which cities choose more entrepreneurial approaches. In the absence of federal resources, more distressed cities tend to be more entrepreneurial in their policy choices, as do cities with strong political leadership and participation in specialized policy networks. These new initiatives appear to be somewhat effective in generating jobs, attracting new, fast-growing companies, and holding down local government taxes and expenditures. Furthermore, there is tentative evidence that specific strategies are associated with positive local economic development impacts.

These transformational efforts entailed not only rethinking local economic development strategies but also redesigning local institutions. Cities faced the need to structure decision contexts in ways that would enable them to mobilize local interests for their economic development goals. These processes can be described only on a city-by-city basis, but our case studies of Cleveland, Tacoma, Jacksonville, and Syracuse underscore the importance of state government and business organizations in shaping these contemporary arenas. Our follow-up survey in 1996 confirmed our hunch that the next wave of policy innovation will center on two aspects of wealth creation that are not fully addressed in current initiatives: the increasing importance of human capital and the need to establish global-local links through information infrastructure as well as trade initiatives.

Rethinking Local Citizenship in a Global Era

Despite these intriguing findings of local inventiveness and tenacity, cities are falling short if we regard the true work of cities as supporting and enabling citizens. The citizens gaining the most from globalization are increasingly distancing themselves from those less fortunate, with the truly rich seceding altogether (Reich, 1991; Kaus, 1992). Although the market-based, entrepreneurial policies discussed in this book may well help cities adjust to economic change in the aggregate, there is little reason to expect this adjustment to promote a "trickle down" of benefits or redistribution of wealth. Indeed, globalization portends further erosion of citizenship. Addressing citizenship issues requires more than enabling market forces.

The Grounds for Citizenship

To bring citizenship concerns into the analysis of globalization and local policy change, it is necessary to recognize that the "work of globalization" involves complex networks of workers not obviously engaged in global enterprises (Sassen, 1996). Globalization is grounded in these workers and their communities; as Sassen (1996) puts it, recognizing the array of local *practices* constituting and enabling globalization pushes us beyond a focus on obviously global cities to a concern with the many types of places in which "the work of globalization gets done" (see also Knox, 1996). It also means attention to the ways in which doing "the work of globalization" precludes the practice of local citizenship. This citizenship can be undermined by compressed wages, reduced social benefits, limited job retraining opportunities, lack of affordable housing, discriminatory housing and employment practices, environmental hazards, inaccessible and unaccountable political processes, unhealthy work conditions, restricted educational opportunities, and other conditions of daily life that hinder citizens from taking on civic responsibilities and participating fully in public life. Redressing these ills is not solely a matter of more public spending, although there is ample evidence that money matters— that we may not understand how to bring about happiness and harmony, but we do know how to "reduce misery," as Barrington Moore (1972) puts it. Even a cursory review of studies of Canadian and European cities reveals the importance of political will in mitigating many of these ills; American citizens' experience with globalization is especially harsh in comparison (Levine, 1995). Although our analyses indicate that "reducing misery" in many of these areas would strengthen the competitiveness of communities—that it is economically rational to do so—we acknowledge the rhetoric and political forces making large national expenditures less likely. Yet we note the local efforts to ensure "living wages," as in Baltimore and Minneapolis; to put policy priority on labor force development, as in Portland, Oregon; to rely on nonprofits to build affordable housing, as in Seattle and San Francisco; to make human capital investment part of economic development planning, as in Tacoma; to provide low-income communities with telecommunications links, as in Oklahoma City's Enterprise Community, Cleveland's Freenet, and Syracuse's Diffusion Fund; to tax central-city and metropolitan residents for support of cultural amenities, as in Denver. Such initiatives begin to mediate the potentially polarizing effects of globalization. They provide the foundation for reconstructing local citizenship by reconnecting the individual with the community, reminding us of the venerable link between city and citizenship.

Reinventing Government or Restoring Citizenship?

This demands more than "reinventing government." The advocates of reinventing government (Osborne and Gaebler, 1992, 20) are careful to note that they do not advocate running government like a business. They urge the design of entrepreneurial government, one using resources in new ways to maximize productivity and effectiveness. This corresponds to the local economic development roles and policies we describe as entrepreneurial. Although many "reinventing government" prescriptions *appear* to address citizenship concerns—homilies to empower communities rather than simply deliver services; to meet the needs of the customer, not the bureaucracy; to invest in prevention, rather than cures; to decentralize authority— none speaks to the rendering of community and citizenship brought out in Reich's account. Reinventing government is an insufficient policy goal;

reinventing local citizenship in a global era is a necessary element in policy frameworks at the national, state, and local levels.

A citizenship focus underscores the continued relevance of classic citizenship notions.[1] In the traditional liberal view of citizenship, civic identity is assumed to supersede all other identities. As Dietz (1987, 2) puts it, context matters little: in these liberal views, individuals are seen as bearing rights independent of their immediate social and political conditions. But as our analyses show, context makes all the difference: globalization affects communities differentially but not mechanically; the importance of political leadership, social mobilization, and local intentionality in mitigating the more deleterious effects of globalization for the most disadvantaged cannot be underestimated. This is especially important in light of the liberal assumption that all citizens enjoy the social and economic independence necessary for democratic political participation. The four-fifths Reich sees as especially vulnerable cannot be characterized as enjoying sufficient economic independence necessary for full participation, nor are their prospects likely to improve without some public intervention.

In contrast to classic liberal notions, more relational notions of citizenship begin with context: they emphasize the ways in which social, economic, and political conditions affect citizenship status by altering the public standing of individuals and social groups (Shklar, 1991; King and Waldron, 1988). This relational perspective introduces greater sensitivity to the changing temporal and spatial nature of citizenship. Citizenship gains are clearly reversible over time, as the global retrenchment of the welfare state makes all too clear. In the context of the local economic and political restructuring processes described here, citizenship status also is increasingly uneven across and within communities. To a disheartening degree, an individual's true citizenship is increasingly a matter of where he or she lives; the rights, entitlements, and opportunities afforded through citizenship are inextricably tied to place (Staeheli and Clarke, 1994).

Bringing a citizenship perspective to the analysis of local economic transformation would encourage a more normative view of local citizenship and urban governance. To some, this is an opportunity to emphasize the obligations citizens share as well as the rights they enjoy. To us, it provides the occasion for debate over a purposeful public philosophy, one in which the state promotes citizenship and justice through attending to the distribution of capabilities to take action in society (e.g., Young, 1990, 1992). Directing attention to who is capable of taking action is another way of thinking about how social capital supports democratic practice and what our public responsibilities are for enhancing those capabilities (Putnam,

1995; Skocpol, 1996).[2] Such a purposeful public philosophy is essential in countering meritocracy trends that restrict these capabilities to the fortunate fifth, as Reich puts it. It also redirects attention to democratic rules, procedures (Mouffe, 1992b), and political forms in which different voices can be heard. A citizenship focus on globalization and cities would return urban analysis to a normative consideration of democratic values and the trends that contribute to uneven local citizenship status.

Localities are the arenas for reconstructing globalization and reinventing citizenship. Although national government is the most able to provide these guarantees of economic and social well-being, we remain skeptical of the willingness of national officials to resist the siren songs of international competitiveness, economic efficiency, and deficit reduction. Given the structural and political constraints on local officials, localities may not be the best places for grappling with globalization and citizenship issues, but they currently offer the greatest potential for making a difference in the everyday lives of citizens. The choices local officials make affect the ways in which local citizens understand and experience globalization. These are not always wise or effective choices, but the local officials we have talked to believe they can and must be engaged in these transformational processes. This intentionality and pragmatism in the face of uncertainty and complexity is the story of globalization and community we hope to do justice to with this account.

Appendix A:
Spatial Statistics

Methodology for Explicitly Incorporating
and Controlling Regional Effects

This study explicitly controls the expected spatial variation in market-based policies and outcomes. A given market-based level of effort in a distressed region should not have the same effect as that same level of effort in a prosperous region. The same strategy should have different effects in Buffalo and San Diego. Identical strategies both may have high effectiveness relative to their regions, but this success will probably be overwhelmed by the statistical noise of regional variations in the overall economy. "Basic statistical theory may indicate the criteria which must be fulfilled in order to measure . . . locational relationships numerically and test hypotheses about them in reliable ways, but conventional statistical methods are often insufficient to fulfill these criteria for geographic data" (Odland, Golledge, and Rogerson, 1989, 719). The use of spatial statistical techniques (Gaile and Willmott, 1984) can identify and control these broad regional variations, because it is within the capacity of these techniques to support explanations in explicitly locational contexts. Spatial autocorrelation analyses (Miron, 1984; Griffith, 1987) and trend surface analyses (Agterberg, 1984) are spatial statistical techniques that allow for the explicit incorporation of spatial variation into the research. Spatial autocorrelation analyses measure the degree to which geographic (spatial) neighbors are related in the sense of having similar values for particular variables.

Trend surface analysis allows for similar identification and measurement of the strength of regional variables and also allows residuals to be used as independent nonautocorrelated variables in further analyses. It differs from spatial autocorrelation analytic techniques in that it uses a smoothed surface to measure broader regional trends versus the more "neighborly" approach of spatial autocorrelation. The technique of trend surface can be simply explained. The location of each city can be expressed in x- and y-coordinates (or latitude and longitude). These coordinates can be used as the only independent variables to explain the dependent variable. These variables (x, y) are orthogonal by definition, so there is no problem of autocorrelation. Simply put, using coordinates elevates the analysis from a nominal scale to a ratio-interval scale of analysis and thereby increases the potential for more powerful statistical analysis.

Trend surface analysis is a straightforward modification of standard regression techniques that allows the explicit incorporation of location into the analyses. The technique uses regression analysis to isolate a variable's locational attributes by disaggregating the variable into a *regional component* described by the regression "surface" and a *local component* described by the residuals from that surface.

For example, in a nationwide analysis of urban economic development, one would expect Detroit and San Francisco to have substantially different net migration and consequent labor market situations. Previous analyses incorporating migration or employment change either (1) ignored the locational differences in these urban situations or (2) tried to control them by using nominal variables for regions (e.g., the U.S. Census "Geographic Areas" can easily be converted into nine dummy variables, each valued at 1 in a given region and 0 in the other eight). In both types of analyses, significant explanatory power is lost.

Trend surface analysis is a simply understood variation of regression techniques. The dependent variable in the analysis can be any variable that has been measured at a set of locations. The independent variables in the analyses are combinations of locational coordinates (e.g., longitude and latitude, or x- and y-coordinates on a grid). The simplest trend surface analysis is provided by a linear surface wherein

$$z_i = a_0 + a_1 x_i + a_2 y_i,$$

where z_i is the value of the dependent variable (e.g., net migration) at the *i*th location (which is measured by its x-, y-coordinates). This analysis produces a simple three-dimensional plane that has a slope whose rate of change is a linear function of the x-, y-coordinates.

More sophisticated surfaces can be generated by simply "powering" the independent locational variables (x, y). Each additional "powering" of the surface allows for one additional point of inflection on the surface. The number of "powerings" possible is limited by the number of points in the analysis.

Most surface phenomena can be described by relatively simple surfaces, and thus most examples of trend surface analyses stop at linear, quadratic, or cubic surface use for both deductive and sample limitation reasons. In the case of the urban system in the United States, the dominant regional trend may be categorized as the "Snowbelt-Sunbelt" phenomenon, which is adequately captured in a quadratic trend surface analysis. The equation for the quadratic analysis is

$$z_i = a_0 + a_1 x_i + a_2 y_i + a_3 x_i^2 + a_4 x_i y_i + a_5 y_i^2,$$

which is a *quadratic polynomial* surface. More complex cubic surfaces could provide greater explanation. In the analyses herein, the quadratic surface is deemed most appropriate. Exploratory attempts to include cubic analyses in several cases did not significantly increase the explanatory power of the analyses: simpler turned out to be better.

The residuals from trend surface analyses are essentially residuals from a regression analysis. In the trend surface case, they have the attribute of being statistically independent from (uncorrelated with) the regional trend described by the surface. In nonstatistical terms, this allows for a fair comparison between Detroit and San Francisco to be made, having controlled for their regional location.

The validity of trend surface results can be judged by using the same appropriateness measures as in simple regression analyses. Thus F tests were performed, and significance levels of the analyses are readily interpretable.

The trend surface technique is interesting in that it has two common uses. The first is the statistical *identification* of a regional trend. The second common use, and the one essential in this work, is the *elimination* of a regional trend so that subsequent statistical analyses can make use of the regionally independent residuals.

Trend surface analysis requires the same assumptions as regression analysis. The technique may be troubled by "edge effects" and other problems due to an unusual distribution of locational points. If the data "cover" is adequate and a reasonably low order of surface is used (e.g., the quadratic), these problems tend to be minimized. All independent and dependent variables used in the analyses were trend surface analyzed. It is important to note that the independent policy variables (based on federal and nonfederal policy use) rarely yielded statistically significant trend surfaces. In the federal case this is to be expected, because an explicitly spatially unbiased federal policy process underlies the dissemination of these funds. The lack of statistically significant trend surfaces for nonfederal policies is less easily explained, although it indicates that the information on such policy use is widely diffused throughout the nation (Morrill, Gaile, and Thrall, 1988) and that these policies are broadly applicable.

The great majority of dependent variables did yield statistically significant trend surfaces. This supports the claim that the predictable regional variation in most relevant variables is quite strong, and could be construed as noise that overwhelms a signal in analyses that fail to control these geographic phenomena explicitly. In the analyses that follow, the standardized residuals from the trend surface analyses are used as the dependent variables. These "region-free" variables allow for greater local differentiation.

Results of Trend Surface Analyses

The principal methodological argument of this study is that regional trends exist in most of the variables. This is especially likely for those variables used to identify the characteristics and effectiveness of local market-based economic development strategies. The hypothesized strength of regional trends is such that they would likely mask or misrepresent significant relationships between the variables related to use of market-based strategies and the characteristic and effectiveness variables.

All variables in this study were subjected to quadratic trend surface analyses. These analyses revealed that most of the characteristic and effectiveness variables have statistically significant regional trends.

Trend Surface Analysis of City Characteristic and Policy Effectiveness Variables

Although the trends in themselves are interesting, the purpose of the trend analysis is to *remove* the regional trends from these variables in order to control more accurately the relationships between the independent variables and the dependent variables. In order to achieve this goal, the residuals from the trend surface were extracted and used as new regional-trend-free variables.

A detailed example of the trend surface analysis for the variable Population Change 1980-1986 illustrates the efficacy of this technique. In the trend surface regression, this variable is used as the dependent variable in the equation. The independent variables in the trend surface regression are the location coordinate variables of latitude (LATD), longitude (LONG), latitude squared (LATD2), longitude squared (LONG2), and the latitude-longitude cross-product (LATDLONG). The population change trend surface uses 178 cases and is significant at the 0.001 level with

$r = 0.46307;$

$R^2 = 0.21444;$

standard error $= 36284.14$.

The trend surface regression equation is

PopChange80-86 = -235417.9 + 11467.3 LATD + 1416.42 LONG + 1.08 LATDLONG - 195.2 LATD2 - 4.131 LONG2.

The residual is saved as a new variable that may be interpreted as population change that is independent of this pronounced regional trend.

All variables in this study have been analyzed through trend surface regression. Table A.1 lists the characteristic and effectiveness variables that had significant regional trends at the 0.05 level of significance. For all these variables, the residuals from the trend surface analysis were used in all subsequent statistical analyses.

Most of the city characteristic and policy effectiveness variables used in the analysis showed statistically significant regional trends. Few city characteristic and policy effectiveness variables analyzed show no statistically significant (<0.05) regional trends (see Table A.2).

The lack of regional trend for some of the variables displayed in Table A.2 is understandable. Professional and technical employment is dominated by service industries geared either to the market (thus being distributed rather evenly on a per capita basis) or to "footloose" activities that do not have explicit locational constraints and that also tend to be broadly distributed (e.g., universities).

Table A.1

Trend surface analyses of city characteristic and policy effectiveness variables: Variables with significant regional trends

R^2	Variable
.200	Population per square mile, 1986
.214	Population change 1980–86
.351	Population % change 1980–86
.191	% white population, 1980
.288	% black population, 1980
.176	% Hispanic population, 1980
.223	% 65 years and over, 1980

Table A.1 *(continued)*

.125	Persons per household, 1980
.348	% households with female householder—no spouse, 1980
.132	One-person households, % of all households, 1980
.250	% of births to mothers <20 years old, 1984
.219	Infant deaths under 1 year per 1,000 live births, 1984
.198	Hospital beds per 100,000 population, 1985
.164	Crimes per 100,000, 1985
.345	Police officers per 10,000 population, 1985
.383	% completing 12 years of school or more, 1980
.091	% completing 16 years of school or more, 1980
.071	Per capita money income, 1979 (current $)
.199	Per capita money income, 1979 (constant 1985 $)
.299	1985–79 per capita money income change (1985 constant $)
.221	% of persons below poverty level, 1979
.254	% of families below poverty level, 1979
.239	% change in housing units 1970–80
.588	% of year-round housing units built before 1940, 1980
.319	Owner-occupied units, % of total occupied units, 1980
.539	Median value of owner-occupied housing units, 1980
.126	New private housing units authorized by permits, 1986
.161	Value of new housing per permit, 1986
.180	New private housing units authorized by permits, 1980–86
.286	New private housing permits per capita, 1980–86
.253	New private housing 1980–86, % of 1980 housing stock
.165	Civilian labor force, % change 1985–86
.072	Civilian labor force, unemployment rate, 1986
.185	Precision production, craft, and operator employees per 1,000 employees, 1980
.302	% of manufacturing establishments with >19 employees, 1982
.248	Manufacturing employees % change 1977–82
.255	Manufacturing wages, average per production worker, 1982, $
.100	New capital expenditures for manufacturing worker, 1982, $
.295	Retail trade sales % change 1977–82
.281	Retail trade sales per capita, 1982, $
.182	Retail trade, general merchandise, sales per capita, 1982, $
.253	Retail trade, food stores, sales per capita, 1982, $
.157	Retail trade, apparel and accessories, sales per capita, 1982, $
.170	Retail trade, eating and drinking, sales per capita, 1982, $

Table A.1 *(continued)*

.219	Retail trade, paid employees, % change 1977–82
.106	Taxable service industries health receipts per capita, 1982
.264	City government general revenue per capita, 1985, $
.218	City government taxes per capita, 1985, $
.383	City government property taxes per capita, 1985, $
.478	City government employees per 10,000 population, 1985
.371	City government general revenue, % from state, 1985
.202	City government sales and gross receipts from taxes per capita, 1985, $
.302	City government general expenditures per capita, 1985, $
.266	City government general expenditures, % for highways, 1985
.213	City government general expenditures, % for police, 1985
.188	City government general expenditures, % for sewers and sanitation, 1985
.358	City government general expenditures, % for parks and recreation, 1985
.089	City government general expenditures, % for housing and community development, 1985
.087	City government debt outstanding per capita, 1985, $
.227	% change 1980–86, typical monthly electric bill
.141	Job generation rate, 1984–88
.329	Business birthrate, 1984–88
.163	Fast-growing companies as % all new firms, 1984–88
.422	% change in CDBG funding, FY 1982–84
.065	Corporate R&D location type
.332	% change 1969–79, real income per capita

Note: Significance level <0.05.

Trend Surface Analysis of City Policy Variables

Very different behavior in response to trend surface analyses was found in the city policy variables used in these analyses. Most of these variables showed no statistically significant regional trends; this is true when federal as well as nonfederal resources were used. It appears that market-based policies have become employed largely on a national basis, without strong regional emphases. This does not support our original expectation that the adoption and implementation of market-based urban economic development strategies would have strong regional effects. Table A.3 lists those specific policy strategies, including combined indices, that displayed no significant regional variation when analyzed by trend surface analysis.

Some specific policy dimensions, however, did show regional variation. Table A.4 shows these results. The variable Total Federal Money per Capita (UDAG, CDBG, EDA) is necessarily regional, given the spatial and sectoral targeting of these programs. Two variables relating to leverage ratios also show statistically significant regional characteristics.

Table A.2

Trend surface analyses of city characteristic and policy effectiveness variables: Variables with no significant regional trend

R^2	Variable
.040	Professional, technical, and specialized employees per 1,000 employees, 1980
.053	Federal procurement and contract awards per capita, 1986
.048	Federal grants per capita, 1986
.071	Federal government employees per capita, 1986
.013	City government capital outlay per capita, 1985
.058	Combined state-local general sales tax rates, 1988
.017	Total revenues, 1985–86
.017	General own source revenues, 1985–86
.023	Total general expenditures, 1985–86
.005	Total debt outstanding, 1985–86
.008	Cash and security holdings, 1985–86

Table A.3

Trend surface analyses of city policy variables: Variables with no significant regional trend

R^2	Variable
.026	UDAG: % entrepreneurial reuse of program income
.071	UDAG: % entrepreneurial net cash participation
.021	UDAG: % entrepreneurial revenue generation

Table A.3 *(continued)*

R^2	Variable
.063	UDAG: % entrepreneurial fiscal conditions
.042	UDAG: % entrepreneurial special conditions
.027	UDAG: combined percentages—entrepreneurial reuse, net cash, revenue, fiscal conditions, and special conditions
.032	UDAG: Fiscal Entrepreneurial Index (entrepreneurial categories of leverage, fiscal conditions, and revenue)
.037	UDAG: Social Entrepreneurial Index (entrepreneurial conditions of leverage, net cash, revenue, and special conditions)
.079	UDAG: leverage ratio per UDAG grant
.082	UDAG: private $ leveraged per UDAG project
.027	UDAG: private $ leveraged per UDAG project, per capita
.057	CDBG: % CDBG funds used for economic development activities
.030	Combined Index: ever used 47 nonfederal economic development strategies

Note: Significance level <0.05.

Table A.4

Trend surface analyses of policy variables: Variables with significant regional trends

R^2	Variable
.381	Total federal $ per capita, 1976-84: UDAG, CDBG, EDA
.127	UDAG: % city UDAG projects with high leverage ratio
.305	UDAG: private $ leveraged per capita, per project

Note: Significance levels <0.05.

Appendix B:
Local Economic Development Strategies Relying on Nonfederal Resources

This study gives a "bottom-up" account of the current "state of the art" in urban economic development policy, as devised and practiced at the community level. The forty-seven strategies listed below represent the range of market-oriented strategies relying on nonfederal resources as reported by officials in 101 communities in response to our inquiries. Following this list are another eighteen additional new strategies that were included in the 1996 survey and are part of the "fourth wave."

Tax abatements, general: Special reduction in, or exclusion or exemption from, or deferment of payment of normal property tax rate for specified period, granted to eligible recipients for specific property; lowers effective tax rate for firm by reducing taxes otherwise due.

Tax abatements, targeted for new business: Special reduction in, or exclusion or exemption from, or deferment of payment of normal property tax rate for specified period, granted to new businesses only; lowers effective tax rate for firm by reducing taxes otherwise due.

Tax abatements, targeted for selected sectors: Special reduction in, or exclusion or exemption from, or deferment of payment of normal property tax rate for specified period, granted to firms in selected sectors only; lowers effective tax rate for firm by reducing taxes otherwise due.

Marketing and promotion: Expenditures aimed at communicating city's special comparative advantages as location for investment or promoting community products and resources in appropriate markets.

Trade missions abroad: Expenditures supporting local delegations' travel to foreign sites to promote trade of local products.

Export production promotion: Expenditures encouraging expansion of local firm export activities.

Streamlining permits: Procedural changes simplifying permit process for local development activities; often establishes "one-stop" permit process, where all city permits for business activities can be obtained through one office.

Procurement assistance: Staff resources dedicated to increasing local firms' contracts with other local and regional facilities to deliver goods and services.

Enterprise funds for public services: Budgeting procedure setting up public services as separate self-financing budget entities.

Capital improvement budgeting: Budgeting procedure setting out separate, long-term, capital improvement plan and budget with multiyear funding commitment, often used to coordinate new development.

Strategic planning: Planning procedure identifying explicit multidimensional policy goals, integrated action plans and budget commitments for achieving goals, and explicit timetables for completion. A future-oriented, long-range, nonincremental approach to all local planning and budgeting functions that emphasizes economic development based on local needs and resources.

Comprehensive planning: Planning procedure that classifies total current and future community land uses in functional terms and establishes staged land use development processes that incorporate location of transportation, infrastructure, and business and residential areas.

Infrastructure as in-kind development contribution: Coordinating provision of public facilities with new development as in-kind public share of total development costs.

Industrial parks: Public provision of improved land parcels, through sale or lease, to encourage industrial development in circumscribed area. Commercial, service, and high-technology parks are now common as well.

Annexation: Adding new land area to city jurisdiction and tax base.

Foreign trade zones: Special land use and zoning designation exempting import/export inventory and in-transit goods from local taxes. Depends on state enabling legislation allowing city to establish foreign trade zone.

Enterprise zones: Special land use and zoning designation to encourage development in defined area by granting firms locating in area various tax exemptions, special incentives, and sometimes removing or streamlining certain statutory or administrative controls. Vary by state and depend on state enabling legislation.

Business incubators: Public provision of facilities, often at below-market rents, and business services to new and start-up businesses.

Special assessment districts: Jurisdictional taxing arrangement in which firms and residents in specified area agree to pay additional assessment for specified purpose. May have authority to borrow funds outside city budgetary limits and controls and to assess members for fees and potential default.

Tax increment financing: Jurisdictional taxing arrangement in which city establishes physical area(s) where tax base is "frozen" at specified point for a set period of time. Future tax revenues above base level gained from new development occurring after the specified time go into special fund to repay any public development costs and finance continued area improvements. Depend on state enabling legislation.

Revenue bonds: Long-term debt instrument in which nonguaranteed debt issued by city is backed by revenues from projects financed through bonding authority. Interest paid to lenders is exempt from federal taxes; recent federal restrictions on amount of revenue bonds issued by state and localities and on purposes of bonded projects have curtailed use.

General obligation bonds: Long-term debt instrument in which repayment of debt issued by city is guaranteed by "full faith and credit" of city. Interest paid to lenders is exempt from federal taxes.

Zero-coupon bonds: Non-interest-bearing bonds sold at discount rate through security dealers authorized by city; income accrued is capital gain for investor.

Taxable bonds: Long-term debt instrument in which nonguaranteed city debt is backed by revenues from projects financed through bonding authority but interest paid to lenders is not tax exempt.

Historical tax credits: Federal tax expenditures creating effective tax rate lower than nominal tax rate on preservation and rehabilitation of buildings meeting historic preservation criteria. Tax savings go to individual investors but cities may facilitate use by necessary inventories, applications for historic designation, and possible participation in syndication arrangements for redevelopment of historic buildings.

Revolving loan funds: Use of public funds to capitalize program to make loans for specific purposes or in particular areas. Loan repayments go into separate fund and are loaned out again; self-financing based on repayments, interest, and fees. Often targeted to certain firms, areas, groups, investment stages.

Below-market-rate loans: Offering of loans to eligible firms or groups at low interest rates and/or with extended repayment terms.

Loan guarantees: Loans made to eligible firms and individuals by private lenders but city partially or fully guarantees repayment if default occurs.

Interest subsidies: Loans made to eligible firms and individuals by private lenders but city makes a grant either to the borrower or on the borrower's behalf to the lender to partially subsidize and lower effective interest rate.

Venture capital funds: Public investment pool available for loans and equity investment in new firms or projects with considerable risk and uncertainty.

Cash-flow participation: Negotiation of share in net cash-flow receipts from a development project; disbursement to city is negotiated in return for public share in development risks and costs.

Equity participation: Investment of public capital in private redevelopment project for specified rate of return; city is shareholder in project.

Equity pools funded by public-private consortia: Investment capital pools created and managed by public-private organizations; funded by corporate and nonprofit donations and public funds for joint investment in redevelopment projects.

Community development corporations: Nonprofit organizations run by neighborhood residents to stimulate social development, economic redevelopment, and physical improvements in area through cooperation with public and private sectors. The first CDCs began in the 1960s in federal programs associated with the War on Poverty; most are based in low-income areas. CDC funds and staff are often provided by city.

Local development corporations: Nonprofit organizations run by neighborhood residents to stimulate business development through cooperation with public and private sectors. Perform tasks delegated by local government, including administering funds, managing and operating facilities and enterprises, entering into contracts, borrowing funds, and marketing and promotion activities. LDC funds and staff are often provided by city.

Industrial development authorities: Special independent agency of local or county government that often possesses special financing authorities beyond those of local government and debt limits independent of city government.

Linked deposits: Financial arrangement in which city deposits public funds in bank(s) willing to participate in city loan and loan guarantee programs.

More metropolitan and regional cooperation: Increased coordination across jurisdictional boundaries on planning, fiscal, and development matters. May include establishment of new organizations and shared functional responsibilities and tax base.

Land acquisition and building demolition: Acquisition of land and clearance of existing buildings in preparation for redevelopment. May be land declared as "blighted" and/or buildings may be on tax delinquency rolls.

Sale-leasebacks: Public property or facilities sold and leased back at modest rates; transfers ownership and maintenance costs to private investor.

Land leases: Leases, rather than sales, of publicly owned land to private developers; may be with or without improvements to land at city cost.

Land banking: Acquisition of land (often contiguous parcels) to be held in reserve for future development, through condemnation, donations, tax delinquency rolls, direct purchase, or annexation.

Donating land: Donation of publicly owned land to private developer for redevelopment project; often in exchange developer cooperates with city on project specifications.

Selling land: Sale of publicly owned land to private developer for redevelopment project; public agency may write down land price to below market rate to lower project costs.

Earmarking tax revenues for economic development: Setting aside of specified share of selected tax revenues for economic development purposes; earmarked taxes often include bed tax, hotel tax, or share of special authority revenues, such as airport or port authority fees.

Use program income for economic development: Recycling of program income—loan repayments, fees, net cash-flow participation income, returns on equity investments in earlier redevelopment projects—to fund other economic development activities. Allocation of program income is often outside of general budgeting procedures.

Use pension funds for economic development: Investment of a portion of city personnel pension funds as part of public share of development costs in local projects. Requires state enabling legislation and is possible only where city employees are not part of state personnel systems.

New Strategies for the Fourth Wave

Globalization

Sister cities: Establishment of formal agreements (often registered with Sister Cities International) with foreign cities to facilitate trade and cultural exchange.

International development planning: Specific planning for globalization effects, including such things as trade relations, technical assistance to business, promoting international direct investment, promoting international tourism, educating local businesspeople, and providing technical assistance to business.

International tourism initiatives: Marketing of city as a tourist destination to targeted international groups. Includes promotion of the city's ability to handle foreign visitors and description of tourist attractions and facilities in the city and region.

Links with universities/colleges on improving global competitiveness: Use of local higher-education resources to provide a variety of global business and cultural information targeted at local enterprises to enable them to do business internationally. City may provide some financial, personnel, and/or publicity resources to the educational institution to facilitate these programs.

Attracting international direct investment: Promotion of the city's foreign investment climate. By arguing that its locale is friendly to foreign investment and that growth and profit are likely, city attempts to expand its financial base.

World trade centers: Concentration of global activity in one office building location to provide some agglomeration economies to firms that may benefit from sharing specific services and interacting with each other. City often facilitates development of such a center.

Telecommunications

Fiber-optic networks: Contracting, subsidizing, and/or entering into partnerships with private providers to "wire" specific neighborhoods and possibly the whole city. Fiber-optic cables have the potential to handle substantially more information with higher accuracy than conventional telephone lines.

Using Internet resources: Use of resources available on the Internet that may be helpful in the practice of running a city.

Home pages on the Internet: Creation of an Internet home page to provide information to diverse audiences—residents, prospective immigrants, local business clients, and nonlocal and foreign business interests. City uses the home page to create a positive image of itself.

Linking government offices via e-mail: Use of e-mail as an efficient communications medium among government offices. E-mail provides advantages of speed, ease of access, ensured access, replicability (forwarding) potential, and accountability.

Public access to job and education information: Use of e-mail and/or a home page to provide a clearinghouse for information on local education and job opportunities.

Public access to the Internet: Use of government facilities (often libraries) to provide public access (at times restricted to residents) to the Internet. This access is often otherwise limited.

Telecommunications access to low-income residents: Provision of special access to e-mail and/or the Internet to qualified low-income residents. May be located either in government office/library facilities or in public housing facilities.

Human Capital

Job training: Provision or subsidization of vocational training, often targeted to specific populations—minorities, welfare recipients, or the recently unemployed. At times, efforts are coordinated with state and/or federal programs.

Job training targeting specific economic sectors: Attempted creation of an additional labor pool for an important specific economic sector (e.g., semiconductors) through the provision or facilitation of job training in that economic sector.

City/college collaboration: Cooperation with local institutions of higher education to facilitate human capital development programs.

Youth internships: Provision of or help in coordinating temporary work experience opportunities for youth in city offices or in local businesses. Such opportunities familiarize youth with labor opportunities and requirements, and in some cases facilitate their future employment.

School-to-work programs: Assistance in linking local students with local employers while students are still in school. Students work part-time while in school and are guaranteed jobs with employers upon graduation.

Notes

Introduction

1. Economic restructuring and globalization processes are often conflated. Restructuring processes are changes in the nature and organization of production processes contributing to capital accumulation and concomitant shifts in class alignments. Current restructuring trends are often identified as becoming manifest in the late 1960s and 1970s; they are often associated with technological changes (see Storper and Walker, 1989; Castells, 1989). Globalization is a spatial process typified, in Amin and Thrift's (1992) account, by trends in the 1980s and 1990s toward the functioning of industries on a world scale through the medium of global corporate networks; increases in oligopolistic, progressively centralized power; and ongoing processes of corporate decentralization through new forms of subcontracting, joint ventures, other networked organizational forms, and strategic alliances. In the 1990s, local officials struggle to adapt to the joint impacts of these trends.

2. It is important to distinguish human capital as an analytic concept from specific programs typically targeted at the unemployed—such as job placement services, training programs, and workfare provisions (King, 1995)—and education and health programs. These programs may aid human capital development, but the concept at issue here concerns the development and improvement of skills and the creation of skills transferable across jobs. These are the intended goals of many government programs, but as King (1995, 17) points out, training programs are often linked to anti-unemployment and workfare schemes.

3. Reich's work builds on and makes accessible an important body of scholarly work on globalization, economic restructuring, and localities: see, for example, Amin (1994); Knox and Taylor (1995); Castells (1989); Drucker (1994); Sassen (1991); Fainstein, Gordon, and Harloe (1992); Mollenkopf and Castells (1991); Piore and Sabel (1984); Porter (1990); Henderson and Castells (1987); Amin and Thrift (1994a, 1994b); Sayer and Walker (1992). We find Reich's approach especially lucid and useful for framing our arguments.

1. Transcending Scale

1. Theories of human capital have been available for decades, most notably Gary Becker's (1964) and Ted Schultz's (1971) approaches, but Reich's (1991) perspective emphasizes the economic and geographic implications of human capital in a global era. There are some analogies between traditional concepts of physical capital and human capital, but human capital enjoys certain distinctive characteristics (see chapter 7). The fact that human capital cannot be "owned" renders it very mobile. Further, rather than experiencing diminishing returns, human capital actually increases in value as it is used, because it gains more knowledge and experience. As a consequence, traditional concepts of investment must be modified to account for the distinctive attributes of human capital in contrast to physical capital.

2. Reich (1991) further characterizes symbolic analysts in terms of their tasks and attributes: they engineer, direct, design, research, coordinate, consult, manage, advise, plan, or entertain. Most are college graduates, and many have postgraduate educations. The vast majority are white males, although representation of females and minorities is slowly increasing. Their incomes are often highly variable and may be based on profit-sharing versus wages. The symbolic analyst need not always be in the category of "professional." Indeed, Reich suggests that professional degrees that stress routine acquisition of knowledge may deter the use of creative talent, which is a critical necessity for the symbolic analyst.

3. More specifically, Reich (1991) describes problem identifiers as having a specialized understanding of the needs of customers and identifying opportunities for marketing among a specialized set of those customers. Problem solvers have the skills and experience needed to form unique combinations to serve customized needs.

4. Michael Porter's (1990) early work, for example, portrays agglomeration economies and local intervention as critical elements of globalization processes and changing competitive advantage.

5. More recently, Krugman (1995) has argued that the policy emphasis on international competitiveness is misplaced, as are policies focused on human capital. Rather, he underscores the importance of increasing productivity in the growing, nontraded service sector as the key to domestic prosperity. From Krugman's perspective, any national policy intervention should focus on opportunities to capture the increasing returns on new technologies and products through supportive subsidies.

6. In the new amalgam of enterprise structures, much of our established information becomes less meaningful. Reich (1991) characterizes the Standard Industrial Classification (SIC) codes used in many classifications of urban function (Nelson, 1955; Scott 1988) as "unhelpful and anachronistic." Today's global economy can no longer be measured adequately based on amounts invested in plants, machinery, and warehouses. Nor can the employment of masses of production workers and middle managers be used as a gauge. Indeed, the accounting of a "national product" is increasingly difficult, as core corporations are no longer wholly American.

7. See note 2 to the introduction.

2. The Changing Work of Cities

1. See Clarke and Saiz (1995) for a similar argument on state economic development policies.

2. Our field interviews suggested this shift away from emulation toward differentiation, although we did not attempt to trace policy learning processes directly. One interpretation of the trend surface analysis presented in later chapters is that we find no statistically significant evidence that cities make policy choices by emulating their neighbors. We argue that cities rely on technical assistance from groups such as the National Development Council to craft contextually sensitive local policies rather than the "blueprint" approach implied in the emulation argument.

3. Useful examples of the path dependency concept are presented by Bryan Jones (1994) and D. Wilsford (1994). We pursue this argument in Clarke and Gaile (1997).

4. An early legislative enactment was even more minimalist: Title VII (Enterprise Zone Development) in the 1987 Housing and Community Development Act provided only for coordination of existing federal programs and encouraged states to provide regulatory relief (Rubin, 1994).

5. Boston, Kansas City (Kansas)/Kansas City (Missouri), Houston, and Oakland were designated as Enhanced Enterprise Communities; they receive $3 million in Title XX Social Service Block Grant funds plus $22 million in Economic Development Initiative Grant funds. A Community Development Bank included as part of this strategy is authorized but not funded.

6. Clinton's empowerment zone strategy also recasts lessons learned from past national programs and state experiences (Green, 1991; Rubin, 1994). It harks back to earlier Model Cities program features: concentrating resources in limited targeted areas; coordinating national, state, and local public and private efforts; and mobilizing local leadership to ensure cooperation on locally prepared programs (Rubin, 1994). Learning from the pitfalls experienced by the Model Cities program (see Haar, 1975), the Clinton administration established the Community Enterprise Board to support the interagency coordination necessary to orchestrate the federal funding to localities, specified the designation criteria in the empowerment zone legislation itself to avoid the "spreading" that bedeviled the Model Cities program, incorporated program evaluation plans in the legislation as well (Rubin, 1994), and required local officials and community groups to be included in the planning process. The emphasis on bottom-up planning, coordination of programs, and neighborhood revitalization is a hallmark of the War on Poverty urban programs of the 1960s (Lemann, 1994).

7. The tax benefits are in the form of wage credits (as in Bush's plan) rather than the capital gains tax relief prominent in many earlier Republican proposals.

8. In FY 1995 these proposals included Neighborhood Challenge Grants ($150 million) for use in neighborhood-based strategic planning; the Economic Development Initiative Grants ($150 million) from recaptured UDAG funds for communities to package with Section 108 guaranteed loans for economic revitalization projects; the Leveraged Investments for Tomorrow (LIFT) ($250 million) grants to encourage cooperation between nonprofit community development corporations and for-profit developers and to allow nonprofit community groups to gain equity in development projects; and Fair Housing and Equal Opportunity Act Section 3 ($25 million) funding to establish Economic Opportunity Centers for basic job training, job referrals, job bank services, and short-term child care for job-related needs.

9. The president's FY 1996 budget incorporated these performance partnerships in six areas, including the Department of Housing and Urban Development. At

HUD, this would mean consolidation of sixty statutory programs into three programs over time; up to 10 percent of formula allocation would be withheld and distributed on the basis of performance.

10. OMB proposes consolidation of funding streams and elimination of overlapping authorities; it also seeks to shift the administrative focus from a traditional cost-reimbursement, "level-of-effort" orientation to a performance contract basis. The partnership element—national, state, and local governments and providers— would occur during the design stage and in efforts to remove barriers to implementation. This includes mutual development of performance measures and targets, although the national government may also provide certain core indicators.

11. Performance rewards could also include greater flexibility or reduced matching requirements; poor performance could prompt federal requirements to shift local funds to use of best practices demonstrated by high-performing states or even reduction or termination of federal funds.

3. The Era of Entrepreneurial Cities

1. We recognize the nomenclature hazards here. We use *federal* and *postfederal* to identify the historical periods in which the intergovernmental system was, respectively, relatively mobilized in support of local economic development activity (our "second wave") and then disengaged from that support (launching the "third wave").

2. Elsewhere (Clarke and Gaile, 1992; Clarke and Saiz, 1995), we identify four attributes as characterizing first-wave or locational orientations: (1) the reduction of capital costs to business (such programs include direct grants, loans, and loan guarantees, and are quite common); (2) reliance on subsidies to induce businesses indirectly, specifically through tax incentives; (3) the granting of subsidies to any firm meeting general criteria (e.g., providing a minimum number of jobs) versus employing spatial or sectoral targeting; and (4) the existence of administratively passive policies that require little initiative on the part of a government agency to implement versus programs that require a more activist stance, such as those targeting high-technology or small business start-ups (Hansen, 1989).

3. Osborne (1988, 249) characterizes entrepreneurial policies in terms of a perception that government has a more central role to play in the creation of jobs and growth. We consider the government role one element of entrepreneurial policies, but this definition overlooks scale issues—Which government level?—and thus blurs important distinctions between the federal and postfederal eras.

4. The analysis required data collection on current and historical local economic development policy activities for the 178 cities above the population threshold during the study period. The data collection efforts brought together (1) federal program information, (2) a survey of local officials on present policies, and (3) historical and current census and nongovernmental data on city demographic, economic, and fiscal characteristics. The unique data set on local economic development policy activities described earlier provides the core of the data used in the following analyses. These data were combined with a previously created data set on UDAG projects that includes data for 373 UDAG cities from 1950 to 1990. Among the data in this data set are all city-level economic, fiscal, demographic, and social data included in U.S. Census reports 1950–80; all political structure measures reported in *Municipal Year-*

book volumes; various federal economic distress indices; indices of past federal program experience; per capita figures on federal aid; and program-specific data for UDAG, EDA, and CDBG allocations.

5. A statistical analysis of the subpopulation of cities receiving UDAG grants indicated that, as might be expected due to the UDAG eligibility criteria, these cities were more economically distressed than the entire population of U.S. cities with populations greater than 100,000 and also showed certain demographic features (higher percentage black, less population growth) that were significantly different from those of the average large U.S. city.

6. The interview goals were (1) to identify approaches fitting the market-based criteria guiding the study, (2) to assess whether it would be possible to determine the level of expenditure or forgone tax revenues for each strategy, and (3) to discover whether local evaluations of outcomes were available. Discussions centered on the approaches currently used and under study as well as other topics. A statistical comparison of this subgroup of respondent cities to the overall population of cities meeting the population threshold showed that the responding cities are representative: they are not significantly different from the overall population on major demographic and economic variables. These variables include per capita income, percentage completing twelve years of school or more, persons per household, percentage of persons below poverty level, percentage black population, percentage sixty-five years old and over, and median value of owner-occupied housing units.

7. In the 101 responses received, timing and overall effectiveness information is reasonably complete. Efforts to collect information on strategy costs and cost-effectiveness proved too burdensome for local officials; most said information is not collected in this form and that it would take too long to respond to such a request. Cost and ranking information was judged not to be complete enough for inclusion. Thus one manner of judging level of effort is not available due to data deficiencies. Additional inquiries concerned (1) distinctive features of current economic development policy orientations, (2) levels of activity, (3) the mayor's and council's orientations, (4) agencies responsible for and active in formulating and implementing policy, (5) revenue sources, (6) intergovernmental linkages, (7) failure rates, (8) effects of federal cuts, (9) evaluation processes, and (10) indicators used in assessing success in economic development.

8. In our surveys we asked for information relative to level of effort and money spent, but we did not include these data in our analyses because most respondents failed to give precise information. Thus our level-of-effort measures do not reflect dollars spent. However, we feel that striving for better financial precision on such a large-scale survey is largely a futile effort. Further, we seek to document a shift in orientation—the entrepreneurial use of a strategy—and our indices are created with this, rather than dollars spent, in mind.

9. Nominal data (e.g., dummy variables for regions) are considered statistically "weak" compared with reasonable interval data (e.g., latitude and longitude) because nominal data contain less information: the ability to use interval data allows the application of more statistically "powerful" techniques.

10. Where the spatial pattern of variables is ignored, there may, in fact, be more explanation provided by the locational variation in these variables than in their relationship with dependent variables; that is, the noise is greater than the signal.

Trend surface analysis eliminates the "regional locational" component of the noise, allowing the residual from the analyses to be used as a new variable that is separate from the regional trend and identifies a more "local" value. This aspect of the technique is often more useful than the identification of the trends themselves.

11. We disaggregate these federal strategies by fiscal and social entrepreneurial use in chapter 4.

12. Our survey shows most cities now rely on local general funds (25 percent), CDBG funds (18 percent), tax increment financing (10 percent), private and corporate donations (8 percent), and program income (7 percent) as the most important sources for supporting economic development.

13. Concerned about the displacement of low-income families caused by the gentrification of older neighborhoods, New York City uses its City Historic Property Fund to provide low-interest loans—essentially below-market-rate loans subsidized by the city—to nonprofit development groups rehabilitating historic buildings in low-income neighborhoods. It matches funds put forward by the National Historic Trust and other conservation groups.

14. This variable (leverage ratio) measures the ratio between the dollar amount of private funds that were invested in UDAG projects and the dollar amount of the federal (UDAG) contribution.

15. A trend surface analysis of the postfederal period policy variables (CURRENT, COMBINDX, NEWINDEX) yielded no statistically significant relationships. The correlation coefficients were not just insignificant, they were minimalist (0.03, 0.02, and 0.02, respectively). This should be interpreted as indicating that neighboring cities, in general, do not mimic each other's policy usage and that, overall, there is no significant regional pattern to policy use.

16. Indeed, a study of urban policy emulation may be quite revealing. It may be that, although cities do not emulate contiguous cities, they do emulate cities placed similarly in the urban hierarchy or similarly with regard to other locational factors.

17. The cluster technique is the agglomerative hierarchical method; we used the Ward's method (also called the minimum-variance method) in order to minimize the internal variance of each cluster and the squared Euclidean distance measure to calculate similarity among the cases. We used the simple matching coefficient method to create a ratio of matching pairs to unmatching pairs in the comparisons between cases; the match could be that two cities use or do not use a particular strategy.

4. Context and Policy Effectiveness

1. These are similar to the fiscal and social conditions—minority employment, services, public amenities, and the like—that some cities imposed on developers as conditions for access to UDAG resources.

2. The null hypotheses are as follows: (1) There are no significant relationships between city socioeconomic features and city policy choices using federal resources. (2) There are no significant relationships between city socioeconomic features and city policy choices using nonfederal resources. (3) There are no significant relationships between city political features and city policy choices using federal resources. (4) There are no significant relationships between city political features and

city policy choices using nonfederal resources. (5) There are no significant relationships between city policy choices using federal resources and city policy choices using nonfederal resources. (6) There is no significant relationship between greater use of market-based approaches using federal resources and present positive city socioeconomic features. (7) There is no significant relationship between use of market-based approaches using nonfederal resources and present positive city socioeconomic features. (8) There is no significant relationship between use of market-based approaches using federal resources and present positive city fiscal features. (9) There is no significant relationship between use of market-based approaches using nonfederal resources and present positive city fiscal features.

3. Selected data on city social, economic, and fiscal characteristics were collected from the following publications of the U.S. Department of Commerce, Bureau of the Census: the *County and City Data Book* (1988, 1994a) in PC-user form, *Census of Manufactures* (1977, 1982, 1987, 1992a), *Economic Census* (1992b), *Census of Population and Housing* (1980a, 1990a) and current annual reports, and *City Government Finances* (various years). Also included were *Inc.* magazine growth dynamics data by city on business birthrates, job growth, percentage of fast-growing companies, and nationwide rankings of city business activity; the Fiscal Austerity and Urban Innovation (University of Chicago) national survey data on local fiscal conditions; the *Urban Underclass Data Base* (Social Science Research Council, 1992); and the Advisory Commission on Intergovernmental Relations's *Significant Features of Fiscal Federalism* for various years. Geographic data on latitude and longitude were added for the spatial statistical analyses. Michael Rich, Emory University, generously provided historical federal program data.

4. Although one never accepts a null hypothesis, the ability to reject a null hypothesis lays the groundwork for further speculation and empirical testing. Other than using trend surface analysis to control for regional effects, we restrict the empirical analyses to simple correlations and t tests to render the analysis more transparent. More longitudinal analyses would have been preferable had appropriate time-series data been available for both dependent and independent variables. Multivariate explorations failed to add significant understanding to the study. Combining all sources, more than five hundred independent variables were at our disposal. From the federal sources on UDAG and EDA and from our survey, more than one hundred dependent variables were available. Numerous attempts to build a multivariate model of either characteristics or effectiveness were thwarted by the generally weak statistical relationships found and the high level of autocorrelation among many of the independent variables. Using multiple regression to "control" for such characteristics as race or political structure also proved futile, again largely due to the weak basic correlations we were working with. As such, we chose simply to report bivariate correlations and t tests.

5. Correlations (r) between the UDAG-based Social Entrepreneur Index and a variety of city characteristics are as follows: -.301, person per household; .272, one person household, percentage of all households; -.291, percentage of births to mothers less than 20 years old; .265, percentage completing twelve years of school; .272, percentage completing sixteen years of school; .384, per capita income 1979; and .300, median value of owner-occupied housing. Correlations (r) between the UDAG-based Fiscal Entrepreneur Index and two city characteristics are: -.284, percentage of

persons below poverty level; and -.289, percentage of families below poverty level. All independent variables are standardized residuals from a trend surface analysis and are based on the 1980 and 1990 censuses. Significance level is <0.05.

6. The nature of these data, however, dictated that use of EDA resources in market-based strategies—revolving loan funds, interest subsidies, joint ventures, and other approaches—are treated as nominal (1, 0) variables. Further, the program data are not complete and the sample included only 44 of the 178 cities in this study. Thus this test of correlates is constrained by limited data availability.

7. Results of the t tests between cities using EDA funds entrepreneurially and those not using them entrepreneurially are significant for the following socioeconomic and fiscal variables (significance level in parentheses): percentage of persons below poverty level, 1980 (0.050); below-average retail trade sales per capita, 1982 (0.033); health receipts per capita, 1982 (0.040); and percentage of city expenditures for highways, 1980 (0.019). All city characteristics are standardized residuals from a trend surface analysis.

8. Correlations (r) between use of CDBG funds for economic development activities (FY 1988) and city characteristics are as follows: -.240, per capita money income 1985; -.211, change in per capita money income, 1985–79; .262, percentage of persons below poverty level, 1980; .238, percentage of families below poverty level, 1980; .186, percentage of households, female head, no spouse, 1982; and -.205, owner-occupied units, percentage of total occupied units, 1982. All independent variables are residuals from a trend surface analysis. Significance level is <0.05.

9. Following are the results of correlation analyses on total federal funds per capita (a trend surface residual)—a variable calculated by summing per capita UDAG, CDBG, and EDA outlays for the period 1976–84 and filtering out geographic variation. This variable was then correlated with the same series of independent variables used in each of the analyses reported above.

r	Independent (characteristic) variable
.266	persons per square mile
-.355	population % change 1980–86
-.444	% white population
.418	% black population
.368	% 65 years and over
.572	% of households with female head—no spouse present
.412	one-person household, % of all households
.399	% of births to mothers under 20 years old
.292	infant deaths per 1,000 live births
.333	hospital beds per 100,000 population
.334	crimes per 100,000 population
.397	police officers per 10,000 population
-.451	% completing 12 years of school
-.419	per capita money income, 1979 (constant 1985 $)
.652	% of persons below poverty level, 1979
.638	% of families below poverty level, 1979
-.415	% change in housing units, 1970–80
.670	% of year-round housing units built before 1940

-.335	owner-occupied units, % of total occupied units
-.260	median value of owner-occupied housing units
-.361	new private housing units authorized by permit per capita, 1980–86
-.341	new private housing units authorized by permit 1980–86, % of 1980 stock
-.241	retail trade sales % change, 1977–82
-.364	retail trade sales per capita, 1982
-.334	retail trade establishments with payroll, paid employees % change 1977–82
.338	taxable service industries, establishments with payroll, legal services per capita, 1982

All independent variables are standardized residuals from a trend. Significance level is <0.05.

10. Note that the two indices are treated as dependent variables in this analysis.

11. Based on our 1989 survey of officials responsible for local economic development, the following shows statistically significant differences in the assessment and evaluation procedures of cities using nonfederal resources for market-based strategies.

Indicators used regularly in assessing economic conditions	Strategy index	*t*-test significance
unemployment rates	CURRENT	0.016
unemployment rates	COMBINDX	0.027
unemployment rates	NEWINDEX	0.039
job creation rates	CURRENT	0.009
job creation rates	COMBINDX	0.042

Indicators used most often in evaluating the success of economic development strategies	Strategy index	*t*-test significance
loan repayments	COMBINDX	0.001
loan repayments	NEWINDEX	0.001
leverage ratios	CURRENT	0.001
leverage ratios	COMBINDX	0.001
leverage ratios	NEWINDEX	0.004
program income	COMBINDX	0.019

12. Begun by Terry Clark, Richard Bingham, and Brett Hawkins in 1982, FAUI has developed over time into one of the most impressive data sets on the urban condition. The core questionnaire used by FAUI is reprinted as an appendix in Clarke (1989); it includes items on fiscal management strategies, revenue forecasting, integrated financial management systems, performance measures, management rights, the sophistication of economic development analyses, local leadership, decision-making patterns, and policy preferences, activities, and impacts on city government.

13. The statistical analyses indicate that the per capita federal local development funds received by the cities in our study are negatively related to the local perception that their financial problems stem from unemployment, loss of federal rev-

enue, or declining tax base. That is, cities receiving more federal funds are less likely to define their problems in these terms. There is, however, a positive relationship with mentioning intergovernmental issues, federal mandates, and employment problems as city concerns.

14. The *t* tests between means for mayor-council ($n = 41$) and council- manager ($n = 51$) forms of government indicate that mayor-council governments had higher per capita federal economic development funding during the peak periods, 1978–84 (*t*-test significance level 0.0000), but they were also more entrepreneurial (OLDINDEX *t*-test significance level 0.0001).

15. The *t* test for significant differences in the average per capita federal economic development funding 1978–84 between nonwhite and white mayors was significant at the 0.0180 level.

16. We should note that a large number of the political characteristics identified for cities in the federal period were not statistically significant in the nonfederal period. Much of this may be attributable to a "low *n*" statistical problem in that the intersection of the FAUI data set and our survey response data set produced an $n = 44$, which, especially when disaggregated, often failed to produce statistically significant results.

17. The *t*-test results for the difference of the statistical means between mayor-council and council-manager forms of government were significant at the 0.0012 level for the Current Index, the 0.0233 level for the New Index, and 0.0001 for the Combined Index.

18. The *t* test for the difference between the means on the Combined Index between nonwhite and white mayors was significant at the 0.0865 level.

19. There is a statistically significant correlation ($r = 0.259$; <0.05) between the Current Index and the proportion of the council that is black.

20. National Development Council involvement was treated as a dummy variable. Of the 177 cities in our sample, 58 cities were noted as working with NDC. We thank Ed Goetz and Mike Rich (1983) for sharing and corroborating these data. The *t* tests showed statistically significant differences in the means of the Combined Index (0.020 level), the Current Index (0.020 level), and per capita federal economic development funding 1978–84 (0.000 level) between cities with NDC involvement and those without it.

21. There was a perceived gap in capital financing of these size firms even though they were seen, by the early 1980s, as important job generators. Through its Neighborhood Business Revitalization Program, NDC sought to devise sufficient incentives using public resources to attract long-term financing of these ventures.

22. Lisbeth Schorr (1993) emphasizes the importance of knowledge transfer and finding "what works."

23. As of 1996, NDC counted more than 140 cities, counties, state agencies, and nonprofit organizations as clients. In addition to technical assistance, it operates the Grow America Fund (since 1992), an SBA nonbank lending company using SBA 7(a) loan guarantees to provide below-market-rate financing for small business expansions and start-ups and the Corporate Equity Fund (1995), an investment fund supplying finance capital through limited partnerships in low-income housing and historic preservation projects that then provide tax credits to CEF investors. NDC is

also currently exploring support of community waste management systems as a sustainable local economic development venture.

24. The multivariate methodologies used were correlation analysis, multiple regression analysis, and trend surface analysis. Specifically, correlations were determined after spatial control variables were entered into stepwise multiple regressions in order to isolate the local effects of the independent variables on the dependent outcome variables. Multiple regressions were used to control for the effects of certain variables. Comparison of means tests were used to analyze the impacts of different individual market-based strategies. Upgrading regional variables from nominal variables to spatially continuous and normalized interval variables through the use of spatial statistics allows for the use of the more powerful statistical methods.

25. Note that market-based strategy use indices, formerly dependent variables, are now the independent variables.

26. There are significant correlations (<0.05) between the Social Entrepreneur Index and civilian labor force unemployment, 1986 ($r = -0.304$); retail trade establishments with payroll, apparel and accessory stores—sales per capita, 1982 ($r = 0.271$); and retail trade establishments with payroll, eating and drinking stores—sales per capita, 1982 ($r = 0.266$). There are also significant correlations (<0.05) between the Fiscal Entrepreneur Index and retail trade sales per capita, 1982 ($r = 0.277$). All dependent variables are standardized residuals from a trend surface analysis.

27. There are statistically significant correlations (<0.05) between the New Index and job growth rate, *Inc.* data ($r = 0.200$); employment change 1977–87 (census) ($r = 0.254$); fast-growing companies as percentage of new firms ($r = 0.191$); city tax per capita, 1990 ($r = -0.186$); property tax per capita, 1990 ($r = -0.200$); city government employees per ten thousand population, 1987 ($r = -0.199$); and city government general expenditure per capita, 1990 ($r = -0.162$). All dependent variables are standardized residuals from a trend surface analysis.

28. As suggested by a reviewer, we ran the data controlling for fiscal status and level of growth prior to the adoption of the strategies. The fiscal health variables, Actual Fiscal Health Index 1972 and Standardized Fiscal Health Index 1972, were from the *Urban Underclass Data Base* (Social Science Research Council, 1992), which sources them from Ladd and Yinger (1986). The growth variables were drawn from U.S. Census data; these included per capita income change 1969 to 1979 and employment change 1967 to 1977. Using various combinations of these variables as controls in multiple regressions, we found none of them to be statistically significant. This helps to rule out the possibility that fiscal health or growth causes entrepreneurial strategy use, versus our conjecture that the likely relationship is the opposite.

5. Cities at Work

1. Although more entrepreneurial strategies and organizations have prompted skepticism and suspicion on the part of some, there is a tendency to conflate the intervention mode with the objectives. Rather than dismiss entrepreneurial approaches as inherently costly and privatistic, we contend that cities can use entrepreneurial intervention strategies for broader public goals, depending on the institutional design.

2. This approach differs from pluralist concerns with interest group bargaining and regime theory concerns with coalitional dynamics (Fainstein and Fainstein,

1983, 1989; Elkin, 1980, 1985; Stone, 1989) in that it emphasizes the importance of institutional arrangements in shaping the political landscape (Ferman, 1996; Horan, 1991, 1997). In contrast to these political process orientations, it directs attention to how institutional design structures the preferences and values of different groups and creates decision arenas more favorable to certain types of economic development policy choices than to others.

3. Williamson (1989) refers to this as the establishment of *negotiated orders*; these negotiated orders can vary over time and across cities.

4. This argument is made more fully in Clarke (1995).

5. Emery Roe (1994) has used the distinction between tightly and loosely coupled systems to explore rural development practices; Charles Perrow (1984) also has developed the concept.

6. We visited fifteen cities during the initial research phase: Tulsa and Oklahoma City, Oklahoma; Cleveland, Columbus, and Dayton, Ohio; Columbus and Macon, Georgia; Seattle and Tacoma, Washington; Fort Wayne and Indianapolis, Indiana; Jacksonville and Miami, Florida; and Albany and Syracuse, New York. We selected these cities for site visits based on their profiles of prior social and fiscal innovations using federal grant resources. Our interviews with local officials and community leaders (an average of twelve interviews per city) centered on their policy orientations in the absence of federal resources. Some of these cities feature in other grants and research projects (Clarke, 1986, 1995).

7. In arriving at these designations, we considered each city in terms of a series of issues addressed in the case studies: how the concertation of business and public interests is achieved; whether there are mechanisms for structuring broad participation in economic development policy making; how broadly these participation rights are defined; how public authority and mutual gain are coordinated; the nature, locus, and range of forums for iterative bargaining, exchange, and deliberation; and the definition of appropriate public roles and the delegation of public authority to intermediary organizations outside the political structure. This checklist does not yield quantitative measures; we did not try to come up with a "score" for each city. Nor does it approximate a theory of political forms of the state that Cox claims is necessary (1988, 33). But it serves, we think, to distinguish among institutional arrangements and policy orientations in the four cities and to indicate how these institutional frameworks mediate development policy choices.

We assigned the four cities to these categories based on interviews with local officials and community leaders during visits to each city, review of local newspapers and documents for a ten-year period prior to the field visits (updated with Nexus searches through 1995), and discussions with local academics. As noted above (note 6), we visited fifteen cities during the original survey period; of the fifteen cities we examined in depth, these four cities best illustrate the argument we are making here.

8. There are ninety foreign-owned firms in the area, and the foreign trade zone at the Port of Cleveland serves more than fifty countries.

9. The city's supplemental empowerment zone encompasses the Hough, Fairfax, and Glenville neighborhoods.

10. Mayor White claims that all tax abatements approved since 1990 have gone to industrial and retail concerns outside of downtown (Gleisser, 1996). He also has noted that 80 percent of the business assistance given out since 1990 has gone to

small businesses in neighborhoods. Other criticisms of the downtown strategy center on the fiscal woes of several of the large projects, notably the Gateway complex.

11. Cleveland also shares in the dispersion of primary office space throughout large American cities. In 1990, it ranked above the national average share growth in primary occupied office space (class A and B buildings housing corporate headquarters, financial institutions, and business services) and its growth rate in primary space outstripped its overall office space growth rate from 1985 to 1990 (Sui and Wheeler, 1993, 39).

12. This federal funding was critical to Cleveland's vaunted turnaround. Rehabilitation of the Terminal Tower in the downtown Union Terminal complex, one of Cleveland's most famous landmarks since the 1930s, was stalled until UDAGs started rolling into the city in the mid-1980s. The Terminal Tower was one of the first downtown revitalization projects; together, the Tower City Center and another UDAG for the Galleria, the first retail venture in Cleveland's downtown in twenty-five years, are seen as the turnaround projects that encouraged reinvestment in downtown.

13. As a private for-profit organization, Cleveland Tomorrow takes equity positions in each project supported and structures revenue streams higher than the rate of returns allowed under UDAG projects. It also utilizes a revolving loan fund and makes use of low-income housing tax credits. The decision rules emphasize efficiency: projects are supported on a "but for" basis with the emphasis on those with multiplier effects; job creation is only one of many decision criteria employed.

14. Given these performance criteria, groups are judged in terms of their capacity (their ability to carry out projects). Increasingly, this becomes an issue of staff size and training: organizations without relatively large, well-trained staff, such as voluntary associations, are less and less able to vie for city funds. This trend is exacerbated by NPI's plans to support professional directors of the groups it works with; the salaries paid these directors dwarf those of any other neighborhood personnel. NPI sees this professionalization of the neighborhood development community as essential to the success of these groups; others see it as another wedge creating rancor among groups and between group leaders and members.

15. By the early 1990s, more than $7 billion had been invested in new office buildings, retail centers, and recreational attractions in Cleveland (Geahigan, 1994, 683). Most of that investment is in the office market; retail remains weaker and in competition with the suburbs. Cleveland's downtown revitalization strategies in a nonfederal era are exemplified by a new baseball stadium (Jacobs Field) and, more recently, by the Rock and Roll Hall of Fame. This long-awaited project was completed in 1995. The delays were unfortunate; the hall missed the UDAG era and is the first project in the city to rely on tax increment financing (TIF). The city views TIF as "an internal UDAG" but is less enthusiastic about its utility because it brings fewer benefits than UDAG.

16. Jacksonville, like Cleveland, ranked above the national average share growth in primary occupied office space (class A and B buildings housing corporate headquarters, financial institutions, and business services) in 1990, but its growth rate in primary space relative to overall office space growth rate slipped significantly from 1985 to 1990 (Sui and Wheeler, 1993, 38).

17. The prevalence of market logic and the norms of market exchange are characteristic of Sunbelt city politics, particularly in fast-growing Florida cities,

where population growth and mobility rates appear to inhibit sentiments of community attachment and investment (Appleton and Williams, 1986).

18. This trust fund is capitalized through capital bond issues and administered by the Economic Development Division of the Planning and Development Department. The trust fund grants require an equity investment by the applicant and the written agreement to provide at least one permanent full-time job for every $6,000 of public investment. Funds can be revoked and repayment required if the job target is not met within a reasonable time.

19. The estimate of JAXPORT's direct and indirect economic impacts in 1991 is more than $2 billion a year (JCCI, 1995b, 15). Unlike the Jacksonville Electric Authority, JPA does not make payments to the city.

20. In 1995, JPA began to seek approval for converting neighboring residential property for industrial use as part of its twenty-year expansion plan.

21. Enterprise Florida's mission is to create 200,000 high-wage jobs in ten years through job training, business financing, manufacturing assistance, and domestic and international business marketing programs. The strategy is to shore up manufacturing and high-wage job creation by working through a network of boards: the Innovation Partnership to support new technology companies and existing manufacturers; the Capital Partnership to raise money for start-up firms; and the Jobs and Training Partnership to train workers at new and expanding companies. Smaller communities, minority groups, international businesses, and new firms feel slighted by this privatization of state job-creation efforts; regional infighting and interjurisdictional competition are causing further difficulties and some legislative resistance to funding (Clough, 1995). In 1994, the state legislature refused to approve transfer of most of the state's business marketing to Enterprise Florida, a key element of Enterprise Florida's strategic plan (DeSimone, 1995). The departing Enterprise Florida president attributed this failure, and the continuing stalemate on Enterprise Florida, to the backbiting, logrolling politics prevalent in the state legislature (DeSimone, 1995). By late 1995, Enterprise Florida was on its third president in three years.

22. There is, however, a Northwest Council Chamber of Commerce. Blacks also have served on the chamber's board and the chamber has a director of minority economic development.

23. Since the mid-1980s the downtown renovations have included the Convention Center, the reopening of Harbormaster's Restaurant and Marina, and the construction of Jacksonville Landing, Southbank Riverwalk, the Automated Skyway Express, Omni Jacksonville, Barnett Center, the American Heritage Life Building, and the Jacksonville Maritime Museum (Crownover, 1991b).

24. In 1992, the city bought eleven waterfront-area acres from a defunct shipyard. In 1994, the remaining forty waterfront acres were purchased by Jacksonville Riverfront Development; the city may participate in this next stage through infrastructure improvement and coordination of land development on its contingent acres.

25. Similarly, efforts to bring in Vistakon, Swisher International, and Coach leather goods ($2.9 million, 1994) entailed complex, expensive deals packaging incentives from state, county, and city provisions.

26. The city supports job training programs at Florida Community College at Jacksonville (FCCJ) and Jacksonville's Center for Economic Development (Clary,

1991). FCCJ alone provides about 60 percent of all business and industry training in Florida, according to school officials (Clary, 1991). Although the targeted public investment in the Northside and these job training initiatives contribute to human capital, the emphasis remains on business development.

27. Two recent state grants provide matching funds to local port authorities for specific capital improvement projects. In 1994 the annual value of this funding to JAXPORT was about $2.4 million (JCCI, 1995b, 12). Even if the state were to provide more port funding, the balance of power in the state legislature favors South Florida (JCCI, 1995b, 14).

6. Different Paths

1. To date, cities in the upstate and central New York regions have not experienced the influx of foreign-born immigrants that has boosted populations in downstate cities.

2. In 1985, Syracuse's proportion of primary occupied office space paralleled the national average share growth (class A and B buildings housing corporate headquarters, financial institutions, and business services), but by 1990 it slipped below the average, and its relative growth rate in primary space declined dramatically from 1985 to 1990 (Sui and Wheeler, 1993, 38).

3. Other city organizations include the city Business Assistance and Retention Team and the Urban Business Opportunity Center, which provides financial support to small businesses conditioned on their training in business management techniques.

4. In addition, there are citywide business organizations such as the Greater Syracuse Chamber of Commerce as well as discrete groups like the James Street Business Association. In 1993, the chamber underwent leadership changes after a twenty-seven-year tenure of one director. Among its specialized units, the chamber includes the Pan-African Business Association and the Greater Syracuse Business Development Center (a nonprofit corporation authorized to guarantee SBA and New York Job Development Authority loans). It is one of two such nonprofit corporations in Onondaga County; it operates through the Greater Syracuse Business Development Corporation, a consortium of five banks whose funding of SBA small business loans for the county contributes to compliance with CRA provisions. At the regional level, business groups are also represented by the Manufacturers Association of Central New York. Upstate utilities formed the Empire State Business Alliance.

5. The state of New York has an extensive, long-standing network of specialized economic development organizations, including the Empire State Development Corporation (formerly the New York Urban Development Corporation), the Central New York Regional Planning and Development Board, the Central New York Minority Economic Development Council, the New York State Job Development Authority, and the New York Department of Economic Development. Governor Pataki also integrated the New York State Science and Technology Foundation into the state Department of Development. Syracuse is also eligible for New York State Job Incentive tax benefits granted to firms locating in the city.

6. Similar to the PILOT approach, the state enterprise zone provisions allow for freezing the current property assessment for seven years, then factoring in the

new increment over four years. There are also substantial rebates on electricity costs and wage tax credits provided for those in job training.

7. Although the buyer of the Hotel Syracuse sank under heavy debt burdens and a moribund downtown economy, the bankruptcy court-appointed manager bought the hotel and captured a restructuring business market in the mid-1990s. In contrast to previous efforts, the new owner did not seek city incentives. But the local downtown area is now almost entirely within the state economic development zone; thus the hotel gets some help on taxes and utility costs.

8. Financing for the stadium came primarily from the state, the city, and the owners of the Toronto Blue Jays, whose Triple A team uses the stadium.

9. The institutional terrain is further fragmented, notably by the Port Authority and the Urban Policy Committee (UPC). The Port Authority is a separate municipal corporation (set up by Pierce County in 1918) with five elected commissioners and its own taxing and bond authority. The port commissioners governing the special-purpose district run in countywide primary and general elections. Although it receives city services, the Port Authority pays no city taxes. The UPC was established as a neighborhood advisory body to the city council during the Model Cities era in Tacoma. Its twenty-five members were originally elected, and the UPC's recommendations tended to be adopted by the council. The council now appoints UPC members; periodically there are attempts to rein in the UPC by narrowing its scope and weakening its advisory role. Its resurgence in the 1990s stemmed in part from its role in the strategic planning processes in growth management and human services demanded by the state.

10. There was a deliberate decision *not* to make these new districts coterminous with the five city council districts. Instead, nine planning areas devised in the early 1950s were adapted and utilized as the base for the eight neighborhood council areas (the port and downtown districts were combined). Each neighborhood elects a board of directors; the neighborhood councils are seen as advisory to the city council for their area. In addition, department heads frequently meet with the neighborhood councils and act as informal liaisons among the line agencies, the city manager's office, and the city council.

11. The Community Council addresses citywide issues. As the city administrator for the program sees it, "If we have not achieved anything else, we have achieved a coming together of people, of one mind in what they envision is good or best for the city."

12. Clustered around Union Station will be the new Washington State Historical Museum, with arches replicating the classic beaux arts Union Station and the expanded University of Washington branch campus, set in one of the oldest warehouse districts in the Pacific Northwest (Kipp Associates, 1985). The campus will be housed in renovated historic warehouses scattered up the hillside above the port. These developments anchor Pacific Avenue at one end, with the Sheraton Hotel (UDAG) and the Broadway Center Theater District, several blocks away, closer to the heart of downtown. Pacific Avenue links the Union Depot/Warehouse Historic District with the original Old City Hall Historic District to the north, with stretches interspersed with small businesses, rescue missions, shelters, and blighted buildings—as in the past, when it was known as "whiskey road" (Kipp Associates, 1985)—and newly gentrified shops and bistros.

7. The Fourth Wave

1. The 1996 follow-up survey of the 101 respondents to the 1989 survey yielded 60 valid questionnaires, for a response rate of 59.4 percent. The 1996 survey consisted of a questionnaire with 216 variables assessing post-1989 strategy choices, policy orientations and institutional settings, and initiatives in the areas of human capital, globalization, and telecommunications.

2. We find no statistical relationships among adoption of human capital policies, telecommunications strategies, and globalization initiatives. Nor is adoption of these strategies associated with earlier policy orientations or the contextual features distinguishing entrepreneurial cities in the federal and nonfederal periods. We suspect the small sample and exploratory nature of the questions in 1996 contribute to the lack of statistically significant relationships. Another interpretation of these "nonfindings" is that these fourth-wave approaches are substantively different from previous orientations; neither learning from the past nor contextual features associated with previous approaches would be expected to shape these new agendas.

3. The original Living Wage Job Resolution would have included an across-the-board requirement that any company receiving more than $100,000 in city assistance pay these wages. Local economic development officials did not support this broader proposal, however; the more limited proposal exempts more than two-thirds of the Minneapolis Community Development Agency's project dollars from these wage guarantees. (Diaz, 1997).

4. Coburn (1997) describes the evolution of Eisenhower's People-to-People program in the 1950s from a citizen diplomacy initiative centered on cultural exchanges between sister cities to an economic development tool aimed at increasing trade links.

5. See "The Good, the Bad, and the Internet" at http://www.cs.uchicago.edu/discussions/cpsr/annual/index.html.

6. See Michael Barndt at http://www.uwm.edu/People/mbarndt/mindex.htm.

7. Popularizers such as Toffler and Toffler (1995) and John Naisbitt (1994) also note trends underscoring the importance of human resources and the local setting.

8. An analogy may help illustrate this approach. In Kenya, the concept of *unmet agricultural potential* was measured through simple comparison of a scientific assessment of agricultural potential of land with current production rates. This was accomplished using agroecological zonation based on such physical factors as rainfall, slope, and soil to estimate the complete range of possible crop yields using varying levels of technological inputs, including a low-input "sustainable" level (Jaetzhold and Schmidt, 1982). These potential yields were then converted to shillings per hectare (using a supply discounter) and the actual current level of agricultural production (also in shillings per hectare) was subtracted from the potential yield to arrive at a figure quantifying unmet agricultural potential (Gaile, 1988).

9. We use the term *evaluate* versus the more common *discount* because human capital may in fact increase in value over time, as it is often not subject to diminishing returns.

10. These hypothetical figures illustrate possible gains from investment in human capital. But what does *capital gains* mean as it is applied to human capital? For most of the twentieth century we have subsidized industry mobility through

both capital investment and capital gains tax breaks (Reich, 1983). The logic of these tax breaks seems eminently transferable to the new economy based on human capital. It would be a simple and logical matter to make some of the costs of education deductible on income taxes, as has been proposed by the Clinton administration. Other measures, including increasing the accessibility to loans for education and providing training vouchers, are also currently debated. Capital gains is another matter. Under current tax law, if a person invests $50,000 in stocks, holds them for a period of more than six months, and realizes a gain from that investment, that person receives a "capital gains" tax break. By analogy, if a person uses $50,000 to invest in his or her own human capital (through education), with an eventual doubling of income subject to taxation as a result, he or she is penalized under current tax law, although one could clearly argue that the individual has simply realized "human capital gains." We are not arguing for a human capital gains tax break, but for considering how the current tax code subsidizes physical capital investment and not investment in human capital.

11. Analytically, the joint decision model assumes that central government decisions on, for example, human capital investment are dependent on the agreement of constituent governments; that this agreement must be unanimous or nearly so (thus giving each a veto power); that actors pursue a bargaining decision style based on the anticipated gains of cooperation; and that composite actors, such as state and local governments, can be treated as unitary actors capable of strategic choices. These ideal conditions are approximated in the United States on human capital issues: the functional responsibilities for human capital investment historically reside at the subnational level, any national human capital initiative depends on joint intergovernmental action and implementation, intergovernmental relations in the United States rely on bargaining rather than hierarchical fiat, and the effectiveness of joint action on human capital investment is undermined by "rogue" subnational governments that refuse to cooperate with or defect from national initiatives. Our thanks to Jens Blom-Hansen, Aarhus University, Denmark, for bringing the relevance of this argument to our attention.

12. In a way, this could clear the decks for a national human capital agenda focused on "lifetime learners" while state and local governments simultaneously struggle with the less employable, less productive segments of the labor market and the imperative to carve out new human capital initiatives.

13. Lehnen and McGregor's (1994) study is flawed in their creation of an index of complex human capital. They use factor analysis to construct this index, which is composed of six variables, and their factor loadings are as follows: percentage college education in 1980 (90), percentage college education in 1988 (89), doctoral production rate (71), median education 1980 (64), 1989 adjusted SAT (63), and 1980 percentage grade school education (-59). One flaw is their use of the same variable for two time periods, which is a factor-analytic way of "stacking the deck" to make sure that a desired factor emerges. A second flaw is their inclusion of adjusted SAT, which is questionable because its factor loading is not very different from its loading (57) on Factor 1 (Basic Learning) and because there are two other SAT variables, one of which is indistinguishable between factors and the other of which loads most heavily on the other Factor 1 (Basic Learning). Median education's factor loading (64) is also not very different than its loading on Factor 1 (57). Third, the grade school education variable should have been excluded because intuitively it is clearly more asso-

ciated with Basic Learning (Factor 1) than with Complex Learning (Factor 2). In our analyses, we restrict our use of percentage college education to a variable indicator of complex human capital. Doctoral production rate would be a further useful variable, but is was not available at the city level.

14. The correlates of complex human capital in America's cities are as follows: unemployment rate 1990 ($r = -0.6424$), median income change 1979–89 ($r = +0.4702$), population change 1980–92 ($r = +0.3165$), employment change 1982–87 ($r = +0.2769$), percentage of population homeworkers ($r = +0.2935$).

15. This may be foreshadowed by the last element in the analyses, the trend toward homeworkers (including telecommuters), which is not predicted by previous research because it is an element of new production structures. If the future labor geography of the United States includes a large telecommuting population, this will prompt localities to reconsider how to link their communities—and homeworkers—to the global web.

16. Many of these human capital strategies differ from past initiatives (see Rich, 1995). They draw on ideas that explicitly reframe local human capital issues in terms of underutilized assets rather than social needs and pathologies. Two divergent strategies are prominent: Michael Porter's (1995) emphasis on local competitive advantage and Kretzmann and McKnight's (1993) asset-based orientation. Porter faults past models for treating the central city as an island isolated from the city and focusing on public subsidies rather than creation of wealth via private investment. He advocates building on the competitive advantage of the central city by identifying the *clusters* of activities that would gain from central-city location. He targets development of critical masses of economic activities that would respond to local demand (such as specialty foods, financial services), link with other regional clusters, and export goods and services to broader markets. Porter argues that private sector models and leadership can build on the competitive advantages and underutilized assets of these distressed areas. Although it could be argued that disinvestment by these private institutions created many of the difficulties facing these areas, Porter relegates government to a supportive role to business leadership.

In contrast, Kretzmann and McKnight's influential model of asset-based community organizing relies on strong public and civic leadership. These authors also reject past policy designs, characterizing them as "needs-driven" deficiency models creating client neighborhoods and ensuring only survival. In their alternative view, poor people are the underutilized assets. Kretzmann and McKnight argue explicitly for shifting attention away from deficiency cues and toward an internal focus on rediscovering local assets as the means to development solutions. This involves mapping and developing strategies to knit together the individual skills, associations, and institutions in the neighborhood.

17. There are now a number of local antipoverty programs (Bendick and Egan, 1993). Although not as grandiose as the War on Poverty, these local initiatives aim at ameliorating poverty through new approaches. These include the Atlanta Project, set up in 1991 in twenty neighborhoods with an initial budget of $20 million; in each neighborhood, volunteer-based coalitions are established to work with corporate sponsors to design context-sensitive strategies. In Providence, Rhode Island, the Providence Plan set up a nonprofit organization in 1992 to direct revitalization efforts from the bottom up. These programs, and similar efforts in other cities, tend to be more comprehensive and holistic than the national antipoverty programs of the

1960s; they are also more family oriented and attempt to integrate people- and place-oriented programs at the neighborhood level (Rich, 1993a). Whereas Type II economic development policies are often project specific and dependent on negotiations with private developers, these are citywide programs drawing on local public funds to address community needs. This is not to argue that these local programs will be effective or even compensatory for lost national funds. But their initiation at the local level and their reliance on local funds suggest new thinking on the integration of human capital and economic development.

18. O'Regan and Conway's (1993) analysis categorizes local programs as self-employment, job training and placement, and job creation and retention goals; they match these programs with different types of beneficiaries, such as the working poor, the unemployed, the persistently unemployed, the dependent poor, and the indigent. They identify more than one hundred local microenterprise programs, for example, that treat the poor as potential entrepreneurs (unmet human capital). The Coalition for Women's Economic Development in Los Angeles, for example, targets microenterprise assistance to very low-income self-employed women and AFDC recipients (10). Other workplace-oriented, localistic strategies include "integrated employment services" (Parker, 1995).

19. Vice President Al Gore is credited with launching the term *information highway* into public discourse in a *Washington Post* article published in July 1990. To make the parallels explicit, Gore introduced his "Supercomputer Network Study Act" on the thirtieth anniversary of the signing of the Interstate Highway Act. Gore's father, Senator Albert Gore Sr., was a major backer of the building of the interstate highway system in the 1950s.

20. See Graham and Marvin (1996) for an extensive analysis of local telecommunication issues, including the notion of "electronic public space" (359).

21. These examples are drawn from Neumann (n.d.).

22. This observation has been made by Al Strock, the chief financial officer of International Communications Services, a firm assisting cities in establishing telecommunication utilities.

23. An analysis that created a "Telecommunications Effort Index" based on a simple additive analysis of "hits" on the telecommunications aspects, with one-half point awarded for "under study" of the most current survey, yielded a nonsignificant (0.05) correlation with complex human capital as measured by percentage of populace over twenty-five years of age with a bachelor's degree.

8. Reinventing Citizenship

1. This section draws on the discussion in Staeheli and Clarke (1995).

2. We are aware of, if not completely persuaded by, arguments that local telecommunication initiatives could open the door to "electronic democracy" in which the costs of information, access, and participation are greatly reduced (e.g., Schuler, 1996). Until the distributional consequences of telematics are more clearly articulated, we reserve judgment on whether local telecommunication efforts will enhance local citizenship capacities. More basic policies that can enhance the skills and social well-being of citizens appear to constitute a more direct route to reinventing local citizenship.

Bibliography

Abbott, Carl. 1987. *The New Urban America: Growth and Politics in Sunbelt Cities,* rev. ed. Chapel Hill: University of North Carolina Press.

Abernathy, William J., Kim B. Clark, and Alan M. Kantrow. 1983. *Industrial Renaissance: Producing a Competitive Future for America.* New York: Basic Books.

Advisory Commission on Intergovernmental Relations (ACIR). Various years. *Significant Features of Fiscal Federalism.* Washington, D.C.: Advisory Commission on Intergovernmental Relations.

Agterberg, Fritz. 1984. "Trend Surface Analysis." In *Spatial Statistics and Models,* edited by Gary L. Gaile and Cort J. Willmott. Dordrecht, Netherlands: D. Reidel.

Alonso, William. 1960. "A Theory of the Urban Land Market." *Papers and Proceedings, Regional Science Association* 6: 149–57.

Ambrosius, Margery, and Susan Welch. 1988. "State Legislators' Perceptions of Business and Labor Interests." *Legislative Studies Quarterly* 13: 199–209.

Amenta, Edwin. 1991. "Making the Most of a Case Study: Theories of the Welfare State and the American Experience." *International Journal of Comparative Sociology* 32, 1–2: 172–93.

Amin, Ash (ed.). 1994. *Post-Fordism: A Reader.* Oxford: Basil Blackwell.

Amin, Ash, and Nigel Thrift. 1992. "Neo-Marshallian Nodes in Global Networks." *International Journal of Urban and Regional Research* 16: 571–87.

———. 1994a. "Living in the Global." In *Globalization, Institutions, and Regional Development in Europe,* edited by Ash Amin and Nigel Thrift, 1–22. Oxford: Oxford University Press.

———. 1994b. "Holding Down the Global." In *Globalization, Institutions, and Regional Development in Europe,* edited by Ash Amin and Nigel Thrift, 257–60. Oxford: Oxford University Press.

Appleton, Lynn M., and Bruce A. Williams. 1986. "Community and Collective Goods: How Sunbelt Cities Respond to Austerity." In *Research in Urban Policy,* vol. 2, edited by Terry N. Clark, 3–24. Greenwich, Conn.: JAI.

Asefa, Sisay, and Wei-Chiao Huang (eds.). 1994. *Human Capital and Economic Development.* Kalamazoo, Mich.: W. E. Upjohn Institute for Employment Research.

Baarsma, William H. 1973. *A Study of Dissension and Conflict over Council-Manager Government in Tacoma, Washington and an Analysis of the Impact of That Dissension and Conflict on Governmental Decision-Making in Policy and Administrative Areas.* Unpublished doctoral dissertation, George Washington University.

Ballman, Barbara. 1991. "Norstar Combination Aimed at Boosting Syracuse Growth." *Capital District Business Review,* January 7: 11.

Barnekov, Timothy K., Robin Boyle, and Daniel Rich. 1989. *Privatism and Urban Policy in Britain and the United States.* London: Oxford University Press.

Barnes, William R., and Larry C. Ledebur. 1991. "Toward a New Political Economy of Metropolitan Regions." *Environment and Planning C: Government and Policy* 9: 127–41.

———. 1998. *The New Regional Economies: The U.S. Common Market and the Global Economy.* Thousand Oaks, Calif.: Sage.

Barrett, Katherine, and Richard Greene. 1991. "The New War between the States." *Financial World,* September 3: 34.

Bartik, Timothy J. 1991. *Who Benefits from State and Local Economic Development Policies?* Kalamazoo, Mich.: Upjohn Institute for Employment Research.

———. 1994. "What Should the Federal Government Be Doing about Urban Economic Development?" *Cityscapes* 1: 267–91.

Batten, David F. 1995. "Network Cities: Creative Urban Agglomerations for the 21st Century." *Urban Studies* 32(2): 313–27.

Beauregard, Robert A. 1995. "Theorizing the Global-Local Connection." In *World Cities in a World-System,* edited by Paul L. Knox and Peter J. Taylor, 232–48. Cambridge: Cambridge University Press.

Becker, Gary S. 1964. *Human Capital: A Theoretical and Empirical Analysis with Special Reference to Education.* Chicago: University of Chicago Press.

———. 1993. *Human Capital: A Theoretical and Empirical Analysis with Special Reference to Education,* 3rd ed. Chicago: University of Chicago Press.

Begg, Iain, and Anna Whyatt. 1994. "Economic Development in London: Institutional Conflict and Strategic Confusion." Paper presented to the Economic and Social Research Council London Seminar series, June.

Bender, Penny. 1992. "New York Business Community, Lawmakers Debate Ways to Keep, Bring Jobs." *States News Service,* August 6.

Bendick, Marc, and Mary Lou Egan. 1993. "Linking Business Development and Community Development in America's Inner Cities." *Journal of Planning Literature* 8(1): 3–19.

Benson, Andrew. 1995. "Cleveland Celebrates Its Bicentennial." *Cleveland Plain Dealer,* December 31: spec. sec. S.

Bingham, Richard D., Edward W. Hill, and Sammis B. White. 1990. *Financing Economic Development.* Newbury Park, Calif.: Sage.

Blair, John P., and Robert Premus. 1987. "Major Factors in Industrial Location: A Review." *Economic Development Quarterly* 1: 72–85.

Blakely, Edward J. 1989. *Planning Local Economic Development: Theory and Practice.* Newbury Park, Calif.: Sage.

Bluestone, Barry. 1995. "The Inequality Express." *American Prospect* 20 (Winter): 81–93.

Bluestone, Barry, and Bennett Harrison. 1982. *The Deindustrialization of America:*

Plant Closing, Community Abandonment, and the Dismantling of Basic Industry. New York: Basic Books.

Bowman, Ann O'M. 1987. *Tools and Targets: The Mechanics of City Economic Development.* Washington, D.C.: National League of Cities.

———. 1988. "Competition for Economic Development among Southeastern Cities." *Urban Affairs Quarterly* 23: 511–27.

Brintnall, Michael. 1989. "Future Directions for Federal Urban Policy." *Journal of Urban Affairs* 9(1): 1–19.

Bromley, Simon. 1996. "Feature Review." *New Political Economy* 1: 129–33.

Brunner, Ronald. 1994. "Myths and American Politics." *Policy Sciences* 27: 1–18.

Budd, Leslie. 1994. "The Growth of Global Strategic Alliances in Different Financial Centres." Paper presented to the ESRC London Seminar series, April.

Burns, Danny, Robin Hambleton, and Paul Hoggett. 1994. *The Politics of Decentralisation: Revitalising Local Democracy.* London: Macmillan.

Buss, Terry F., and Steven Redburn. 1983. *Mass Unemployment: Plant Closings and Community Mental Health.* Beverly Hills: Sage.

Cafazzo, Debbie, and Jim Szymanski. 1995a. "Restarting the Heart of the City." *News Tribune,* January 29: A1.

———. 1995b. "Waking Up Downtown: Investors Ask 'Who's in Charge Here?' The Answer: Everybody." *News Tribune,* January 29: A9.

Castells, Manuel. 1989. *The Informational City.* Oxford: Basil Blackwell.

Castells, Manuel, and Peter Hall. 1994. *Technopoles of the World: The Making of 21st Century Industrial Complexes.* New York: Routledge.

Castro, Hector. 1995. "Wapato Hills Neighbors Offer 6 Development Options for Coveted Acreage." *News Tribune,* March 9: B1.

"Charlotte's Virtual Community." 1996. *Governing* 10 (October): 53.

Christopherson, Susan. 1989. "Flexibility in the U.S. Service Economy and the Emerging Spatial Division of Labour." *Transactions of the Institute of British Geographers* 14: 131–43.

Cisneros, Henry G. 1993. *Interwoven Destinies: Cities and the Nation.* New York: W. W. Norton.

———. 1995. *Urban Entrepreneurialism and National Economic Growth.* Washington, D.C.: U.S. Department of Housing and Urban Development.

City of Syracuse. 1982. *Community Development Program: Proposed Annual Program.* Syracuse, N.Y.: Mayor's Office.

City of Tacoma. 1980. *Neighborhoods: A Glimpse at Tacoma's History.* Tacoma, Wash.: Department of Community Development.

———. 1993. *Economic Development Plan* (draft). Tacoma, Wash.: Planning and Development Services Department.

Clark, Terry N. (ed.). 1985. *Research in Urban Policy,* vol. 1. Greenwich, Conn.: JAI.

Clark, Terry N., and Lorna C. Ferguson. 1983. *City Money.* New York: Columbia University Press.

Clarke, Susan E. 1986. "Urban America, Inc.: A Corporatist Convergence of Power in American Cities?" In *Local Economies in Transition,* edited by Edward Bergman. Durham, N.C.: Duke University Press.

——— (ed.). 1989. *Urban Innovation and Autonomy: Political Implications of Policy Change.* Newbury Park, Calif.: Sage.

————. 1995. "Institutional Logics and Local Economic Development: A Comparative Analysis of Eight American Cities." *International Journal of Urban and Regional Research* 19: 513–33.

————. 1998. "Economic Development Roles in American Cities: A Contextual Analysis of Partnership Arrangements." In *Public-Private Partnerships in Local Economic Development,* edited by Norman Walzer. Westport, Conn.: Greenwood.

Clarke, Susan E., and Gary L. Gaile. 1989a. *Assessment of the Characteristics and Effectiveness of Market-Based Urban Economic Development Strategies.* Washington, D.C., U.S. Department of Commerce, Economic Development Administration.

————. 1989b. "Moving Towards Entrepreneurial Local Development Strategies: Opportunities and Barriers." *Policy Studies Journal* 17(3): 574–98.

————. 1992. "The Next Wave: Local Economic Development Strategies in the Post-Federal Era." *Economic Development Quarterly* 6: 189–98.

————. 1997. "Local Politics in a Global Era: Thinking Locally, Acting Globally." *Annals of the American Academy of Political and Social Science* 551: 27–42.

Clarke, Susan E., and Andrew Kirby. 1990. "In Search of the Corpse: The Mysterious Case of Local Politics." *Urban Affairs Quarterly* 25(3): 389–412.

Clarke, Susan E., and Michael J. Rich. 1985. "Making Money Work: The New Urban Policy Arena." In *Research in Urban Policy,* vol. 1, edited by Terry Nichols Clark. Greenwich, Conn.: JAI.

Clarke, Susan E., and Martin Saiz. 1995. "Economic Development and Infrastructure Policy." In *Politics in American States,* 6th ed., edited by Herbert Jacob and Virginia Gray. Washington, D.C.: Congressional Quarterly Press.

Clary, Mike. 1991. "America's Back Office." *Florida Trend* 34 (June): 24.

Clavel, Pierre, and Nancy Kleniewski. 1990. "Space for Progressive Local Policy: Examples from the United States and the United Kingdom." In *Beyond the City Limits: Urban Policy and Economic Restructuring in Comparative Perspective,* edited by John R. Logan and Todd Swanstrom, 199–234. Philadelphia: Temple University Press.

Clay, Phillip. 1988. *Transforming Cleveland's Future: Issues and Strategies for a Heartland City.* Cleveland, Ohio: Cleveland State University.

Clements, Barbara. 1995a. "Future Home of Up to 80 Jobs; $2.7 Million Auto Service to Boost Hilltop." *News Tribune,* April 27: A1.

————. 1995b. "$2.7 Million Auto Service Mall to Offer Jobs on Tacoma's Hilltop." *News Tribune,* April 27: B1.

Clough, Alexandra. 1995. "Legislators Wary of Group Touted as State's Job-Creator." *Palm Beach Post,* February 28: 1A.

Cloward, Richard A., and Frances Fox Piven. 1998. "Poor People and Power: Lessons from the Industrial Age." In *Reflections on Community Organizing,* edited by Jack Rothman and John Turner. New York: Peacock.

Coburn, Karen Ann. 1997. "The Joys of Sisterhood." *Governing* 10(March): 32–34.

Cochrane, Allan. 1993. *Whatever Happened to Local Government?* Buckingham: Open University Press.

Cohen, Stephen S., and John Zysman. 1987. *Manufacturing Matters: The Myth of the Post-Industrial Economy.* New York: Basic Books.

Coletti, Richard J. 1994. "Regional Outlook—Northeast: Recovery Brings the Bite, Jaguars Bring the Roar." *Florida Trend* 36(April): 89.

Committee for Economic Development. 1986. *Leadership for Dynamic State Economies*. New York: Committee for Economic Development.

Conroy, Thomas F. 1992. *Markets of the U.S. for Business Planners*. Detroit, Mich.: Omnigraphics.

Cook, R. 1997. "Cities: Decidedly Democratic, Declining in Population." *Congressional Quarterly*, July 12: 1645–52.

Cooke, Philip. 1989. *Localities*. London: Unwin Hyman.

Cordeau, David. 1996. "International Trade Councils." *CNY Business Journal*, April 29: 11.

Cox, Andrew. 1988. "Neo-Corporatism Versus the Corporate State." In *The Corporate State*, edited by Andrew Cox and Neal O'Sullivan, 27–47. Cambridge: Edward Elgar.

Cox, Andrew, and Neal O'Sullivan (eds.). 1988. *The Corporate State*. Cambridge: Edward Elgar.

Cox, Kevin. 1997. "Governance, Urban Regime Analysis, and the Politics of Local Economic Development." In *Reconstructing Urban Regime Theory: Regulating Urban Politics in a Global Economy*, edited by Mickey Lauria, 99–121. Thousand Oaks, Calif.: Sage.

Crockett, Richard W. 1974. *Institutionalized Political Conflict: The Tacoma City Council Recall Election of 1970*. Unpublished doctoral dissertation, University of Washington.

Crouch, Colin, and Ronald Dore. 1990. *Corporatism and Accountability*. Oxford: Clarendon.

Crownover, Catherine. 1991a. "Ronnie Ferguson: Deputy Mayor Targets Business." *Jacksonville Business Journal*, October 18: 8.

———. 1991b. "Thomas Klechak: Sinking His Teeth into Downtown." *Jacksonville Business Journal*, November 29: 8.

———. 1991c. "The Magnificent Seven Are Key to Future Economic Development." *Jacksonville Business Journal*, December 6: 8.

Cunningham, William C., and Todd H. Taylor. 1985. *Private Security and Police in America*. Portland, Ore.: Chancellor.

Danielson, Michael S., and Paul G. Lewis. 1996. "City Bound: Political Science and the American Metropolis." *Political Research Quarterly* 49: 203–20.

Danzinger, Sheldon H., Gary D. Sandefur, and Daniel H. Weinberg (eds.). 1994. *Confronting Poverty: Prescriptions for Change*. Cambridge: Harvard University Press.

Davis, Mike. 1992. *Cities of Quartz: Excavating the Future in Los Angeles*. New York: Vintage.

"The Death of Distance." 1995. *Economist*, September 30.

Debo, David. 1996. "Region's Trade Gates Open Wide." *Business First—Buffalo* 12(May 3): 1.

DeLeon, Richard E. 1992. *Left Coast City: Progressive Politics in San Francisco*. Lawrence: University Press of Kansas.

de Neufville, Judith I., and Stephen E. Barton. 1987. "Myths and the Definition of Policy Problems." *Policy Sciences* 20: 181–206.

DeParle, J. 1993. "How Jack Kemp Lost the War on Poverty." *New York Times Magazine*, February 28.

Dertouzos, Michael, Richard K. Lester, and Robert Solow. 1989. *Made in America: Regaining the Competitive Edge*. Cambridge: MIT Press.

DeSimone, Jim. 1995. "Stephen Buttress, Glad to Leave Florida Behind." *Orlando Sentinel*, November 19: 4.

Diaz, Kevin. 1997. "Minneapolis Aims for Compromise on Living-Wage Rule." *Minneapolis Star-Tribune*, March 5: B1.

Dicken, Peter. 1994. "Global-Local Tensions: Firms and States in the Global Space Economy." *Economic Geography* 70(2): 101–28.

Dietz, Mary. 1987. "Context Is All: Feminism and Theories of Citizenship." In *Learning about Women: Gender Politics and Power*, edited by J. Conway, S. Bourque, and J. Scott, 1–24. Ann Arbor: University of Michigan Press.

DiMaggio, Paul J., and Walter W. Powell. 1991. "Introduction." In *The New Institutionalism in Organizational Analysis*, edited by Walter W. Powell and Paul J. DiMaggio, 1–38. Chicago: University of Chicago Press.

Downtown Committee. 1996. "$425 Million Invested in Downtown in 10 Years." *Downtown*, November: 1: 8.

Dreyfus, Claudia. 1995. "Present Shock." *New York Times Magazine*, June 11: 46–50.

Drier, Peter. 1995. "Putting Cities on the National Agenda." *Urban Affairs Review* 30: 645–56.

Drier, Peter, and Dennis W. Keating. 1990. "The Limits of Localism: Progressive Housing Policies in Boston, 1984–1989." *Urban Affairs Quarterly* 26: 191–216.

Drucker, Peter F. 1994. "The Age of Social Transformation." *Atlantic Monthly*, November: 53–80.

Dubnick, Melvin J., and Barbara A. Bardes. 1983. *Thinking about Public Policy*. New York: Wiley.

Dunning, J. H. 1993. *Multinational Enterprises and the Global Economy*. Reading, Mass.: Addison-Wesley.

Economics Research Associates (ERA). 1985. *K/J Street Market Analysis*. Tacoma, Wash.: Department of Community Development.

Edsall, Thomas. "What Clinton Won." *New York Review of Books*, December 3: 43.

Eisinger, Peter K. 1988. *The Rise of the Entrepreneurial State: State and Local Economic Development Policy in the United States*. Madison: University of Wisconsin Press.

Elkin, Stephen L. 1980. "Cities without Power: The Transformation of American Urban Regimes." In *National Resources and Urban Policy*, edited by Douglas Ashford, 265–93. New York: Methuen.

———. 1985. "Twentieth Century Urban Regimes." *Journal of Urban Affairs* 7(2): 11–28.

Elkins, David. 1995. "Testing Competing Explanations for the Adoption of Type II Policies." *Urban Affairs Review* 30(6): 809–39.

Ettlinger, Nancy. 1994. "The Localization of Development in Comparative Perspective." *Economic Geography* 70(2): 144–66.

Fagan, Robert H., and Michael Webber. 1994. *Global Restructuring: The Australian Experience*. Melbourne: Oxford University Press.

Fainstein, Norman I., and Susan S. Fainstein. 1983. "Regime Strategies, Communal Resistance, and Economic Forces." In *Restructuring the City*, edited by Susan S. Fainstein et al. 245–82. New York: Longman.

———. 1989. "The Ambivalent State: Economic Development Policy in the U.S. Federal System under the Reagan Administration." *Urban Affairs Quarterly* 25: 41–62.

Fainstein, Susan S., Ian Gordon, and Michael Harloe (eds.). 1992. *Divided Cities: New York and London in the Contemporary World*. Cambridge: Basil Blackwell.

Fainstein, Susan S., and Norman Fainstein. 1995. "A Proposal for Urban Policy in the 1990s." *Urban Affairs Review* 30: 630–34.

Ferman, Barbara. 1996. *Challenging the Growth Machine*. Lawrence: University Press of Kansas.

Fitting, Beth. 1996. "Economic Development: Utilities Get in the Act." *CNY Business Journal*, March 4: 1.

Fosler, R. Scott (ed.). 1988a. *The New Economic Role of American States*. New York: Oxford University Press.

———. 1988b. "The New Economic Role of American States." In *The New Economic Role of American States*, edited by R. Scott Fosler, 311–29. New York: Oxford University Press.

———. 1991. "Human Capital Investment and Federalism." In *Human Capital and America's Future: An Economic Strategy for the '90s*, edited by David W. Hornbeck and Lester M. Salamon. Baltimore: Johns Hopkins University Press.

Frieden, Bernard J., and Lynn B. Sagalyn. 1989. *Downtown, Inc*. Cambridge: MIT Press.

Friedland, Roger, Frances Fox Piven, and Robert R. Alford. 1978. "Political Conflict, Urban Structure, and the Fiscal Crisis." In *Comparing Public Policies*, edited by Douglas Ashford, 197–25. Beverly Hills: Sage.

Friedland, Roger, and Robert Alford. 1991. "Bringing Society Back In: Symbols, Practices and Institutional Contradictions." In *The New Institutionalism in Organizational Analysis*, edited by Walter W. Powell and Paul J. DiMaggio, 232–63. Chicago: University of Chicago Press.

Friedmann, John. 1992. *Empowerment: The Politics of Alternative Development*. Cambridge: Basil Blackwell.

———. 1995a. "Where We Stand: A Decade of World City Research." In *World Cities in a World-System*, edited by Paul L. Knox and Peter J. Taylor, 21–47. Cambridge: Cambridge University Press.

———. 1995b. "The World City Hypothesis." In *World Cities in a World-System*, edited by Paul L. Knox and Peter J. Taylor, 317–31. Cambridge: Cambridge University Press.

Friedmann, John, and Goetz Wolff. 1982. "World City Formation: An Agenda for Research and Action." *International Journal of Urban and Regional Research* 6: 309–44.

Fuchs, G., and A. M. Cox. 1991. "Corporatism and 'Political Context' in the Federal Republic of Germany." *Government and Policy* 9: 1–14.

Fysh, Graham. 1994. "Group Works to Foster Harmony on Community's Future." *News Tribune*, November 10: B12.

———. 1995. "Study Group: Lower Taxes Will Boost City." *News Tribune*, June 30: C1.

Gaile, Gary L. 1988. "Kenya's Rural Trade and Production Centers." Development Discussion Paper No. 263. Cambridge: Harvard Institute for International Development.

Gaile, Gary L., and Dean M. Hanink. 1985. "Relative Stability in American Metropolitan Growth." *Geographical Analysis* 17(4): 341–48.

Gaile, Gary L., and Cort J. Willmott (eds.). 1984. *Spatial Statistics and Models*. Dordrecht, Netherlands: D. Reidel.

Gallagher, Jay. 1991. "Retail Use of IDA Subsidies Questioned." *Gannett News Service*, October 21.

Galster, George (ed.). 1996. *Reality and Research: Social Science and U.S. Urban Policy since 1960*. Washington, D.C.: Urban Institute Press.

Garreau, Joel. 1991. *Edge City: Life on the New Frontier*. New York: Doubleday.

Geahigan, Priscilla C. 1994. *American Business Climate and Economic Profiles*. Detroit, Mich.: Gale Research.

Glazer, Nathan. 1993. "A Human Capital Policy for the Cities." *Public Interest* (Summer): 27–49.

Gleisser, Marcus. 1996. "Mayor White Hails Jobs, Development throughout City," *Cleveland Plain Dealer*, May 10: 1C.

Goetz, Edward. 1990. "Type II Policy and Mandated Benefits in Economic Development." *Urban Affairs Quarterly* 26: 170–90.

———. 1993. *Shelter Burden*. Philadelphia: Temple University Press.

———. 1994. "Expanding Possibilities in Local Development Policy: An Examination of U.S. Cities." *Political Research Quarterly* 47: 85–109.

Goetz, Edward, and Susan E. Clarke (eds.). 1993. *The New Localism: Comparative Urban Politics in a Global Era*. Newbury Park, Calif.: Sage.

Goetz, Edward, and Michael J. Rich. 1983. "Coordinating Urban Economic Development: Assessing the Neighborhood Business Revitalization Program." Center for Urban Affairs and Policy Research Working Paper 83–20. Evanston, Ill.: Northwestern University.

Goldsmith, Michael. 1990. "Local Autonomy: Theory and Practice." In *Challenges to Local Government*, edited by Desmond S. King and Jon Pierre. London: Sage.

Gore, Al. 1990. "Communications Networking the Future: We Need a National 'Superhighway' for Computer Information." *Washington Post*, July 15: B3.

Gottdiener, Mark. 1988. "The Paradigm Shift in Urban Sociology." *Urban Affairs Quarterly* 24(2): 163–87.

Graham, Stephen, and Simon Marvin. 1996. *Telecommunications and the City: Electronic Spaces, Urban Places*. New York: Routledge.

Green, Roy (ed.). 1991. *Enterprise Zones: New Directions in Economic Development*. Newbury Park, Calif.: Sage.

Griffith, Daniel. 1987. *Spatial Autocorrelation: A Primer*. Washington, D.C.: Association of American Geographers.

Grossman, Naomi. 1994. "GATT Seen Bringing Opportunities, Challenges to Central NY Business." *CNY Business Journal*, December 26: sec. 1, 1.

Gurr, Ted R., and Desmond S. King. 1987. *The State and the City*. Chicago: University of Chicago Press.

Haar, Charles. 1975. *Between the Idea and the Reality: A Study in the Origin, Fate, and Legacy of the Model Cities Program*. Boston: Little, Brown.

Hadley, Mark. 1996. "CNY Nurtures Info-Tech Growth." *Central New York Business Journal*, May 13: 1.

Hall, Peter, and Ann Markusen (eds.). 1985. *Silicon Landscapes*. Winchester, Mass.: Allen & Unwin.

Hambleton, Robin. 1994. "Lessons from America." *Planning Week*, June 16, 16–17.

Hansen, Susan. 1989. "Industrial Policy and Corporatism in the American States." *Governance* 2: 172–97.

Hanson, Russell. 1993. "Bidding for Business: A Second War between the States?" *Economic Development Quarterly* 7: 183–98.

Hanson, Russell, and Michael B. Berkman. 1991. "Gauging the Rainmakers: Toward a Meteorology of State Legislative Climates." *Economic Development Quarterly* 5: 213–28.

Harding, Alan. 1994. "Urban Regimes and Growth Machines: Towards a Cross-National Research Agenda." *Urban Affairs Quarterly* 29: 356–82.

Hardley, Mark. 1995. "Luring New Companies to Central New York Takes Teamwork, Utility Says." *Central New York Business Journal*, January 9: 6.

———. 1996. "CNY Nurtures Info-Tech Growth." *Central New York Business Journal*, May 13: 1.

Harrington, J. W., and Barney Warf. 1995. *Industrial Location: Principles, Practice, and Policy*. New York: Routledge.

Harris, Chauncy. 1943. "A Functional Classification of Cities in the United States." *Geographical Review* 33: 86–99.

———. 1954. "The Market as a Factor in the Localization of Industry in the United States." *Annals of the Association of American Geographers* 44: 315–31, 341–48.

Harrison, Bennett, Maryellen R. Kelley, and Jon Gant. 1996. "Specialization versus Diversity in Local Economies: The Implications for Innovative Private-Sector Behavior." *Cityscape* 2: 61–93.

Harvey, David. 1989. "From Managerialism to Entrepreneurialism: The Transformation in Urban Governance in Late Capitalism." *Geografiska Annaler* 71B: 3–17.

Heclo, Hugh. 1994. "Poverty Politics." In *Confronting Poverty: Prescriptions for Change*, edited by Sheldon H. Danziger, Gary D. Sandefur, and Daniel H. Weinberg. Cambridge: Harvard University Press.

Henderson, Jeffrey, and Manuel Castells (eds.). 1987. *Global Restructuring and Territorial Development*. London: Sage.

Henderson, Rex. 1995. "Floridians' Incomes Barely Keep Up." *Tampa Tribune*, April 28: A1.

Hessel, Arthur R. 1988. "Special Report: Communities Expand UDAG Aid with Creative Repayment Use, Study Finds." *Housing and Development Reporter*, January 25: 659–61.

Hollingsworth, J. R., and E. J. Hollingsworth. 1972. "Expenditures in American Cities." In *The Dimensions of Quantitative Research in History*, edited by W. O. Aydelotte, A. C. Bogue, and R. W. Fogel. Princeton, N.J.: Princeton University Press.

Horak, Kathy. 1992a. "Computer Power: Nero's Hard Sell." *Jacksonville Business Journal*, September 18: 5.

———. 1992b. "AHL Decides to Join Others in the Suburbs." *Jacksonville Business Journal*, November 13: 1.

———. 1994. "Duval Leads in Securing State Road Money." *Jacksonville Business Journal*, October 28: 2.

Horan, Cynthia. 1991. "Beyond Governing Coalitions: Analyzing Urban Regimes in the 1990s." *Journal of Urban Affairs* 13: 119–35.

———. 1997. "Coalition, Market, and State: Postwar Development Politics in

Boston." In *Reconstructing Urban Regime Theory: Regulating Urban Politics in a Global Economy*, edited by Mickey Lauria, 149–70. Thousand Oaks, Calif.: Sage.

Hornbeck, David W., and Lester M. Salamon (eds.). 1991. *Human Capital and America's Future: An Economic Strategy for the '90s*. Baltimore: Johns Hopkins University Press.

Hudson, Ray. 1994. "Institutional Change, Cultural Transformation, and Economic Regeneration: Myths and Realities from Europe's Old Industrial Areas." In *Globalization, Institutions, and Regional Development in Europe*, edited by Ash Amin and Nigel Thrift, 196–216. Oxford: Oxford University Press.

Hughes, David W., and David W. Holland. 1994. "Core-Periphery Economic Linkage: A Measure of Spread and Possible Backwash Effects for the Washington Economy; Washington State." *Land Economics* 70: 364–81.

Hughes, Kyle. 1992. "Enterprise Zones No Miracle Cure." *Gannett News Service*, May 21.

Hwang, Sung-Don, and Virginia Gray. 1991. "External Limits and Internal Determinants of State Public Policy." *Western Political Quarterly* 44: 277–98.

International City Management Association. Various years. *The Municipal Yearbook*. Washington, D.C.: International City Management Association.

Jacksonville Community Council Inc. (JCCI). 1993. *Planning for Northeast Florida's Uncertain Military Future*. Jacksonville, Fla.: Jacksonville Community Council Inc.

———. 1995a. *People Working Together for a Better Jacksonville: 1994–95 Annual Report*. Jacksonville, Fla.: Jacksonville Community Council Inc.

———. 1995b. *JAXPORT: Improvement and Expansion*. Jacksonville, Fla.: Jacksonville Community Council Inc.

———. 1996. *Leadership: Meeting Community Needs*. Jacksonville, Fla.: Jacksonville Community Council Inc.

Jacobs, Jane. 1961. *The Death and Life of Great American Cities*. New York: Random House.

———. 1967. *The Economy of Cities*. New York: Random House.

———. 1984. *Cities and the Wealth of Nations*. New York: Random House.

Jaetzhold, B., and H. Schmidt, 1982. *Farm Management Handbook of Kenya*, vol. 2, *Natural Conditions and Farm Management Information*. Nairobi: Ministry of Agriculture, Government of Kenya.

Jaffe, Adam. 1989. "Universities and Regional Patterns of Commercial Innovation." *REI Review* (Case Western University), September.

Jessop, Bob. 1993. "Towards a Schumpeterian Workfare State? Preliminary Remarks on Post-Fordist Political Economy." *Studies in Political Economy* 40: 7–39.

———. 1997. "A Neo-Gramscian Approach to the Regulation of Urban Regimes: Accumulation Strategies, Hegemonic Projects, and Governance." In *Reconstructing Urban Regime Theory: Regulating Urban Politics in a Global Economy*, edited by Mickey Lauria, 51–73. Thousand Oaks, Calif.: Sage.

Jezierski, Louise. 1990. "Neighborhoods and Public-Private Partnerships." *Urban Affairs Quarterly* 26: 217–49.

Johnson, Anne M. 1995. "The Power of Diversity: The Region's Balanced Economy Is Expanding as Pro Sports and Urban Renewal Play Larger Roles." *Florida Trend*, April 37: 120 ff.

Johnson, James H., Jr., Warren C. Farrell Jr., and Maria-Rosario Jackson. 1994. "Los

Angeles One Year Later: A Prospective Assessment of Responses to the 1992 Civil Unrest." *Economic Development Quarterly* 8(1): 19–27.

Jones, Bryan. 1994. *Reconceiving Decision-Making in Democratic Politics.* Chicago: University of Chicago Press.

Jones, Bryan, and Lynn Bachelor. 1986. *The Sustaining Hand.* Lawrence: University Press of Kansas.

Jones, Robin R. 1994. "Civic Capacity and Urban Education: Pittsburgh." Paper presented at the annual meeting of the Urban Affairs Association, New Orleans, March 3–5.

Judd, Dennis, and Randy L. Ready. 1986. "Entrepreneurial Cities and the New Policies of Economic Development." In *Reagan and the Cities,* edited by George Peterson and Carole Lewis. Washington, D.C.: Urban Institute.

Juffras, Jason, and Isabel V. Sawhill. 1991. "Financing Human Capital Investment." In *Human Capital and America's Future: An Economic Strategy for the '90s,* edited by David W. Hornbeck and Lester M. Salamon. Baltimore: Johns Hopkins University Press.

Kanter, Rosabeth Moss. 1995. *World Class.* New York, Simon & Schuster.

Kantor, Paul. 1995. *The Dependent City Revisited: The Political Economy of Urban Development and Social Policy.* Boulder, Colo.: Westview.

Kantor, Paul, with Stephen David. 1988. *The Dependent City.* Glenview, Ill.: Scott, Foresman.

Kantor, Paul, and H. V. Savitch. 1993. "Can Politicians Bargain with Business?" *Urban Affairs Quarterly* 29: 230–55.

Kaplan, Marshall. 1995. "Urban Policy: An Uneven Past, an Uncertain Future." *Urban Affairs Review* 30: 662–80.

Katz, Jeffrey L. 1996. "Education Programs Get Big Boost in Spending." *Congressional Quarterly,* October 5, 2867–69.

Kaus, Mickey. 1992. *The End of Equality.* New York: New Republic Books.

Keating, Dennis. 1996. *Revitalizing Urban Neighborhoods.* Lawrence: University Press of Kansas.

Keating, Dennis, Norman Krumholz, and John Metzger. 1989. "Cleveland: Post-Populist Public-Private Partnerships." In *Unequal Partnerships: The Political Economy of Urban Redevelopment in Postwar America,* edited by Gregory Squires. New Brunswick, N.J.: Rutgers University Press.

Kerstein, Robert. 1995. "Political Exceptionalism in Sunbelt Cities." *Journal of Urban Affairs* 17(2): 143–63.

King, Desmond S. 1990. "Economic Activity and the Challenge to Local Government." In *Challenges to Local Government,* edited by Desmond S. King and Jon Pierre. London: Sage.

———. 1995. *Actively Seeking Work?* Chicago: University of Chicago Press.

King, Desmond S., and J. Waldron. 1988. "Citizenship, Social Citizenship, and the Defence of Welfare Provision." *British Journal of Political Science* 18: 415–43.

Kipp Associates. 1985. *Tacoma Rediviva: Tacoma's Downtown Rehabilitated Buildings.* Tacoma, Wash.: Department of Community Development.

Knox, Paul L. (ed.). 1993. *The Restless Urban Landscape.* Englewood Cliffs, N.J.: Prentice Hall.

———. 1995. "World Cities in a World-System." In *World Cities in a World-System,* edited by Paul L. Knox and Peter J. Taylor. New York: Cambridge University Press.

———. 1996. "Globalization and Urban Change." *Urban Geography* 17: 115–17.

Knox, Paul L., and Peter J. Taylor (eds.). 1995. *World Cities in a World-System.* New York: Cambridge University Press.

Kotlowvitz, Alex. 1991. *There Are No Children Here.* New York: Anchor.

Kozol, Jonathan. 1991. *Savage Inequalities: Children in America's Schools.* New York: Crown.

Kresl, Peter Karl, and Gary Gappert. 1995. *North American Cities and the Global Economy: Challenges and Opportunities.* Thousand Oaks, Calif.: Sage.

Kretzmann, John P., and John L. McKnight. 1993. *Building Communities from the Inside Out: A Path toward Finding and Mobilizing a Community's Assets.* Chicago: ACTA.

Krugman, Paul. 1995. *Geography and Trade.* Cambridge: MIT Press.

Krumholz, Norman. 1982. "A Retrospective View of Equity Planning: Cleveland, 1969–1979." *Journal of the American Planning Association* 52: 133–41.

Kuttner, Robert. 1997. *Everything for Sale: The Virtues and Limits of Markets.* New York: Knopf.

Ladd, Helen. 1994. "Spatially Targeted Economic Development Strategies: Do They Work?" *Cityscapes* 1: 193–218.

Ladd, Helen, and John Yinger. 1986. *America's Ailing Cities: Fiscal Health and the Design of Urban Policy.* Baltimore: Johns Hopkins University Press.

Lasswell, Harold D. 1965. "The World Revolution of Our Time: A Framework for Basic Policy Research." In *World Revolutionary Elites,* edited by Harold D. Lasswell and Daniel Lerner. Cambridge: MIT Press.

Lauria, Mickey (ed.). 1997. *Reconstructing Urban Regime Theory: Regulating Urban Politics in a Global Economy.* Thousand Oaks, Calif.: Sage.

Lehnen, Robert G., and Eugene M. McGregor Jr. 1994. "Human Capital Report Card for American States." *Policy Sciences* 27: 19–35.

Leicht, Kevin T., and J. Craig Jenkins. 1994. "Three Strategies of State Economic Development: Entrepreneurial, Industrial Recruitment, and Deregulation Policies in the American States." *Economic Development Quarterly* 8: 256–69.

Leitner, Helga. 1990. "Cities in Pursuit of Economic Growth: The Local State as Entrepreneur." *Political Geography Quarterly* 9: 146–70.

Lemann, Nicholas. 1994. "The Myth of Community Development." *New York Times Magazine,* January 9: 26–33.

Leslie, Stuart W. 1990. "From Backwater to Powerhouse: Stanford Engineering and Silicon Valley." *Stanford,* March.

Levin, Al. 1996. "Lakefront Development Will Finally Take Off, Spurred by Thruway Money." *Syracuse Business,* May: 1.

Levine, Marc. 1995. "Globalization and Wage Polarization in U.S. and Canadian Cities: Does Public Policy Make a Difference?" In *North American Cities and the Global Economy,* edited by P. K. Kresl and G. Gappert. Thousand Oaks, Calif.: Sage.

Lindblom, Charles E. 1977. *Politics and Markets.* New York: Basic Books.

"Local Economic Developers Pursue Canadian Plastic Industry Based on NY's Tax Advantage." 1992. *Syracuse Business,* August: 1.

Logan, John R., and Harvey L. Molotch. 1987. *Urban Fortunes: The Political Economy of Place.* Berkeley: University of California Press.

Logan, John R., and Todd Swanstrom (eds.). 1990. *Beyond the City Limits: Urban Policy and Economic Restructuring in Comparative Perspective.* Philadelphia: Temple University Press.

"Long Term Shifts Will Burden Cities." 1996. *Nation's Cities Weekly,* March 25.

Longman, Phillip. 1991. "Amid Good News, Some Ominous Trends." *Florida Trend* 33 (12): 89–93.

Lowery, David, and Virginia Gray. 1990. "The Corporatist Foundations of State Industrial Policy." *Social Science Quarterly* 71: 3–23.

Lugar, Michael I. 1985. "Explaining Differences in the Use and Effectiveness of State Industrial Policies." Working Paper, Institute of Policy Sciences and Public Affairs, Duke University, January.

Lynn, Laurence E. 1994. "Social Structures as Economic Growth Tools." *Cityscapes* 1: 245–65.

Marshall, Ray, and Marc Tucker. 1992. *Thinking for a Living.* New York: Basic Books.

Martin, Roscoe C., Frank J. Munger, et al. 1961. *Decisions in Syracuse.* Bloomington: Indiana University Press.

Massey, Douglas S., and Nancy A. Denton. 1993. *American Apartheid: Segregation and the Making of the Underclass.* Cambridge: Harvard University Press.

Mayer, Margit. 1994. "Post-Fordist City Politics." In *Post-Fordism: A Reader,* edited by Ash Amin, 316–37. Oxford: Basil Blackwell.

———. 1995. "Urban Governance in the Post-Fordist City." In *Managing Cities: The New Urban Context,* edited by Patsy Healy et al., 231–49. Oxford: Basil Blackwell.

McGregor, Eugene M., Jr. 1994. "Economic Development and Public Education: Strategies and Standards." *Educational Policy* 8(3): 252–71.

McLennan, Douglas. 1993. "It's Show Time Downtown." *News Tribune,* December 5: A1 ff.

McLuhan, Marshall, and Bruce R. Powers. 1989. *The Global Village.* New York: Oxford University Press.

Metropolitan Development Association, Downtown Committee. 1996. "$425 Million Invested in Downtown in 10 Years." *Downtown* (newsletter), November.

Mincy, Ronald B. (ed.). 1994a. *Nurturing Young Black Males: Challenges to Agencies, Programs and Social Policy.* Washington, D.C.: Urban Institute.

———. 1994b. "The Underclass: Concept, Controversy and Evidence." In *Confronting Poverty: Prescriptions for Change,* edited by Sheldon H. Danziger, Gary D. Sandefur, and Daniel H. Weinberg, 109–46. Cambridge: Harvard University Press.

Miranda, Rowan, and Donald Rosdil. 1995. "From Boosterism to Qualitative Growth: Classifying Economic Development Strategies." *Urban Affairs Review* 30(6): 868–79.

Miron, John. 1984. "Spatial Autocorrelation." In *Spatial Statistics and Models,* edited by Gary L. Gaile and Cort J. Willmott. Dordrecht, Netherlands: D. Reidel.

Mollenkopf, John H., and Manuel Castells (eds.). 1991. *Dual City: Restructuring New York.* New York: Russell Sage Foundation.

Molotch, Harvey. 1976. "The City as a Growth Machine: Toward a Political Economy of Place." *American Journal of Sociology* 82: 309–30.

Moore, Barrington. 1972. *Reflections on the Causes of Human Misery and upon Certain Proposals to Eliminate Them*. Boston: Beacon.

Morrill, Richard L. 1965. "The Negro Ghetto: Problems and Alternatives." *Geographical Review* 55: 335–61.

Morrill, Richard L., Gary L. Gaile, and Grant I. Thrall. 1988. *Spatial Diffusion*. Newbury Park, Calif.: Sage.

Mouffe, Chantal. 1992a. "Preface: Democratic Politics Today." In *Dimensions of Radical Democracy*, edited by Chantal Mouffe, 1–14. London: Verso.

———. 1992b. "Democratic Citizenship and the Political Community." In *Dimensions of Radical Democracy*, edited by Chantal Mouffe, 225–39. London: Verso.

Mumphrey, Anthony, and Krishna Akundi. 1995. "Intrametropolitan Location of Industry: A Study of Eight MSAs, 1967–1992." Paper presented at the annual meeting of the Urban Affairs Association, Portland, Ore., May.

Naisbitt, John. 1994. *Global Paradox*. New York: Morrow.

Nathan, Richard P. 1992. "Needed: A Marshall Plan for Ourselves." *Economic Development Quarterly* 6: 347–55.

Navarro, Mireya. 1995. "Jacksonville Journal: Panting for Football and Standing Tall." *New York Times*, August 22: A8.

Nelson, Howard. 1955. "A Service Classification of American Cities." *Economic Geography* 31: 189–210.

Neumann, Stephanie. n.d. "Telecommunication: The Experience of Other Cities." Unpublished manuscript, Littleton, Colo.

"New DED Commish Gargano Says Millions Have Been Wasted under the Name of Economic Development." *Syracuse Business* 10(1): 1–2.

Newton, P. 1991. "The New Urban Infrastructure: Telecommunications and the Urban Economy." *Urban Futures* 5: 54–75.

Norton, R. D. 1995. "Reader's Guide: How 3 Policy Waves Overlap Today." *Economic Development Horizon* 1: 1.

O'Brien, Richard. 1992. *Global Financial Integration: The End of Geography*. New York: Royal Institute for International Affairs, Council on Foreign Relations Press.

Odland, John, Reginald G. Golledge, and Peter A. Rogerson. 1989. "Mathematical and Statistical Analysis in Geography." In *Geography in America*, edited by Gary L. Gaile and Cort J. Willmott, 719–45. Columbus, Ohio: Merrill.

Okin, Susan Moller. 1992. *Justice, Gender, and the Family*. New York: Basic Books.

Olson, Mancur. 1965. *The Logic of Collective Action*. Cambridge: Harvard University Press.

Omerod, Paul. 1996. "National Competitiveness and State Intervention." *New Political Economy* 1: 119–28.

O'Regan, Fred, and Maureen Conway. 1993. *From the Bottom Up: Toward a Strategy for Income and Employment Generation among the Disadvantaged*. Washington, D.C.: Aspen Institute.

Organization for Economic Cooperation and Development (OECD). 1983. *Managing Urban Change: Policies and Finance*. Paris: OECD.

Orr, Marion. 1992. "Urban Regimes and Human Capital Policies: A Study of Baltimore." *Journal of Urban Affairs* 14: 173–87.

Ortega, Bob. 1991. "Old Theater's Glory Nearly Restored—Success Story for Tacoma." *Seattle Times*, September 26: C1.

Osborne, David. 1988. *Laboratories of Democracy*. Boston: Harvard Business School Press.

Osborne, David, and Ted Gaebler. 1992. *Reinventing Government: How the Entrepreneurial Spirit Is Transforming the Public Sector*. Reading, Mass.: Addison-Wesley.

Pagano, Michael A., and Ann O'M. Bowman. 1995. *Cityscapes and Capital: The Politics of Urban Development*. Baltimore: Johns Hopkins University Press.

Painter, Joe. 1995. "Regulation Theory, Post-Fordism and Urban Politics." In *Theories of Urban Politics*, edited by David Judge, Gerry Stoker, and Harold Wolman, 276–95. London: Sage.

Parker, John. 1995. "Turn Up the Lights." *Economist*, July 29: 1–17.

Peck, Jamie. 1996. *Work Place*. New York: Guilford.

Peck, Jamie, and Martin Jones. 1994. "Training and Enterprise Councils: Schumpeterian Workfare State, or What?" *Environment and Planning A* 27(9): 1361–96.

Peck, Jamie, and Adam Tickell. 1994. "Searching for a New Institutional Fix: The *After*-Fordist Crisis and the Global-Local Disorder." In *Post-Fordism: A Reader*, edited by Ash Amin, 280–315. Oxford: Basil Blackwell.

Perrow, Charles. 1984. *Normal Accidents: Living with High Risk Technologies*. New York: Basic Books.

Persky, Joseph, and Wim Wiewel. 1994. "The Growing Localness of the Global City." *Economic Geography* 70(2): 129–43.

Peterson, Paul E. 1981. *City Limits*. Chicago: University of Chicago Press.

———. 1995. *The Price of Federalism*. New York: Twentieth Century Fund.

Peterson, Paul E., and Mark C. Rom. 1990. *Welfare Magnets: A New Case for a National Standard*. Washington, D.C.: Brookings Institution.

Pierce, Neil R. 1995. "The Power of Empowerment Zones." *National Journal*, February 2: 315.

Pierce, Neil R., Curtis W. Johnson, and John Stuart Hall. 1993. *Citystates: How Urban America Can Prosper in a Competitive World*. Washington, D.C.: Seven Locks.

Piore, Michael, and Charles Sabel. 1984. *The Second Industrial Divide*. New York: Basic Books.

Piven, Francis Fox, and Richard A. Cloward. 1993. *Regulating the Poor: The Functions of Public Welfare* (rev. ed.). New York: Vintage.

Plaut, Thomas, and Joseph Pluta. 1983. "Business Climate Taxes and Expenditures, and State Industrial Growth in the United States." *Southern Economic Journal* 50: 99–119.

Pollard, Jane, and Michael Storper. 1996. "A Tale of Twelve Cities: Metropolitan Employment Change in the Dynamic Industries in the 1980s." *Economic Geography* 72(1): 1–22.

"The Poor and the Rich." 1996. *Economist*, May 25–31: 23–25.

Popham, Art. 1995. "Downtown Tacoma's Losing Its Loser Complex." *News Tribune*, January 29: G1.

Porter, Michael E. 1990. *The Competitive Advantage of Nations*. New York: Macmillan.

———. 1995. "The Competitive Advantage of the Inner City." *Harvard Business Review* 73(May–June): 55–71.

"Portrait of the Electorate." 1992. *New York Times*, November 5: 9.

Pred, Alan R. 1965. "The Concentration of High-Value-Added Manufacturing." *Economic Geography* 41: 110–25.

Preteceille, E. 1990. "Political Paradoxes of Urban Restructuring: Globalization of the Economy and Localization of Politics?" In *Beyond the City Limits: Urban Policy and Economic Restructuring in Comparative Perspective,* edited by John R. Logan and Todd Swanstrom, 27–59. Philadelphia: Temple University Press.

Putnam, Robert D. 1993. *Making Democracy Work.* Princeton, N.J.: Princeton University Press.

———. 1995. "Bowling Alone: America's Declining Social Capital." *Journal of Democracy* 6(1): 65–78.

———. 1996. "The Strange Disappearance of Civic America." *American Prospect* 24 (Winter): 34–48.

Reese, Gary F. 1973. "Centennial Sagas." Unpublished manuscript, Tacoma City-County Public Library.

Reich, Robert. 1983. *The Next American Frontier.* New York: Times Books.

———. 1991. *The Work of Nations: Preparing Ourselves for 21st Century Capitalism.* New York: Knopf.

Rich, Michael J. 1993a. "Riot and Reason: Crafting an Urban Policy Response." *Publius* 23: 115–34.

———. 1993b. *Federal Policymaking and the Poor: National Goals, Local Choices, and Distributional Outcomes.* Princeton, N.J.: Princeton University Press.

———. 1995. "Empower the People: An Assessment of Community-Based, Collaborative, Persistent Poverty Initiatives." Paper presented at the annual meeting of the Midwest Political Science Association.

Rivlin, Alice M. 1995. *Performance Partnerships: Summary and Guiding Principles.* Memorandum: U.S. Executive Office of the President, Office of Management and Budget, March 28, 1995.

Roberts, Susan M., and Richard H. Schein. 1993. "The Entrepreneurial City: Fabricating Urban Development in Syracuse." *Professional Geographer* 45: 21–33.

Roe, Emery. 1994. *Narrative Policy Analysis.* Durham, N.C.: Duke University Press.

Rogers, Everett M. 1983. *Diffusion of Innovations* (3d ed.). New York: Free Press.

Rubin, Herbert J. 1988. "Shoot Anything That Flies; Claim Anything That Falls: Conversations with Economic Development Practitioners." *Economic Development Quarterly* 2: 236–51.

Rubin, Irene, and Herbert Rubin. 1987. "Economic Development Incentives: The Poor (Cities) Pay More." *Urban Affairs Quarterly* 23: 37–62.

Rubin, Marilyn Marks. 1994. "Can Reorchestration of Historical Themes Reinvent Government? A Case Study of the Empowerment Zones and Enterprise Communities Act of 1993." *Public Administration Review* 54: 161–69.

Rushton, Bruce. 1994. "Land Plan Impact May Take 2 Years." *News Tribune,* December 13: B1.

Rusk, David. 1993. *Cities without Suburbs.* Washington, D.C.: Woodrow Wilson Center Press.

Sabel, Charles F. 1994. "Flexible Specialisation and the Re-emergence of Regional Economies." In *Post-Fordism: A Reader,* edited by Ash Amin, 101–56. Oxford: Basil Blackwell.

Saiz, Martin. 1991. *Determinants of Economic Development Policy Innovation among the U.S. States.* Unpublished doctoral dissertation, University of Colorado at Boulder.

Salamon, Lester. 1991. "Why Human Capital? Why Now?" In *Human Capital and America's Future: An Economic Strategy for the '90s,* edited by David W. Hornbeck and Lester M. Salamon, 1–39. Baltimore: Johns Hopkins University Press.

Sass, Steven A. 1990. "The U.S. Professional Sector: 1950 to 1988." *New England Economic Review* (January/February): 37–55.

Sassen, Saskia. 1991. *The Global City: New York, London, Tokyo.* Princeton, N.J.: Princeton University Press.

———. 1996. "Cities and Communities in the Global Economy: Rethinking Our Concepts." *American Behavioral Scientist* 39: 629–39.

Savitch, H. V. 1988. *Post-industrial Cities: Politics and Planning in New York, Paris and London.* Princeton, N.J.: Princeton University Press.

Savitch, H. V., David Collins, Daniel Sanders, and John P. Markham. 1993. "Ties That Bind: Central Cities, Suburbs, and the New Metropolitan Region." *Economic Development Quarterly* 7: 341–58

Savitch, H. V., and Ronald K. Vogel (eds.). 1996. *Regional Politics: America in a Post-city Age.* Thousand Oaks, Calif.: Sage.

Saxenian, AnnaLee. 1994. *Regional Advantage: Culture and Competition in Silicon Valley and Route 128.* Cambridge: Harvard University Press.

Sayer, A., and R. Walker. 1992. *The New Social Economy: Reworking the Division of Labor.* Oxford: Basil Blackwell.

Sbragia, Alberta. 1996. *Debt Wish.* Pittsburgh: University of Pittsburgh Press.

Scharpf, Fritz W. 1988. "The Joint-Decision Trap: Lessons from German Federalism and European Integration." *Public Administration* 66: 239–78.

Schneider, M., and P. Teske. 1992. "Toward a Theory of the Political Entrepreneur." *American Political Science Review* 86: 737–47.

Schnore, L. F. 1972. *Class and Race in Cities and Suburbs.* Chicago: Markham.

Schnorr, Alvin J. 1991. *Cleveland Development: A Dissenting View.* Cleveland, Ohio: David.

Schorr, Lisbeth B. 1993. "What Works: Applying What We Already Know about Successful Social Policy." *American Prospect* 13(Spring): 43–54.

Schuler, Douglas. 1996. *New Community Networks: Wired for Change.* New York: Addison-Wesley.

Schultz, Judith L. 1990. "CityWide OKs Assistance Plan for Center City." *Dayton Daily News,* May 1: 6B.

Schultz, T. Paul. (ed.). 1995. *Investment in Women's Human Capital.* Chicago: University of Chicago Press.

Schultz, Theodore W. 1971. *Investment in Human Capital: The Role of Education.* New York: Free Press.

Scism, Leslie. 1990. "Hotel to Rise, after 25 Years." *New York Times,* August 26: 35.

Scott, Alan J. 1988. *New Industrial Spaces: Flexible Production, Organization and Regional Development in North America and Western Europe.* London: Pion.

———. 1992. "The Roepke Lecture in Economic Geography: The Collective Order of Flexible Production Agglomerations: Lessons for Local Economic Development Policy and Strategic Choice." *Economic Geography* 68: 219–33.

Sen, Amartya. 1982. *Choice, Welfare, and Measurement.* Oxford: Basil Blackwell.

Shearer, D. 1989. "In Search of Equal Partnerships: Prospects for Progressive Urban Policy in the 1990s." In *Unequal Partnerships: The Political Economy of Urban*

Redevelopment in Postwar America, edited by Gregory Squires, 289–307. New Brunswick, N.J.: Rutgers University Press.

Shklar, Judith. 1991. *American Citizenship: The Quest for Inclusion*. Cambridge: Harvard University Press.

Shlay, Anne, and R. Giloth. 1987. "The Social Organization of a Land-Based Elite: The Case of the Failed Chicago 1992 World's Fair." *Journal of Urban Affairs* 9: 305–24.

Skocpol, Theda. 1992. *Protecting Soldiers and Mothers*. Cambridge: Harvard University Press.

———. 1996. "Unravelling from Above." *American Prospect* 25(March–April): 20–25.

Smith, Michael Peter. 1992. "Postmodernism, Urban Ethnography, and the New Social Space of Ethnic Identity." *Theory and Society* 21: 503–22.

———. 1995. "The Disappearance of World Cities and the Globalization of Local Politics." In *World Cities in a World-System*, edited by Paul L. Knox and Peter J. Taylor, 249–66. Cambridge: Cambridge University Press.

Social Science Research Council. 1992. *Urban Underclass Data Base*. New York: Social Science Research Council.

Staeheli, Lynn A. 1994. "Restructuring Citizenship in Pueblo, Colorado." *Environment and Planning A* 26: 849–71.

Staeheli, Lynn A., and Susan E. Clarke. 1995. "Gender, Place and Citizenship." In *Gender and Urban Research*, edited by Judith Garber and Robyne Turner, 3–23. Thousand Oaks, Calif.: Sage.

Stanfield, Rochelle L. 1993. "The Ward Healers." *National Journal*, June 5: 1344–48.

———. 1996. "Rising from the Ashes?" *National Journal*, June 8: 1244–48.

Steiner, Michael. 1985. "Old Industrial Areas: A Theoretical Approach." *Urban Studies* 22: 387–98.

Sternberg, Ernest. 1987. "A Practitioner's Classification of Economic Development Policy Instruments, with Some Inspiration from Political Economy." *Economic Development Quarterly* 1: 149–61.

Stewart, Mizell. 1990. "Business-Civic Group Takes Downtown's Reins." *Dayton Daily News*, December 19: 12C.

Stoffel, Jennifer. 1990. "City Offered Portside Mall." *New York Times*, January 28: 31.

Stoker, Gerry. 1995. "Regime Theory and Urban Politics." In *Theories of Urban Politics*, edited by David Judge, Gerry Stoker, and Harold Wolman, 54–71. London: Sage.

Stone, Clarence. 1980. "Systemic Power in Community Decision Making." *American Political Science Review* 74: 978–90.

———. 1989. *Regime Politics*. Lawrence: University Press of Kansas.

Stone, Clarence, et al. 1994. *Civic Capacity and Urban Education*. Washington, D.C.: National Science Foundation.

Storper, Michael, and Richard Walker. 1989. *The Capitalist Imperative: Territory, Technology, and Industrial Growth*. Oxford: Basil Blackwell.

Sudjik, Deyan. 1992. *The 100 Mile City*. London: Andre Deutsch.

Sui, Daniel Z., and James O. Wheeler. 1993. "The Location of Office Space in the Metropolitan Service Economy of the United States." *Professional Geographer* 45: 33–43.

Swanson, Bert. 1995. "Mayors, Patterns of Community Power, and Urban Reform: Consolidation in Jacksonville from 1949 to 1993." Unpublished manuscript.

————. 1996. "Consolidation and Regional Governance: The Emergence of a Growth Machine and Its Efforts and Impact to Build a Metropolity." In *Regional Politics: America in a Post-city Age*, edited by H. V. Savitch and Ronald K. Vogel. Thousand Oaks, Calif.: Sage.

Swanstrom, Todd. 1985. *The Crisis of Urban Politics*. Philadelphia: Temple University Press.

————. 1996. "Ideas Matter: Reflections on the New Regionalism." *Cityscape* 2: 5–21.

Szymanski, Jim. 1994. "I-5: The Cash Corridor." *News Tribune*, August 23: G1.

————. 1995. "Tax Breaks Give Baker the Dough for New Jobs." *News Tribune*, April 26: D1.

Tacoma-Pierce County Commission on Children, Youth, and Their Families. 1992. *Charting Our Children's Future: A 3-Year Strategic Plan for the Tacoma-Pierce County Community*. Tacoma, Wash.: Tacoma-Pierce County Commission on Children, Youth, and Their Families.

Theiss, Evelyn. 1996. "School Reform Hamstrung by Players' Political Naivete." *Cleveland Plain Dealer*, January 7: 1A.

Thelen, Kathleen, and Sven Steinmo. 1992. "Historical Institutionalism in Comparative Politics." In *Structuring Politics: Historical Institutionalism in Comparative Analysis*, edited by Sven Steinmo, Kathleen Thelen, and Frank Longstreth, 1–32. New York: Cambridge University Press.

Thomas, Jim. 1991. "NFL Expansion Becomes Serious Race." *St. Louis Post-Dispatch*, September 29: 1.

Thottam, Jyoti. 1994. "Chamber Going to Members to Up Ante for Cornerstone." *Jacksonville Business Journal*, July 29: 4.

Thuermer, Karen E. 1991. "A Sunny Disposition for Florida Ports." *Global Trade* 111: 10 ff.

Tiebout, Charles M. 1962. *The Community Economic Base Study*. Washington, D.C.: Committee for Economic Development.

Tobin, James. 1994. "Poverty in Relation to Macroeconomic Trends, Cycles and Policies." In *Confronting Poverty: Prescriptions for Change*, edited by Sheldon H. Danziger, Gary D. Sandefur, and Daniel H. Weinberg, 147–67. Cambridge: Harvard University Press.

Toffler, Alvin, and Heidi Toffler. 1995. *Creating a New Civilization: The Politics of the Third Wave*. Atlanta, Ga.: Turner.

Tolbert, Caroline Joan. 1995. *Direct Democracy and State Governance Policies: Dismantling the Administrative State*. Unpublished doctoral dissertation, University of Colorado.

"Tomorrow's Second Sex." 1996. *Economist*, September 28.

Turner, Robyne. 1992. "Growth Politics and Downtown Development." *Urban Affairs Quarterly* 28(1): 3–21.

Uchitelle, L. 1994. "The Rise of the Losing Class." *New York Times*, November 20: 1, 5.

United Nations Development Programme. 1994. *Human Development Report 1994*. New York: Oxford University Press.

Urban Institute et al. 1983. *Directory of Incentives for Business Investment and Development in the United States*. Washington, D.C.: Urban Institute.

U.S. Department of Commerce, Bureau of the Census. 1990a, 1980a. *Census of Population and Housing*. Washington, D.C.: U.S. Government Printing Office.

———. 1990b, 1980b. *City Government Finances.* Washington, D.C.: U.S. Government Printing Office.

———. 1992a, 1987, 1982, 1977. *Census of Manufactures.* Washington, D.C.: U.S. Government Printing Office.

———. 1992b. *Economic Census.* Washington, D.C.: U.S. Government Printing Office.

———. 1994a, 1988. *County and City Data Book.* Washington, D.C.: U.S. Government Printing Office.

———. 1994b. *Statistical Abstract.* Washington, D.C.: U.S. Government Printing Office.

———. 1996. *What's It Worth? Field of Training and Economic Status: Spring 1993.* Washington, D.C.: U.S. Government Printing Office.

U.S. Department of Housing and Urban Development. 1988. *1988 Consolidated Annual Report to Congress on Community Development Programs.* Washington, D.C.: HUD, Office of Community Planning and Development.

———. 1989. *Report to Congress on Community Development Programs.* Washington, D.C.: HUD, Office of Community Planning and Development.

———. 1995. *Empowerment: A New Covenant with America's Communities. President Clinton's National Urban Policy Report.* Washington, D.C.: HUD, Office of Policy Development and Research.

U.S. Executive Office of the President. Office of Management and Budget. 1995. *The Budget for Fiscal Year 1996.* Washington, D.C.: U.S. Government Printing Office.

U.S. Office of Management and Budget. 1995. *The Budget for Fiscal Year 1996.* "Building on our Economic Record." Washington, D.C.: U.S. Government Printing Office.

Valente, Mickie. 1995. "Mallot Finds Success in Jacksonville." *Tampa Tribune,* January 31: A1.

Van Fleet, Mark. 1992. "The U.S. Chamber of Commerce: The Voice of Business." *Business America,* November 16: 18.

Vaughn, Roger J., and Robert Pollard. 1986. "Small Business and Economic Development." In *Financing Economic Development in the 1980s,* edited by Norman Walzer and David Chicone. New York: Praeger.

Vidal, Avis. 1992. *Rebuilding Communities: A National Study of Urban Community Development Corporations.* New York: New School for Social Research.

Walker, Christopher, and Patrick Boxall. 1996. "Economic Development." In *Reality and Research: Social Science and U.S. Urban Policy since 1960,* edited by George Galster, 13–37. Washington, D.C.: Urban Institute Press.

Warren, R. 1990. "National Urban Policy and the Local State: Paradoxes of Meaning, Action, and Consequence." *Urban Affairs Quarterly* 25(4): 541–61.

Warson, Albert. 1995. "Building Telecommunities." *Urban Land,* May: 37–39.

Waters, Malcolm. 1995. *Globalization.* New York: Routledge.

Weaver, R. Kent. 1996. "The Politics of Welfare Reform." In *Looking Before We Leap: Social Science and Welfare Reform,* edited by R. Kent Weaver and W. T. Dickens, 91–108. Washington, D.C.: Brookings Institution.

Webber, Michael. 1984. *Industrial Location.* Beverly Hills: Sage.

Weinstein, Bernard L., and Robert E. Firestine. 1978. *Regional Growth and Decline in the United States: The Rise of the Sunbelt and the Decline of the Northeast.* New York: Praeger.

Weir, Margaret. 1992. *Politics and Jobs*. Princeton, N.J.: Princeton University Press.
———. 1996. "Central Cities' Loss of Power in State Politics." *Cityscape* 2: 23–40.
White, J. 1996. "Old Wine, Cracked Bottle? Tokyo, Paris and the Global City Hypothesis." Unpublished paper, American Political Science Association.
White House, Office of the Press Secretary. 1994. "White House Data on Washington Empowerment Zones and Enterprise Communities." Press release.
Wilkie, Curtis. 1994. "Boom Times Arrive in the Southeast." *Boston Globe*, January 24: 1.
Williamson, J. G., and J. A. Swanson. 1966. *The Growth of Cities in the American Northeast, 1820–1870: Explorations in Entrepreneurial History*. Madison: University of Wisconsin Press.
Williamson, Peter J. 1989. *Corporatism in Perspective: An Introductory Guide to Corporatist Theory*. London: Sage.
Wilsford, D. 1994. "Path Dependency, or Why History Makes It Difficult but Not Impossible to Reform Health Care Systems in a Big Way." *Journal of Public Policy* 14: 251–83.
Wilson, William Julius. 1996. *When Work Disappears: The World of the New Urban Poor*. New York: Knopf.
Wolman, Harold. 1988. "Local Economic Development Policy: What Explains the Divergence between Policy Analysis and Political Behavior?" *Journal of Urban Affairs* 10: 19–28.
Wolman, Harold, with David Spitzley. 1996. "The Politics of Local Economic Development." *Economic Development Quarterly* 10(2): 115–50.
Wolman, Harold, Royce Hanson, Edward Hill, Marie Howland, and Larry Ledebur. 1992. "National Urban Economic Development Policy." *Journal of Urban Affairs* 14(3/4): 217–38.
Wong, Kenneth. 1988. "Economic Constraint and Political Choice in Urban Policymaking." *American Journal of Political Science* 32: 1–18.
World Bank. 1994. *World Development Report 1994: Infrastructure for Development*. New York: Oxford University Press.
World Resources Institute. 1994. *World Resources 1994–95*. New York: Oxford University Press.
Young, Iris. 1990. *Justice and the Politics of Difference*. Princeton, N.J.: Princeton University Press.
———. 1992. "Social Groups in Associative Democracy." *Politics and Society* 20: 529–34.

Index

Susan E. Clarke is professor of political science at the University of Colorado. Her publications include *The New Localism* and *Urban Innovation and Autonomy*.

Gary L. Gaile is professor of geography at the University of Colorado. Among his publications are *Spatial Diffusion* and *Geography in America*.